Springer Texts in Business and Economics

Springer Texts in Business and Economics (STBE) delivers high-quality instructional content for undergraduates and graduates in all areas of Business/Management Science and Economics. The series is comprised of self-contained books with a broad and comprehensive coverage that are suitable for class as well as for individual self-study. All texts are authored by established experts in their fields and offer a solid methodological background, often accompanied by problems and exercises.

More information about this series at https://link.springer.com/bookseries/10099

Amy Van Looy

Social Media Management

Using Social Media as a Business Instrument

Second Edition

 Springer

Amy Van Looy
Faculty of Economics and Business Administration
Ghent University
Ghent, Belgium

ISSN 2192-4333   ISSN 2192-4341 (electronic)
Springer Texts in Business and Economics
ISBN 978-3-030-99093-0   ISBN 978-3-030-99094-7 (eBook)
https://doi.org/10.1007/978-3-030-99094-7

This Springer imprint is published by the registered company Springer Nature Switzerland AG
The registered company address is: Gewerbestrasse 11, 6330 Cham, Switzerland

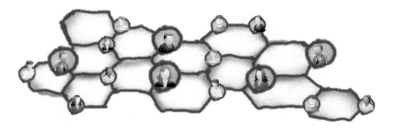

Fictive social media network representation. This simplified image illustrates how the social media profiles of individuals and organizations can be connected to enable a social ripple effect between different communities and potentially link users who do not even know each other. Social media management heavily relies on network mechanisms. Courtesy: Amber E. D. M.

To inspire and be inspired by technology.

Preface

Before getting started, the reader is invited to consider what can be expected from this book. It is also explained how this edition differs from the previous one.

Who This Book Is For

This book is written as an international handbook and primarily targets students in economics and business administration. Other students interested in the organization's way of working or social media management in general are encouraged to read the book as well.

Additionally, business people (ranging from employees to managers and CxOs) who wish to be acquainted with the diverse business aspects of social media will profit from the book, the more since we link social media to strategies for creating business value.

How This Book Differs from Other Social Media Books

This book takes the perspective of organizations (not individuals) and clarifies the impact of social media on the different departments or disciplines in an organization. This multidisciplinary approach differs from other books on social media which deal with a single topic and/or a single focus (e.g., limited to marketing or IT). As this book intends to offer an introduction to a wide range of business-related social media topics, it serves as a complement to the more specialized books that elaborate on each topic separately.

The unique selling points of this book are as follows.

- Basic concepts and practices on social media management are explained in order to introduce the reader to the business essentials of social media.
- The reader is offered critical reflections on a recent and hyped phenomenon, based on a combination of academic insights and practical tips and tricks.

- By taking a multidisciplinary approach, the reader gets to know a wide range of organization-relevant topics in order to put social media into an appropriate business perspective.
- The point of departure concerns potential social media strategies that help achieve organizational strategies and business objectives, derived from an organization's mission statement. It is shown that social media are not a solution to all business problems, and their use should be well considered to avoid failures or too high expectations.
- Each chapter in the book offers a self-test and suggests further readings to learn and better comprehend the material. At the start of each chapter, teaser questions are presented that will gradually be demystified. Additionally, the wrap-up chapter is dedicated to case studies and assignments covering social media management in practice.

How This Book Is Organized

After the introductory chapters, different chapters elaborate on relevant business topics that cope with social media management in an organization. For each chapter, it is explained which departments are primarily involved in the topic and to which degree.

- Chapter 1—Introduction to social media management
- Chapter 2—Definitions, social media types, and tools
- Chapter 3—Social media strategy and return on investment
- Chapter 4—Online advertising and viral campaigns
- Chapter 5—Social customer relationship management
- Chapter 6—Search engine optimization
- Chapter 7—Sentiment analysis and opinion mining (Business intelligence 1)
- Chapter 8—Social network data and predictive mining (Business intelligence 2)
- Chapter 9—e-Recruitment
- Chapter 10—Crowdfunding
- Chapter 11—Legal and ethical issues in social media
- Chapter 12—Wrap-up: integration exercises

Each chapter is organized as follows. It starts with an abstract that summarizes the chapter's outline, followed by teaser questions. The body of the text is written to be accessible to a wide audience and contains a plethora of links and references that enable further readings for those who are eager to delve into the chapter's topic. Each chapter ends with recapping the takeaways, supplemented by a self-test to challenge the reader's understanding of the topic.

Disclaimer and Trademarks

This book intends to give an objective state of the art of the social media landscape at a certain moment in time, without supporting one or another social media tool or online service. Being an international handbook, the book neither intends to give specific advice to organizations. This book is an independent publication and has not been authorized, sponsored, or otherwise approved by any organization, product, or vendor mentioned in the book. All trademarks are the property of their respective owners.

How This Edition Differs from the Previous One

Every edition is characterized by the era in which it is published. While the first edition was written when social media were still emerging, the number of current social media tools has significantly increased and their users have become much more diverse. Consequently, knowledge about the subject has advanced, including the impact from newly emerging technologies in Industry 4.0 (or the Fourth Industrial Revolution). Also, the COVID-19 pandemic (i.e., with worldwide lockdowns) has accelerated the digitalization efforts in organizations, with people becoming more acquainted with social media use for telework or just for getting together.

This second edition differs from the first one in terms of various extensions, but keeping the original business angle. The book's multidisciplinary approach has been retained and updated with recent sources. Interestingly, some predictions in the first edition have come true, such as the increased relevance of video and audio messages, the changing popularity of specific social media tools along a hype cycle or evolution graph, and the need for strong passwords with potentially multifactor authentication. More attention has been paid to the changing legal restrictions, for instance, with GDPR affecting social media efforts and decreasing the risks of information abuse via informed consents. The latter triggers novel perspectives on privacy concerns and social engineering for combining online data from different origins for the sake of knowledge creation. The power of knowledge is also one of the driving forces for critically approaching the business models behind social media tools. Upgrades have been made with respect to the strategic level of social media initiatives, and extensions formulated regarding the business models of more innovative organizations. Furthermore, the increasing role of influencers has been recognized. Throughout the different chapters, reflections have been made about the latest opportunities of emerging technologies, such as artificial intelligence (AI) or Internet of Things (IoT), for letting social media tools further evolve. Finally, the wrap-up chapter consists of extra exercises that comprehensively integrate the different topics of prior chapters.

We Would Like to Hear from You

As social media are a new and rapidly evolving domain, we are interested in your feedback to prepare the next version of this book (Amy.VanLooy@UGent.be).
   Enjoy reading!

Ghent, Belgium   Amy Van Looy

Acknowledgments

I would like to thank Ghent University for giving me the opportunity to teach a novel course on social media management (3 credits) for international bachelor's students in economics and business administration. The course is titled: "*Creating value by using social media.*"

After having received many positive messages about the first edition, I feel grateful to share this second edition with a warm audience.

Contents

List of Abbreviations

24/7	24 hours a day, 7 days a week (round-the-clock, nonstop)
Ad	Advertisement
AI	Artificial intelligence
AIDA	Awareness, interest, desire, action
AIDAL	Awareness, interest, desire, action, loyalty
App	Application
AR	Augmented reality
ATS	Applicant tracking system
B2B	Business-to-business
B2C	Business-to-consumer or business-to-customer
BI	Business intelligence
C2C	Consumer-to-consumer or customer-to-customer
CEO	Chief Executive Officer
CRM	Customer relationship management
CSO	Chief Social Media Officer or Chief Social Officer
CV	Curriculum vitae
CxO	Chief x Officer (i.e., a generic term to indicate a corporate officer. The letter "x" is to be replaced by a specific organizational domain, e.g., Chief Executive Officer, Chief Financial Officer, Chief Operations Officer, Chief Information Officer, Chief Marketing Officer, Chief Social Media Officer)
DAU	Daily active users
DFV	Desirability feasibility viability
E-A-T	Expertise-authority-trustworthiness
ECSP	European Crowdfunding Service Providers
e.g.,	Exempli gratia (Latin for: "for example")
et al.	Et alii (m)/Et aliae (f) (Latin for: "and others")
EU	European Union
eWOM	Electronic word of mouth
FAQ	Frequently asked questions
FOMO	Fear of missing out
FTC	Federal Trade Commission
GDPR	General Data Protection Regulation

GIF	Graphics Interchange Format
GSP	Generalized second-price
HR	Human resources
HTML	HyperText Markup Language
HTTP	HyperText Transfer Protocol
HTTPS	HTTP Secure
ICT	Information and communications technology
ID	Identification
i.e.,	Id est (Latin for: "that is")
iOS	iPhone™ Operating System
IoT	Internet of Things
IP	Internet Protocol
IPO	Initial public offering
IT	Information technology
JOBS	Jumpstart Our Business Start-Ups
KPI	Key performance indicator
MarCom	Marketing and communications
MAU	Monthly active users
mDAU	Monetizable daily active users
NLP	Natural language processing
OSM	OpenStreetMap
P2P	Peer-to-peer
p.	Page
PDF	Portable Document Format
PGC	Publisher-generated content
Q&A	Questions and answers
R&D	Research and development
ROI	Return on investment
RSS	Really Simple Syndication
RTBF	Right to be forgotten
SCRM	Social customer relationship management (or social CRM)
SEA	Search engine advertising
SEM	Search engine marketing
SEO	Search engine optimization
SERP	Search engine results page
SMART	Specific, measurable, attainable, relevant, timely
SMARTER	SMART, evaluate, reevaluate
SME	Small and medium-sized enterprise
SWOT	Strengths, weaknesses, opportunities, threats
UCC	User-created content
UGC	User-generated content
UK	United Kingdom
UN	United Nations

URL	Uniform Resource Locator (also known as a link or a website address)
US	United States (of America)
VC	Venture capitalist (or venture capital investor)
VCG	Vickrey–Clarke–Groves
VR	Virtual reality
WOM	Word of mouth
WWW	World Wide Web
XML	Extensible Markup Language
YMYL	Your money or your life

Introduction

1

This chapter introduces the role of the Internet and particularly social media in today's digital economy. The reader gets an overview of the topics covered in the subsequent chapters and of the extent to which these topics relate to the different departments in an organization. Evidence is given that social media are not limited to marketing or information technology (IT), but that a multitude of departments are involved. This multidisciplinary approach of social media constitutes the main thread of the book in order to determine, execute, and evaluate social media strategies that help achieve business objectives and create business value.

1.1 Introduction to the Internet

1.1.1 What Happens on the Internet?

Nowadays, children are part of a digital generation, and they can hardly imagine a world without the Internet, smartphones, tablets, games, and apps. Still, only a few decades ago, this was normal business. See, for instance, the following video in which children of today react to computers from the 1980s: https://www.youtube.com/watch?v=PF7EpEnglgk#t=440#t=25.

Instead, social media can be seen as part of the Internet evolution. While the first Internet generation primarily looked for information in the 1990s, we now use the Internet to share information and opinions and to collaborate or participate in online content. Given its high impact on our daily lives and on today's economy, the Internet can also be called a revolution instead of only an evolution.

The Internet impacts on both online and offline relationships. For instance, more people meet online and dating sites are flourishing, whereas the content of social media tools (e.g., Instagram™, TikTok™, Twitter™, Facebook™, YouTube™) might get censored to some degree in certain countries (e.g., China). Many people have already shared online pictures of offline events, possibly without well considering who might actually see those pictures. For instance, what if anyone can see pictures of your holiday or party (let us say your ex-partner, your parents, or total strangers)? Blunders are easily made if the access rights are not strictly defined, for instance.

Social media may also have a business impact. For instance, regarding someone's career, what if a (current or future) employer can see personal pictures of employees or candidates on social media? Furthermore, organizations seem forced to adopt social media and even to adapt to social media content, because people tend to have more trust in online recommendations about a brand and its products or services rather than in traditional advertisements.

Given the impact of social media on offline relationships and organizations, it seems that the concept of "word of mouth" (WoM) is changing toward "world of mouth." The former refers to people talking to each other and influencing each other, which is relevant as people tend to believe their friends and family more than an organization that tries to sell its products or services. By changing the term "word" to "world," it is emphasized that the Internet allows us to potentially reach out to almost everyone around the globe. The latter also counts for organizations, e.g., by means of viral campaigns which take advantage of a wider spread.

Infographics can be found with a snapshot of what an Internet user will miss of new content (e.g., posts, videos, comments, news alerts, e-mails, swipes, search queries, and GIFs) when one shuts down the Internet for only 60 seconds. Such infographics illustrate why many people become almost addicted to the Internet. Every free minute, they check their mailbox, browse the Internet, or participate on social media due to a so-called fear of missing out (FOMO). The Internet may even distract you while studying for an exam or while working. It might be tempting to open a web browser and start browsing, looking for what others are currently doing. In response, new terms arise for potential solutions, such as the hype of digital detoxing (i.e., not using any digital device for a while).

1.1.2 Could You Live Without the Internet?

Already in 2012, an American journalist decided to find out what his life would look like without the Internet. He was tired of the modern way of living with its constant impulses from the Internet. Hence, *The Verge* magazine paid him to stay off the Internet during a whole year and to report on his findings. After 1 year offline, he did not feel better. He disagreed with the assumption that the Internet would make people "lonely" and/or "stupid," as the Internet is "where people are" and allows them to keep in touch with people. For instance, the journalist missed the regular video chats with his family and the pictures of his rapidly growing nieces and nephews that were usually shared. To conclude, he explained that it is a matter of finding the right balance between a digital identity and a real identity, since the Internet will never replace personal relationships (The Verge 2013). If this experiment were repeated today, the findings would probably have been more strongly worded because of our ever-increasing dependence on the Internet for work, study, and private life.

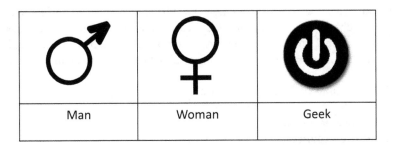

Man	Woman	Geek

Fig. 1.1 The gender-neutral category of "geek"

The Internet has become so ingrained in our daily lives that we might not always realize its omnipresence. For instance, take a moment to look at your own environment and find out how many people have a smartphone or a tablet, in addition to or in place of a traditional computer or laptop. The power of the Internet has also challenged the typical distinction between men and women, resulting in a third and gender-neutral category, called "geek."

Figure 1.1 shows that the "geek" category can be symbolized by the typical power button of electronic devices. Similarly, it refers to those men and women who are extremely interested in IT (which also comprises new technologies, such as social media). For instance, "geek" people will be the first to know whenever a new smartphone is released. They are typically highly active on social media tools (e.g., Instagram™), and many geeks have their own blog to share their experience. These examples illustrate that geeks are not limited to technical profiles (e.g., software developers), but may involve anyone (even you?) who agrees that IT and social media are exciting and fun with a lot of opportunities.

Unfortunately, the word "geek"still has a negative connotation, and it is frequently seen as a synonym for "freak," "fool," or "nerd." Think, for instance, about a character like Sheldon Cooper in the television sitcom "The Big Bang Theory." Nevertheless, when looking in Wikipedia (2021), the word "geek" also has positive meanings, namely, "eccentric or nonmainstream people," ranging from (1) "a peculiar person, especially one who is perceived to be overly intellectual, unfashionable, boring, or socially awkward," to (2) "an expert or enthusiast obsessed with a hobby or intellectual pursuit" and (3) "a member of some fandom." Examples of technologically oriented geeks who "exert a powerful influence" in the twenty-first century are social media founders or app developers (i.e., young billionaires), such as Mark Zuckerberg. In sum, although often considered as a pejorative word, the term "geek" should rather be used self-referentially, namely, as a way to refer to oneself as being a believer in or an early adopter of (technological) innovations.

The latter is an illustration of the theory on the diffusion of innovations (Rogers 2003). According to this theory, innovations in general are gradually adapted by different groups in society, typically starting with a small group of believers (i.e., "innovators" and "early adopters"), followed by the mass (i.e., "early majority" and "late majority"), and finally also nonbelievers or latecomers (i.e., laggards). Since IT and social media (i.e., social technologies) can be seen as innovations in society, in particular technological innovations, the theory can also be applied to this topic.

In order to find out whether you are rather an early adopter or a laggard, the following questions on the use of IT and social media may give an indication:

- **Which computing device do you use?**
  - (a) A traditional desktop or notebook.
  - (b) A tablet or smartphone.
- **How do you connect?**
  - (a) With a traditional telephone and with wires.
  - (b) With a wireless cell phone or smartphone.
- **How do you share memories or life stories?**
  - (a) In written letters, printed books, or exhibitions.
  - (b) In personalized media that are widely accessible (e.g., a Facebook™ timeline).
- **How do you share news?**
  - (a) In a printed newspaper.
  - (b) In news feeds with digital breaking news (e.g., on a website or a Twitter™ page).
- **How do you take notes in class or during a meeting?**
  - (a) Using pencil and paper.
  - (b) Using a word processor (e.g., MS Word) that you possibly share in the cloud (e.g., Dropbox or Evernote) to be in synch on multiple devices.
- **How do you navigate?**
  - (a) Using physical, printed copies of a map or traffic information reported on television or radio.
  - (b) Using a navigation system with a digital map, possibly with live crowdsourced traffic data (e.g., Waze™ or Coyote™).
- **How do organizations collaborate?**
  - (a) In a physical meeting room with whiteboards.
  - (b) In a virtual meeting room, using tools to collaborate remotely, to share data, to chat, and to send instant messages (e.g., Skype™, Yammer™, Zoom™, MS Teams™).

The second options of the questions above refer to more innovative technologies or trends in the domain of IT and social media. The more questions you answered with the second option, the more likely it is that you are an early adopter and thus a geek (whether you like the term or not). If so, then studying informatics or IT management and working in the IT sector might be something for you? Maybe you are even a future innovator, such as Steve Jobs (founder of Apple Inc.™), Marc Zuckerberg (founder of Facebook™), Bill Gates (founder of Microsoft™), or Larry Page and Sergey Brin (founders of Google™)?

Despite the fact that many people make use of the Internet and social media, the IT industry faces an important challenge to recruit IT-minded candidates. Although IT jobs are characterized by a dynamic work environment (e.g., not in a typical work office, with possibilities to travel and a competitive salary), the need for more IT professionals is increasingly growing. This worldwide labor shortage ranges from Chief Information Officers (CIOs) and managerial roles to business or functional analysts, developers, and IT support staff, among others. For instance, different talent shortage surveys of international recruiting firms put IT skills in the list of global skills that are in the greatest demand (Hays 2021) or IT and data roles in the top 5 of jobs that are globally most difficult to fill (Manpower Group 2021). The need for digital skills is especially growing when entering a digital economy that is triggered by emerging technologies (e.g., AI and robotics, IoT, and blockchain), and so realizing Industry 4.0 (or a fourth industrial revolution). The COVID-19 pandemic only accelerated this trend because of the global lockdowns with mandatory telework.

Moreover, as women are generally underrepresented in the IT industry, specific initiatives have been launched to promote IT courses and jobs for female candidates in particular (e.g., https://girlgeekdinners.com/, https://inspiringfifty.org/).

The subsequent sections and chapters will narrow the scope from IT in general to social media in particular.

1.2   Introduction to Social Media

Many social media tools (or platforms) already exist for different purposes, as illustrated in Table 1.1. Similar infographics exist for drinking, peeing, eating donuts or bacon, etc. (instead of drinking in Table 1.1). They can be found by using the search query "social media explained" in a search engine (e.g., Google™, Bing™, or Yahoo!™). These and more social media tools will also be explained in Chap. 2.

This book does not intend to give statistics per social media tool, e.g., the number of users, posts, images, and videos. Although such statistics are remarkably high, they are also rapidly out of date and may vary from region to region, and different sources tend to give varying numbers (which makes it difficult to compare). If

Table 1.1   An example of the different purposes of social media tools

Twitter™	I need to #drink	Spotify™	Now listening while I am drinking
LinkedIn™	I am good at drinking	YouTube™	Here is a video of how drinks are made
Facebook™	I just drank	Pinterest™	Here are good recipes of drinks
Swarm™	This is where I like to drink	Quora™	Where did this drink get invented?
Instagram™	Here is a vintage picture and a story of my drinks	Flickr™	I take pictures while I am drinking
		TikTok™	Watch me as I drink and dance

Table 1.2 Social media explained by social actions and business actions

Social actions	Business actions
Like	Click
Follow	Visit
Retweet	Subscribe
Blog post	Join
Post a comment	Register
Rate this	Take a survey
Bookmark	Qualify a lead
Recommend	Purchase
Etc.	Etc.

interested, the following websites regularly monitor and provide a summary of social media statistics:

- Worldwide and regional data: http://www.statista.com/
- Worldwide and regional data: http://www.internetworldstats.com/

When comparing numbers, please note that such statistics can refer to different measures, such as the number of daily active users (DAU), monthly active users (MAU), and monetizable daily active users (mDAU, e.g., for showing ads). Nevertheless, the following trends are confirmed by the abovementioned sources and provide the reader with some idea about the emergence and relevance of social media tools:

- Facebook™ is still the largest social media tool in the world, e.g., in terms of user accounts and the number of daily active users. Facebook™ had approximately 100 million users in 2008, while this number grew to almost 1.1 billion users at the time of its initial public offering (IPO) in May 2012. About ten years later (in 2021), this number has further increased up to 2.8 billion active users. To give the reader a relative idea about the impact of Facebook™, this number is approximately 35% of the world population with circa 8 billion people (although organizations can also have an account and the same person may have multiple accounts).
- Other social media tools, such as Instagram™, YouTube™, and TikTok™, are increasingly growing in the last few years. As they have fewer accounts, their yearly growth tends to exceed.

If you take a few moments to visit some websites, you will soon observe that most websites incorporate some form of social media use. Particularly, websites can apply social media by means of social actions and business actions. A social action refers to sharing an opinion, while a business action refers to a desired action that an organization wants website visitors to do because it involves a business return.

As shown in Table 1.2, examples of business actions are clicking on an online advertisement to reach the company website (e.g., for brand awareness), visiting the

Table 1.3 The advantages and disadvantages of social media

Social media advantages	Social media disadvantages
Speed	Learning curve for more advanced use
Scalability	Transparency
Analytics	Undeletable
Interactivity	Privacy
Etc.	Etc.

company website, subscribing to a newsletter, joining a corporate community, registering for an account on the company web shop, taking a survey, being an influencer who creates leads with product information, or purchasing a product or a service online. The distinction between social actions and business actions shows how social media can create business value for an organization, i.e., by sharing content and, most importantly, by providing business returns.

Table 1.3 summarizes the main advantages and disadvantages of social media.

- A first advantage is speed. Social media can be used to react to or share content faster than traditional media (e.g., television, radio, and postal letters). They are also less limited by geographical distances. For instance, the minimum response time for an electronic message on social media is much lower than for a postal letter, independent of the location of the sender and the receiver (e.g., Europe versus Australia).
- The second advantage, scalability, means that organizations can potentially reach out to more people with a lower budget. This advantage gives new opportunities to organizations with budget constraints or small and medium-sized enterprises (SMEs).
- Thirdly, analyzing and monitoring social media use are less expensive than, for instance, collecting customer data in face-to-face interviews at a railway station or at a supermarket. The big data that are sent and shared by social media tools can also be (quantitatively) analyzed by means of business intelligence (see Chaps. 7 and 8) and IT support tools (see Chaps. 3 and 5).
- The final advantage refers to interactivity between multiple parties instead of two-way communication. For instance, by using social media, customers can give their opinions about a brand, product, or service whenever they want or ask questions to organizations whenever they feel the need to do so (i.e., also known as the "pull" principle). This contrasts from only receiving product information when an organization launches an advertisement or publishes information on the company website (i.e., the "push" principle).

Social media are, however, also confronted with disadvantages:

- As social media become more advanced, many organizations continue to learn how to properly take advantage of the full potential of social media in order to create business value. The wrap-up chapter of this book will illustrate some bloopers or common mistakes that organizations have made while using social media.

- Secondly, social media are transparent in the sense that they are traceable (i.e., it can be tracked who posted which comments, when, where, etc.). As social media are accessible to the crowd, people may also risk revealing too much private information (e.g., secret business information) and may need to take responsibility for the consequences (e.g., by resigning, when it is clear who revealed the business secret).

- Thirdly, social media content is to some degree undeletable because of the possibility to take electronic backups. Even when posts or pictures are not visible anymore for the crowd (i.e., and thus assumed to be deleted), social media tools or individuals might have stored a copy elsewhere. For instance, in the Terms of Service of social media tools, it can be mentioned that a profile picture is reusable for campaigns, even after deleting it from the profile. A separate chapter of this book will deal with such ethical and legal issues (see Sect. 11.2.2). Some attempts to remove yourself from the Internet can be found here: http://www.wikihow. com/Delete-Yourself-from-the-Internet. Besides trying to delete information from websites and social media tools yourself, search engines can be contacted to request a removal of information from the search engine results pages. The latter is, however, only allowed in a few cases, as stipulated in the removal policies of particular search engines (e.g., https://blog.google/products/search/ when-and-why-we-remove-content-google-search-results/, https://www.bing. com/webmaster/tools/eu-privacy-request -request) and following a 2014 decision of the European Court of Justice about the European citizen's "right to be forgotten" (RTBF) and (later on) the GDPR privacy legislation (article 17— "right to erasure").

- Finally, one of the biggest concerns of social media remains privacy. Also, this topic deals with ethical and legal issues and will be discussed in the remainder of the book (Chap. 11). For instance, is it ethically correct to post a picture of a Chief Executive Officer (CEO) in a swimming pool? Furthermore, as people tend to release much (private) information, real risks are created in the domain of IT security (e.g., identify theft, fraud, or combining information of different social media tools by social engineering) or regarding selling big data about customers to third parties.

One possibility to predict the future of social media (i.e., as social technologies) is by relying on the technological evolution graph of Gartner, Inc. (2021). This graph assumes that every technology follows a similar evolution over time. Based on this technology evolution graph, we may suppose that social media already passed their highest point of visibility (i.e., leading to social media acceptance and high expectations) as well as their lowest point of visibility (i.e., with organizations getting disillusioned after losing money in projects that use social media in an inappropriate way). Instead, in the 2020s, more advanced and mature social media usage will bring social technologies toward a steadier plateau of productivity. For instance, the technology evolution graph can explain both the initial social media hype and the past social media bloopers (see also Chap. 12).

Following the above, we may expect that social media will rather stay in the future than totally disappear. In the opinion of Royer (2012), the productivity level of social media will even remain relatively high because human nature is characterized by a certain degree of curiosity and exhibitionism: (1) curiosity, because many people want to see what others have or do, and (2) exhibitionism, because many people also want to show what they have or do. Nonetheless, based on the traditional product life cycle (Levitt 1965), specific social media tools (i.e., as concrete applications of social media technologies) may come and go, while the principles or common characteristics remain. For instance, we expect that particular social media may disappear over time and be replaced by other more advanced social media tools. For instance, in the early 2020s, we already experienced a growing criticism of Facebook™ (e.g., regarding privacy issues) while observing a rise in popularity for other tools (e.g., Instagram™ and TikTok™).

1.3 Social Media as a Multidisciplinary Approach

This book intends to take a holistic view on social media from the perspective of organizations, particularly by discussing how organizations can create business value by taking a multidisciplinary approach. In order to introduce this multidisciplinary approach of social media, the current section first shows the usefulness of social media for various specialization areas of a business student, before turning to the typical departments in an organization.

The examples in Table 1.4 illustrate that social media should not be examined by marketing or IT students only, but should be part in the curriculum of every business student.

Furthermore, the multidisciplinary approach of social media can be explained by using a typical organization chart (i.e., organogram). Therefore, Fig. 1.2 distinguishes management departments from operational or core departments and supporting departments.

In many organizations, the marketing and communications (MarCom) department and/or the IT department are responsible for managing and implementing social media initiatives. Both are supporting departments. On the other hand, organizations are also increasingly adopting a dedicated social media department or cross-functional team. This option is shown in Fig. 1.2 as a new management department, called a "social media task force," which is led by a "Chief Social Media Officer" or a social media manager.

The business title of "Chief Social Media Officer" or "Chief Social Officer" (CSO) (or equivalent, e.g., Chief Digital Officer) refers to one of the highest level executives in senior management, who typically reports to the Chief Executive Officer (CEO). The CSO is usually ranked on a similar level as other CxOs in the organization—such as the Chief Information Officer (CIO) or the Chief Marketing Officer (CMO)—and works cross-functionally with them. In sum, a CSO is a senior

Table 1.4 Examples of social media use in specialization areas for a business student

Domain	Social media use	Examples
Accountancy and taxation	For knowledge sharing	How do organizations or accountants experience the influence of (new) taxation rules?
		How can social media be used to create a specific community to explain and to talk about issues and regulation regarding accountancy and taxation?
Finance and risk management	For sentiment analysis	Will negative or positive messages in social media influence the value (i.e., rise or fall) of stocks and market shares of a certain organization?
	For social network mining	How can social media data be used to predict the risk of an investment, a loan, or an insurance?
	For crowdfunding	How can social media be used to help finance an organization's projects?
Marketing management	For online advertising	On which social media tools should an organization advertise and how (e.g., pay-per-click versus pay-per-view)?
	For viral campaigns	How can an organization create a popular YouTube™ commercial, i.e., that viewers are eager to share with friends, colleagues, and family?
	For employer branding	How can an organization improve its image of being a good employer?
	For crisis communication	How can social media help an organization when a crisis arrives?
Strategic management and human resources	For a social media strategy	How do social media fit within an organizational strategy?
	For e-recruitment	How do human resources (HR) managers make use of LinkedIn™ to screen potential employees?
	For internal communication	How can an organization connect with its employees by using social media, e.g., to stimulate team spirit?
Public administration	For citizen participation (e-government, e-democracy)	How can a government inform, consult, or advise its citizens or let them collaborate in decision-making through social media?
IT management	For all the applications in the previous domains	IT is the foundation for all social media applications. Hence, all previous examples require people aware of IT management
	For supporting the previous domains	How can an organization monitor social media to calculate the return on investment (ROI) of social media investments (i.e., with analytical techniques of social actions and business actions, e.g., how many clicks, how many messages spread over time, how long do visitors stay on a website, and how many

(continued)

Table 1.4 (continued)

Domain	Social media use	Examples
		members/topics/comments does a blog have)?
		How can an organization screen large amounts of data and get the right information to the right people at the right time through the right channel (i.e., business intelligence, particularly data mining for sentiment analysis or social network mining)?
		How can an organization improve its visibility and rank of its social media use in a search engine such as Google™, Bing™, or Yahoo!™, thus appearing as unpaid search results (i.e., search engine optimization or SEO)?
		Etc.

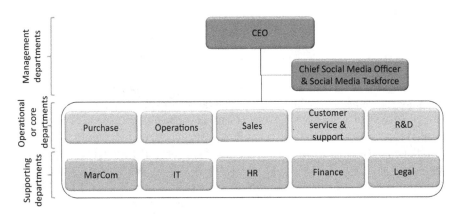

Fig. 1.2 A typical organization chart

manager who is typically responsible and accountable for all social media initiatives in the organization. Although supported by a task force and other departments, this role has to deal with all social media topics discussed in this book (i.e., with regard to determining, executing, and evaluating the overall social media strategies; see also Sect. 1.4, Fig. 1.3) and focuses on the integration of social media into the functions of each employee.

Since this book presents a multidisciplinary approach of social media, a cross-functional task force consisting of one manager per department (as shown in Fig. 1.2 as the "social media task force") seems to be the best solution. Consequently, not a single department should own social media in an organization, and social media has to be part of every department to create business value across departments. With regard to value creation, social media help to significantly raise the productivity of knowledge workers, and many organizations are now changing their business

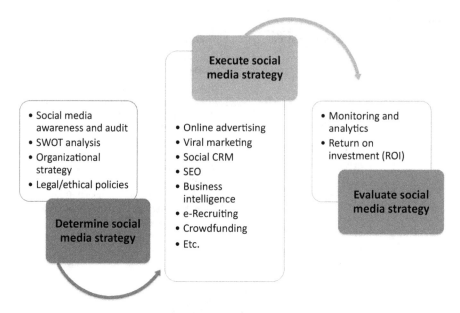

Fig. 1.3 An overview of the topics in this book

processes and organizational structure accordingly. Moreover, social media technologies are becoming integrated into organizations' day-to-day work, and the next generation of more advanced tools focus on enhancing collaboration (e.g., also more project based rather than being limited to teams or functions) (McKinsey 2017). To overcome any difficulty in creating an open, nonhierarchical culture of trust, each specific organization should adopt the role of a CSO depending on its particular context. For instance, the initial view of Altimeter Group (2013) presenting different organization charts is still original, ranging from a traditional and centralized chart to a so-called hub and spoke model which acts as a central Center of Excellence for social activities in order to support the other departments (i.e., comparable to the task force in Fig. 1.2, but without hierarchical relationship).

Figure 1.2 will be used throughout the book to specify in which departments social media have the potential to create business value for recent business topics. Depending on the chapter topic, one or more departments are primarily involved. By combining all topics together, this book addresses the different departments and thus gives evidence of the multidisciplinary approach of social media from the perspective of organizations.

1.4   Learning Objectives of this Book

This book is not about an individual reader who can apply social media for personal use in one's spare time. Thus, this book does not intend to explain how the reader can socialize or create a personal social media page, tweet, keep a personal blog up to date, vlog, or create an electronic résumé for future jobs, etc. Instead, this book is written from the perspective of (public or private) organizations (i.e., primarily targeting readers in their role of business students and—future—employees or employers). It intends to answer the question: "How can organizations create business value by using social media?"

The **main learning objectives** of this book are as follows:

- **Proper use.** Being able to use social media management in a proper way, taking into account the dos and don'ts.
- **Knowledge.** Obtaining knowledge of the impact of social media management for organizations, namely, by (1) understanding the theories and applications of social media and (2) understanding which social media tools are appropriate for which situations.
- **Strategic insights.** Acquiring insight into the social media strategies of organizations, for instance, regarding collecting and analyzing information on the social media use of a specific organization.
- **Critical reasoning.** Sharpening critical reflection and reasoning skills, particularly by (1) evaluating how value can be created from social media and (2) formulating suggestions for improvement.
- **Lifelong learning.** Stimulating lifelong learning by illustrating recent developments in IT management, particularly social media.

The practical relevance of this book can be explained by the way people communicate with each other and the differences over time. In particular, the following evolution has taken place: (1) from "people as people" in ancient times (i.e., one-to-one communication), (2) over "people as mass" as from the fifteenth century (i.e., mass communication, such as printed books, newspapers, radio, and television), (3) to "people as data" and "people as designers" in the twenty-first century. Similar to the first evolution phase, the third phase refers to more personalized communication, albeit now via online activities such as (un)subscribing, (de)friending, and (un)liking. The focus is on sending and receiving messages relevant to the people involved (instead of to the mass) and on "pulling" instead of "pushing" information (see Table 1.3).

- **People as data.** Social media can reveal much personal information about its users (e.g., hobbies on Facebook™ and job experience on LinkedIn™). Organizations can use this background information to provide the Internet user with information that is most relevant to one's profile in order to better meet specific needs. This evolution relates to topics such as targeted marketing with online advertisements or viral campaigns (see Chap. 4) and social customer relationship management (see Chap. 5), but also business intelligence with opinion mining (see Chap. 7) and social network analysis with predictive mining (see Chap. 8), as well as crowdfunding (see Chap. 10). Social media also allow targeting future employees by means of e-recruitment (see Chap. 9).

- **People as designers.** Since content has become increasingly important, power is
rather within social media communities than within an organization. For instance,
new products or services are more likely to survive the first year after having
received community feedback during the conception phase (R&D). Instead of
controlling the message in a top-down hierarchy, organizations should rather
involve and collaborate with all parties in an equal partnership as good ideas
may come from everywhere. Some examples of co-design or co-creation are
"bring your own device" (BYOD) to give employees the freedom to choose the
type of laptop or cell phone they want (instead of standardization) or fine-tuning
products to individual customer needs (e.g., giving the choice between either a
weekend trip or a midweek with 40% off). Other real-life examples are (1) Ice
Watch™, which started as an SME but with millions of Facebook™ "likes" and
which proved that user feedback can lead to more enthusiastic followers;
(2) LEGO™, the producer of toy building bricks, which proved that enthusiastic
fans can propose new product ideas with profit sharing; and (3) Nike™, which let
customers customize their ideal pair of shoes, e.g., by choosing the color. In these
examples, employees, customers, and Internet users in general can become
co-owners or co-creators and are thus sources of value creation because they
are more likely to become advocates of the organization and its products and
services. For more information, see Chap. 5 on social customer relationship
management. Before people may become co-designers, however, they must be
aware of the organization's existence and related initiatives. Therefore, an organization can apply search engine optimization (see Chap. 6) to help Internet users
find the corporate web pages. Finally, ideas that are collected from the crowd
might also be sponsored by means of crowdfunding based on early promotion and
public discussion (see Chap. 10).

The social purpose or strength of social media is that they are able to unite people
based on common ground (e.g., the reasons why like-minded people love a certain
product or service), with common ground being a better motivator than money. For
instance, fans of a brand may influence other people to buy certain products or
services and become brand advocates as such. Enthusiastic fans are also more likely
to voluntarily manage a community, which can reinforce employer branding and
product branding, among others. Furthermore, by means of social media, SMEs may
appear bigger (e.g., by increasing their voice), while larger organizations may appear
smaller (i.e., more accessible and responsive). Independent of the organization size,
social media might help organizations survive or become more competitive by being
more responsive to change after listening to customers and collecting innovative
ideas from the crowd.

1.5   Overview of the Book Chapters

The topics in this book are summarized in Fig. 1.3 and aim to determine, execute, and evaluate a social media strategy. The figure shows that social media use by organizations should follow one or more social media strategies, which in turn should be in line with the overall organizational strategy. In particular, social media actions should not be separated from other business actions, as organizations should act in accordance with their overall strategy in order to support the organization's mission and business objectives.

Subsequently, an overview of the different book chapters is given.

- **Social media definitions, types, and tools.** Chapter 2 introduces the reader to the mainstream social media tools (e.g., Instagram™, TikTok™, Facebook™, Twitter™, and LinkedIn™) and how they can be classified in social media types. This chapter defines what is actually meant by social media and what not. It also gives an idea about which social media types are more suited for certain purposes or business goals.
- **Social media strategy and return on investment (ROI).** Chapter 3 allows the reader to strategically think about social media, to derive business actions in order to realize a social media strategy, and to evaluate whether the business goals have been reached. This chapter emphasizes that social media should not be used ad hoc, but should serve a broader organizational strategy, which in turn contributes to the higher vision, values, and mission of the organization. Regarding the multidisciplinary approach, the CEO together with the MarCom department usually copes with strategy setting. The CEO is also responsible for communicating about policies and organizational goals. Social media monitoring and analytics can be done by the MarCom and/or the IT department, whereas an evaluation of the return on investment (ROI) also involves the finance department. The subsequent chapters present possible social media strategies involving different departments.
- **Online advertising and viral campaigns.** Chapter 4 is typically situated in the MarCom department for executing a social media strategy by means of online ads or viral marketing campaigns. This chapter does not intend to elaborate on general marketing insights that relate to ads and campaigns, but will rather focus on those aspects typical for an online context. Furthermore, the chapter explains how the corresponding social media monitoring and analytics are typically done by the MarCom and/or the IT department.
- **Social customer relationship management (CRM).** As social CRM is the collection of social media initiatives in an organization that try to enhance customer satisfaction and ultimately loyalty, Chap. 5 deals with all forms of direct contact between an organization and its customers and suppliers. Social CRM is broader than advertisements or viral campaigns and also gives an important role to helpdesks, among others. Regarding the multidisciplinary approach, typical CRM departments are closely linked to customers, particularly (1) the MarCom for organizing marketing activities, (2) the sales department for

those activities to sell products or services, and (3) the customer service and support department, also called after-sales, with a helpdesk to respond to customer inquiries or questions and to handle requests or complaints. Other departments linked to social CRM are (1) the research and development (R&D) to innovate in close collaboration with stakeholders (e.g., employees, suppliers, or customers) from idea generation to the final development of products and services, (2) the operations department for internal collaboration with social media (e.g., internal social media use, e.g., Yammer™; see Chap. 2) and for changing business processes or the organization's way of working based on customer feedback received by social media, (3) the purchase department for business-to-business social media (as the organization itself is also a customer of its suppliers) and for better forecasting, (4) the IT department for monitoring and social media analytics, and (5) the finance department for evaluating ROI (similar to Chap. 3).

- **Search engine optimization.** In Chap. 6, the reader will learn how to make a website, blog, or social media page more visible and thus more accessible to people. It is shown that if a page appears higher on a search engine results page (e.g., Google™, Bing™, or Yahoo!™), significantly more people will click on the URL and visit the web page. Tips and tricks are explained that facilitate a higher ranking for websites, blogs, or other social media pages in search engines. Regarding the multidisciplinary approach, SEO is generally situated in the IT department.
- **Opinion mining and sentiment analysis (Business intelligence 1).** Chapter 7 deals with the first part of business intelligence, in which social media content is analyzed as big data in order to elicit knowledge. This chapter investigates the degree to which customer reviews and ratings may affect the behavior of others and thus business outcomes (e.g., sales). Regarding the multidisciplinary approach, this chapter is mainly situated in the IT department.
- **Social network data (Business intelligence 2).** The business intelligence approach is further explained in Chap. 8, which focuses on identifying and analyzing how people profiles or client types are linked to each other. For instance, it can be used to predict trends like future sales or customer retention by answering a question such as "Given that a particular person—say John—has bought a service (or churned), what is the probability that his friends or people with similar characteristics as John will buy the same service (or churn)?" As in the previous chapter, social network mining is mainly related to the IT department. The mining results can be input for targeted marketing, e.g., to increase sales, but also for other domains such as fraud detection and credit risk scoring.
- **e-Recruitment.** Chapter 9 clarifies how organizations can recruit and how people can get recruited via social media. Social media tools, e.g., Facebook™ or Twitter™, can be used to find the right people for a job vacancy, but also specialized professional communities exist, such as LinkedIn™. Legislation regarding e-recruitment is briefly discussed in this chapter. For instance, can someone get fired because of the content one writes in social media posts?

Regarding the multidisciplinary approach, this chapter is mainly situated in the human resources (HR) department.

- **Crowdfunding.** How can we convince other people to invest in our projects or ideas, for instance, if we are a starting company, an SME, an artist, etc.? Chapter 10 shows how social media can help organizations raise money from the crowd and ultimately relates to the finance department.
- **Legal and ethical issues in social media.** Chapter 11 elaborates on the dos and don'ts regarding social media use in organizations. By focusing on the legal department, this chapter tries to clarify who is responsible for social media content written by an employee (i.e., the employee or the employer?), what are the possible consequences for hiring and firing, who is the owner of social media content when getting fired or after death (i.e., the employee, the employer, or the social media tool?), etc. Concepts such as privacy, anonymity, confidentiality, intellectual property, Terms of Service, and digital afterlife are discussed.
- **Wrap-up.** Chapter 12 reconsiders the main learning objectives of this book, as previously stipulated in this chapter. It concludes with multidisciplinary case studies and assignments to apply the insights and knowledge obtained throughout the different chapters. The purpose of this final chapter is to encourage the reader to critically reflect on how specific organizations can combine the different perspectives discussed in this book in order to take advantage of social media and create business value.

Each chapter is associated with a teaser question, as one of the central elements to be demystified per topic (Table 1.5).

1.6   Takeaways

Social media are omnipresent and affect online relationships between people, as well as their offline relationships. Since many people use one or another social media tool, organizations continue to use social media to create business value.

The major value-increasing factor for social media is content (see Fig. 1.4). The more relevant social media content is to people, the more likely they will share and talk about it, which may lead to diverse business outcomes (e.g., increasing sales or customer loyalty, acquiring new customers, image building, brand recognition, and employer branding). Ideally, a snowball effect starts with a dialogue between two parties, e.g., formal business-to-consumer (B2C) communication, and may evolve toward conversations with other parties (C2C), e.g., informal consumer-to-consumer communication. Nonetheless, since a lot of social media content is directly created in a C2C context, organizations can try to monitor relevant conversations, react (if needed), and take advantage (if possible and appropriate).

As it is all about good and relevant content, content management has become a real currency for organizations (instead of only money). This way, social media can give new opportunities to small and medium-sized enterprises (SMEs) that have smaller budgets than, for instance, internationals. It is, however, increasingly

Table 1.5 Teaser questions per chapter

Topic	Chapter	Example of possible teaser questions
Definitions, Social Media Types, and Tools	Chap. 2	• Why are traditional e-mails not seen as social media? • Why is it better not to rely on Wikipedia™ for a dissertation or student group work?
Social Media Strategy and Return on Investment	Chap. 3	• Why are social media so important for organizations anyway? • Why is this book titled "social media management," and not just "social media"?
Online Advertising and Viral Campaigns	Chap. 4	• What do cookies and social media have in common? • How do I know what you did last night?
Social Customer Relationship Management	Chap. 5	• How can customers gain more power, even if this is sometimes to the detriment of businesses?
Search Engine Optimization	Chap. 6	• What do spiders and hats have in common with social media?
Sentiment Analysis and Opinion Mining (Business Intelligence 1)	Chap. 7	• How can social media adjust your opinion?
Social Network Data and Predictive Mining (Business Intelligence 1)	Chap. 8	• How can social media help predict the future?
e-Recruitment	Chap. 9	• Which of your private behaviors could jeopardize your job?
Crowdfunding	Chap. 10	• Is it legal for me to borrow some money?
Legal and Ethical Issues in Social Media	Chap. 11	• What is the best age for a social media manager or Chief Social Media Officer?
Wrap-up	Chap. 12	• Can you give me social media advice?

Fig. 1.4 The value-enabling effect of social media

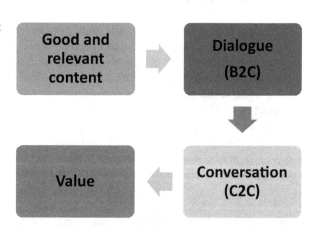

important that customers and prospects follow an organization before a snowball effect with content sharing and talking can take place. Hence, organizations should also pay attention to conversation management (i.e., to properly communicate with customers and prospects) as well as knowledge management (i.e., to gather information about customers and prospects in order to determine what they find relevant) and this among others by combining information from different social media tools through so-called social engineering.

Value creation happens across the departments of an organization and is not limited to marketing (e.g., for online ads or viral campaigns) or IT (i.e., in the sense of social technologies). Although social media ownership is still mainly located at these departments, a better alternative would be to create a social media task force as a cross-functional team with one manager per department and a Chief Social Media Officer.

One final example to illustrate the multidisciplinary approach of social media concerns monitoring complaints on social media and web care (i.e., IT department) for customer support (i.e., after-sales department), the insights of which can be used in future marketing efforts (i.e., marketing department) and/or to improve products or services accordingly (i.e., R&D and the operations department). This kind of interconnectivity is facilitated by IT and social media, but is not necessarily restricted to the boundaries of a single organization. Also, collaboration between organizations can be facilitated in connected networks or partnerships, which allows organizations to specialize themselves and act in so-called ecosystems. The latter is of particular interest for SMEs which may not have a large budget to invest in all departments.

1.7   Self-Test

- Can you explain FOMO?
- Can you explain how social media relate to the theory on the diffusion of innovations?
- Do you think social media will stay or not? Give a rational argumentation to motivate your choice.
- Can you explain how social media tools relate to emerging technologies by relying on the technology evolution graph?
- Can you explain why and to what extent social media require a multidisciplinary approach? Which departments are involved when?
- How would you describe the role and profile of a Chief Social Media Officer? And in your opinion, to which degree does this role differ from the role of CIO and CMO?
- Can you specify how the different chapters in this book relate to each other?
- In order to test whether you have clearly understood the main ideas in this chapter, you can fill out the crossword puzzle in Fig. 1.5. The central keyword (i.e., in column I) is a central construct for the next chapter (Chap. 2).
    1. Negatively perceived synonym for a (digital) innovator (I–L).
    2. Example of a new role for people and customers (C–D + F–L).
    3. Example of a social action (E–L).
    4. Example of a social media disadvantage (G–M).

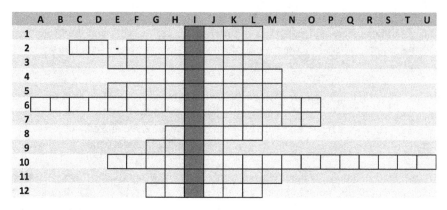

Fig. 1.5 Crossword puzzle

5. Name for an organizational unit that coordinates social media efforts (E–M).
6. A crucial point in the evolution of new technology (A–O).
7. Example of a key obstacle for (digital) transformation and innovation (I–O).
8. The main purpose of social media management is to create ... (H–L).
9. In many social media tools, people are the product by means of their ... (G–J).
10. The discipline to which social media belong (E–U).
11. Author of the theory on the diffusion of innovations (H–M).
12. Screening large amounts of data for information and business insights (G–L).

Bibliography

Altimeter Group. (2013). *The evolution of social business: Six stages of social business transformation.* Retrieved November 27, 2014, from http://www.Slideshare.net/Altimeter/the-evolution-of-social-business-six-stages-of-social-media-transformation

Gartner, Inc. (2021). *Hype cycle.* Retrieved July 14, 2021, from https://www.gartner.com/en/research/methodologies/gartner-hype-cycle

Hays. (2021). *The most in-demand skills for 2021.* Retrieved July 28, 2021, from https://www.hays.com.au/blog/insights/skills-in-demand-2021

Levitt, T. (1965). Exploit the product life-cycle. *Harvard Business Review, 43*(6), 81–94.

Manpower Group. (2021). *The talent shortage.* Retrieved July 19, 2021, from https://go.manpowergroup.com/talent-shortage

McKinsey. (2017). *Advanced social technologies and the future of collaboration.* Retrieved July 19, 2021, from https://www.mckinsey.com/business-functions/mckinsey-digital/our-insights/advanced-social-technologies-and-the-future-of-collaboration#

Rogers, E. M. (2003). *The diffusion of innovations* (5th ed.). Free Press.

Royer, C. (2012). *Guest lecture of Cédric Royer in the course Creating Value Using Social media at Ghent University,* December 2012.

The Verge. (2013). *I'm still here: Back online after a year without the internet.* Retrieved July 19, 2021, from http://www.theverge.com/2013/5/1/4279674/im-still-here-back-online-after-a-year-without-the-internet

Wikipedia. (2021). *Geek.* Retrieved July 19, 2021, from http://en.wikipedia.org/wiki/Geek

Definitions, Social Media Types, and Tools

2

Before discussing the multidisciplinary approach of social media in subsequent chapters, this chapter provides the reader with a common understanding. The most important concepts are defined, such as social media, social media management, user-generated content, and Web 2.0. The latter concept is also situated in a broader Internet evolution (until Web 4.0 and beyond), including emerging technologies. It is shown how and to which degree traditional communication models and theories apply to social media and how a social ripple effect can be created. Furthermore, social media tools are classified in social media types. This chapter also reflects on community management, blogging/vlogging , social bookmarking, and gamification. By discussing different characteristics of social media, the reader gets an idea about which social media types are more suited for which purposes or business goals.

> **Teaser Question**
> - Why are traditional emails not seen as social media?
> - Why is it better not to rely on Wikipedia™ for a dissertation or student group work?

2.1 Defining Social Media

While Chap. 1 mentioned the existence of different social media tools, this chapter continues with a clarification of the differences or purposes of these tools. Afterward, the subsequent chapters will show how organizations can use such tools to create business value. Moreover, social media tools themselves are also likely to fight against each other, figuratively speaking, in order to obtain more user accounts or posts and thus to obtain more power for selling advertisements or data to other organizations or third parties, among others. In the end, social media tools belong to organizations (e.g., Alphabet™ Inc. for Google™ or Meta™ Platforms Inc. for Facebook™) that want to make profit (possibly at the expense of their users).

As a metaphor, Director Clément Morin translated the opening sequence of the television series "Game of Thrones" to some frequently used social media tools (i.e., based on the concept of Hootsuite™). A video illustrates some battles in which social media tools build walls and block access between their different websites and applications: https://www.stashmedia.tv/clament-morin-game-social-thrones-hootsuite/.

One example is a battle between Facebook™ and Twitter™ that started mid-2012, when Facebook™ acquired the social media tool Instagram™ to share photos and videos. In response, Twitter™ decided that Instagram™ photos were no longer fully appearing in tweets but that only a link to the web version of the photo would be displayed. Only after clicking on that link, the full picture would appear. In turn, Facebook™ reacted by blocking access to full Instagram™ pictures for tweets. Instead, after clicking on the link, a Twitter™ user would only see a cropped version of the picture (Forbes 2012; TechCrunch 2012). Further on, when Twitter™ launched Vine™ (i.e., a former social media tool for sharing six-second videos) in 2013, Facebook™ disabled Vine™ to automatically find friends on Facebook™, and Vine™ users would have to manually search for other users they know (The Huffington Post 2013). Meanwhile, the battles between social media competitors continue. More recently, also a series of public issues appeared on how to deal with fake news, privacy concerns, and the use of artificial intelligence (AI) to gain more insight into users' social lives (i.e., for social engineering purposes) (Cnet 2018). As a result, in 2020, public voices criticized Facebook™'s expansive power, calling for spinning off Instagram™ and WhatsApp™ (i.e., the messaging service owned by Facebook™).

This example also refers to different functionalities of social media tools, such as creating and sharing text, images, and videos. But what is actually meant by social media? The subsequent sections clarify the main concepts that are related to social media.

2.1.1 The Concept of Web 2.0

Social media are often associated with the term Web 2.0. See, for instance, Chap. 1 in which social media have been described as a next step in the Internet evolution.

Web 2.0 refers to the use of the Internet (or the World Wide Web, WWW) in order to create content, share, and collaborate among Internet users. In particular, Web 2.0 is the technical platform for the evolution of social media, as it allows online content and applications (e.g., blogs or wikis) to be modified by all users in a rather participatory and collaborative way.

Web 2.0 follows Web 1.0. Compared to Web 2.0, Web 1.0 allows that online content and applications (e.g., a personal web page, an online encyclopedia, or newspaper) are created and published by individuals in a unidirectional way. Web 1.0 started in the early 1990s, namely, with the official birth of the (commercial)

Internet, available to the general public, and thus the start of the information age (Wikipedia 2021a). This means that the Internet was initially limited to providing information as one-way communication (and possibly with feedback by email or postal letter) for Web 1.0, while Web 2.0 can be seen as the second generation of the Internet with multi-way communication in the 2000s.

Nowadays, Web 3.0 and Web 4.0 are more advanced ways of using the Internet and social media (Aghaei et al. 2012). In these terms, the Internet has evolved from a "read-only" or static web (Web 1.0) over a "read-write" or participating web (Web 2.0) to a "read-write-execute" or semantic web (Web 3.0) and a "read-write-execute-concurrency" or symbiotic web (Web 4.0). Some works also start referring to Web 5.0 as an "open, linked, and intelligent" or emotional web, which will be developing in the coming years (e.g., by 2030), or even Web 6.0 as the future generation with a more independent existence from humans (Benito-Osorio et al. 2013; Business2Community 2019; Król 2020).

The following example of a library website clarifies the different functionalities of the evolving Internet:

- Web 1.0 includes online shopping carts or browsing in online catalogues (e.g., a library website).
- Web 2.0 also gives library users the opportunity to review books online (e.g., by means of liking, sharing, or commenting on book entries in the online catalogues).
- Web 3.0 enhances a library website by automatically recommending books that an individual user might like, based on the earlier searches and preferences of that particular user, as well as based on the reviews by other users with a similar profile. Web 3.0 is called the semantic web (also smart or intelligent web) because it allows contextual, personalized searches by giving meaning to words in response to the typical information overload in search engines. Particularly, Web 3.0 applications are able to provide context to data in order to understand what is relevant to a certain user and what is not. This can be realized by means of data integration (among web pages and social media posts), which structures data by labels. For instance, if you follow someone on Instagram™, then that link or relationship can be considered as data. Similarly, if you tag someone's photo, the name in that tag is also data. By integrating all data available about an individual Internet user, semantic search engines become able to make recommendations (e.g., books) that might be of particular interest for you. For instance, if you search for books on the topic "jaguar," a semantic search engine knows whether you search for a car or an animal (e.g., based on your interests or posts on social media tools, your social media connections, previous searches).
- Web 4.0 or the symbiotic web goes a step further by proactively recommending new types of books on a library website, even before a user has searched for that book type. Web 4.0 can also introduce you to other users with a similar profile and thus having similar interests. Or it can give you news about your favorite authors or books, e.g., when they are granted a literature reward or appear in a news feed. The symbiotic web refers to a linked web which will communicate

with people, similar to people communicating with each other. For instance, as an intelligent personal assistant, a Web 4.0 application on an electronic device will recognize the person that is in front of the machine and might say "good morning" (i.e., based on the time zone),"put a coat on today, because it will be rainy today" (i.e., based on the person's geographical location and the online weather forecast), "your flight of today has been canceled" (i.e., based on a personal agenda, flight details, and an online timetable of the airline company), "you need to leave now to arrive on time for your next meeting" (i.e., based on the personal agenda, location, and online traffic information), etc. One early example of an intelligent personal assistant was Google™ Now (launched in 2012), which was available in the Google™ search mobile application for proactively showing potentially relevant information based on one's search habits and other factors. For instance, a virtual assistant can look into your emails for appointments and to find reservations or travel information. Meanwhile, Google™ Now is replaced by Google™ Assistant (launched in 2016), which enables two-way conversations with the Internet user based on AI (i.e., keyboard-based but also through natural voice) and which is also available for smart home functionalities. Consequently, a personal or virtual assistant has become part of the so-called Internet of Things (IoT) or Cloud of Things, which refers to a network of connected objects (e.g., devices, systems, services). For instance, based on someone's location, a smartphone may know when the smartphone owner leaves home, alert him or her when domestic appliances (e.g., heating or a television) are still on, and offer a remote to switch the appliances off. Thus, Web 4.0 refers to a symbiotic relationship between the Internet user and the Internet by equally depending on each other. This evolution is linked to a fourth industrial revolution in the 2020s (also called Industry 4.0), and which recognizes the adoption of emerging technologies that help advance social media (e.g., AI, robotics, IoT, blockchain technology, virtual reality, and augmented reality).

- The next web generation of Web 5.0 is still a vison for the future, but we can already reflect on how it might look like given the rising opportunities of emerging technologies. For instance, based on AI, the Internet might work more telepathically, with microchips (e.g., in your brain or hand) or a headset allowing the Internet to understand and respond to human thoughts and feelings (instead of just using an emoji). For instance, once you think of a specific book you would like to read, the webpage with this information would open. Alternatively, certain book types would be advised based on how you feel. And websites would offer a more individual experience by adapting their colors or details based on the user's emotions. This evolution responds to the fact that the intelligence levels of robots increase, making us able to have more complex conversations with smart devices (i.e., including cognitive and emotional interpretations). Nevertheless, current AI technology is not yet that far in the early 2020s.

In sum, as from Web 2.0, one talks about the influence of social media. Web 3.0 and Web 4.0 (or later evolutions) are more advanced ways of using the Internet and

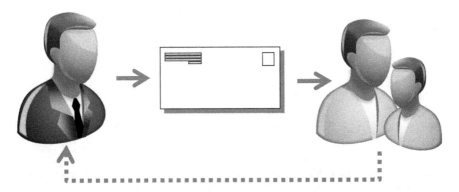

Fig. 2.1 The traditional communication model

Fig. 2.2 The new communication model, characterized by communities

social media to better serve the users. As such new ways of communicating have drastically changed the way humans typically communicate, the traditional communication model of Fig. 2.1 seems no longer valid.

Figure 2.1 distinguishes a sender (on the left, e.g., an organization), sending a message (in the middle) to a receiver (on the right, e.g., a customer) and possibly including a feedback loop. This traditional communication model reflects the typical way of communicating for Web 1.0 but does not allow multi-way communication as from Web 2.0. A new communication model seems required, as proposed in Fig. 2.2.

Figure 2.2 consists of networks or communities that are linked to each other. The networks can be intertwined, which means that a person (or Internet user) can be simultaneously part of multiple networks (e.g., professional or private networks and networks such as Instagram™, TikTok™, Facebook™, Twitter™, LinkedIn™).

In this new communication model, communication is frequently not initiated by an organization itself. For instance, end users or customers can create leads about a brand, product, or service by sharing (positive or negative) comments and so influencing other users inside and outside their networks. Namely, this message will first spread within a user's own networks, and then possibly reach other networks due to sharing and commenting on activities of others. The latter is called

Table 2.1 The functionalities of the traditional marketing funnel translated to Web 2.0 and social media tools

AIDA	Translated to a social media context
Attract **A**ttention/ **A**wareness	See (e.g., banner, link)
Attain **I**nterest	Click (e.g., banner, link)
Create **D**esire	Like (e.g., home page)
Get **A**ction	Use (e.g., subscriptions, online sales, or shop locator for offline sales)

the **social ripple effect**. A ripple refers to the circles or waves that are created when a raindrop reaches the surface of water. The ripple becomes larger and larger, and so reaching other ripples. Translated to social media and Web 2.0, it means that once a message is posted on social media tools, it may spread from the sender's networks to other networks, and so reaching the connections of connections.

Furthermore, the traditional marketing funnel, called AIDA, can be translated to the functionalities of Web 2.0 and social media tools (Table 2.1).

AIDA describes the behavior from prospects to actual customers. First, people have to be aware that a certain brand, product, or service exists. Then, they may become interested in the product or service and start looking for more information. They might even consider buying the product or service if they like the information they found earlier and if they can use the product or service themselves. Such a desire to buy may eventually lead to actual buying.

Translated to a social media context, Table 2.1 shows which actions or functionalities may apply to the AIDA thinking. Attention or awareness can be facilitated by seeing an online ad or a link to a web page, e.g., on a search engine results page. Interest refers to clicking on the ad or link, and so reaching the corporate web page. Desire means that people start liking the web page or its profile on social media tools such as Facebook™. Finally, action should be enabled by the website. For instance, it can be an online shop or just a list of offline shops. Actions do not necessarily include sales but all desired business actions, e.g., also the registration for an online newsletter. Furthermore, Chap. 5 on social CRM will extend AIDA with the concept of customer loyalty (i.e., AIDAL, with the letter "L" referring to "loyalty").

2.1.2 The Concept of User-Generated Content

The previous section focused on the Internet evolution (in particular the meaning of Web 2.0) and how it affects traditional communication models. As being the technical platform for the evolution of social media, Web 2.0 allows users to create and share content or to "generate" content. Or as Kaplan and Haenlein (2010) briefly stated: "User-generated content (UGC) can be seen as the sum of all ways in which people make use of social media" (p. 61). The present section turns to defining the concept of user-generated content (UGC) in order to show that social media are more than UGC (i.e., social media involve UGC but are not limited to UGC).

UGC literally refers to content that is generated by Internet users (as opposed to publisher-generated content or PGC). Some early definitions assume that UGC can entail various forms of media content, as long as this content satisfies two assumptions: (1) **being publicly available** and (2) **created by end users** (Webopedia 2014). The first assumption correctly excludes emails, but it also seems to exclude all private communication (e.g., videoconferencing) and which is thus restrictive regarding the classification of social media tools. Hence, this first assumption contrasts with Sect. 2.2, in which Safko (2012) classifies interpersonal tools (e.g., Skype™ or Zoom™ for videoconferencing) as social media. The second assumption suggests that UGC would be a synonym for consumer-generated content or consumer-generated media. Also, this assumption is restrictive, as Chap. 4 will show that viral campaigns are inherently initiated by an organization and that end users or consumers can share this content or post comments. Such refinements should be considered when looking for a general definition for social media in the next section.

Further on, in an attempt to define UGC, the OECD (2007) proposed three requirements that should be satisfied before content can be called user generated: (1) published, (2) creative effort, and (3) created outside the professional routines and practices.

- **UGC must be published**. This requirement is in line with the previous assumption which refers to publicly available content and thus involves the same critical reflections.
- **UGC must be the result of a creative effort**. This requirement emphasizes that content must be created, instead of merely being a replication of existing content. The question, however, raises whether merely sharing content (which is frequently done by social media) can thus be seen as UGC in the sense of a creative act of (let us say) self-expression. Nevertheless, according to the OECD (2007), sharing or copying content is not considered as UGC.
- **UGC must be created outside the professional routines and practices**. This requirement excludes, for instance, communication between an organization and a commercial market to gain profit. It rather refers to (unpaid) users that generate content in order to connect with peers, to become recognized as an expert, to express oneself, etc. Also, this requirement needs some critical reflections in the context of social media, as it seems to exclude social media use for professional purposes (e.g., viral campaigns, videoconferencing, or internal social media use to increase productivity).

More recently, Santos (2021) conducted a literature review to systematically derive a UGC definition as "any kind of text, data or action performed by online digital systems users, published and disseminated by the same user through independent channels, that incur an expressive or communicative effect either on an individual manner or combined with other contributions from the same or other sources" (p. 1). In this definition, content is widely interpreted (e.g., as text, data, or any meaningful action such as sharing or reacting by an emoji), and thus extending the OECD's second assumption. The reference to independent channels excludes moderation by interested parties, even though Santos (2021) claims that political or economic actors (e.g., organizations) do not operate as gatekeepers or editors in social media and can thus also be seen as users (e.g., in viral campaigns) (i.e., in contrast to the OECD's third assumption). Finally, the generation of content is confirmed as being the publication and diffusion of an entangled action in a digital creative process (i.e., confirming the first and second OECD assumption).

The comments discussed above should be taken into account when looking for a general social media definition.

2.1.3 The Concept of Social Media

If social media are not a synonym for user-generated content or Web 2.0, then what are social media? Different definitions exist, ranging from more limited to broader interpretations of social media. One example of a limited interpretation was an initial definition of Kaplan and Haenlein (2010), who defined social media as "a group of internet-based applications that build on the ideological and technological foundations of **Web 2.0**, and that allow the creation and exchange of **UGC**" (p. 61). This definition seems to restrict social media to Web 2.0 and UGC, but more general definitions exist. For instance, Wikipedia (2021c) adds that social media include **interactive** technologies used to create and share information (or other forms of expression) and thus turning communication into **interactive** dialogue, while Safko (2012) refers to media that people can use to be social or "the story is in the tactics of each of the hundreds of technologies, all of the tools that are available for you to **connect** with your customers and prospects, and the strategies necessary to use these tactics and tools effectively" (p. 3). In the end, social media are about online interactions and connections.

In an attempt to examine the evolution of social media definitions over time (i.e., starting from the mid-1990 s), Aichner et al. (2021) observed four common themes in current social media definitions. First, social media **enable** human interaction and act as an avenue to **connect** with other users. Over the years, the emphasis has changed from "people" to "**users**" in particular (e.g., to also include organizational users). Secondly, a social media definition should refer to "**sharing**" content, rather than uploading. Thirdly, the authors uncovered that recent definitions refer to "user-supplied" content or "**user-driven**" platforms in addition to UGC. And, finally, since social media are powerful tools for organizations but also influencers and celebrities, they link users based on **common interests** and so reaching out to the mass.

For the purpose of this handbook, we comprehensively define social media as follows:

> **Social media** are a group of **interaction-enabling** tools (i.e., based on the foundations of **Web 2.0** and later web evolutions) to **connect** Internet **users** (e.g., people, organizations) based on **common interests** by creating and **sharing user-driven** content (e.g., within a specific group or by triggering a social ripple effect to the mass) in order to create **value** (e.g., self-expression or a feeling of belonging for people, and business value for organizations and influencers).

Since this handbook mainly focuses on how organizations can create business value from social media, we also provide a definition for social media management.

> **Social media management** is the art and science of how organizations should strategically apply social media across their different disciplines (or departments) by performing social actions and business actions in order to help create business value and realize the organization's mission.

For more information about possible types of business value that can be targeted and the alignment of social media strategies to higher-level corporate strategies, we refer to Chap. 3.

2.2   Social Media Types and Tools

This section elaborates on the different social media types and the tools per social media type. Classifying existing social media tools is useful given the many tools that exist, and it also allows us to gain insight into the way of working of individual social media tools. Two classifications are discussed: (1) based on theories and (2) based on common characteristics.

The first classification relies on theories in the field of media research (in the columns of Table 2.2) and theories on social processes (in the rows of Table 2.2) and is based on the original view of Kaplan and Haenlein (2010). According to theories in the field of media research, one can better influence the behavior of someone else with personalized and synchronous communication than with mediated and

Table 2.2   A theoretical classification of social media tools, applied to a case study

		Instant contact		
		Low	Medium	High
Image building	High (individually)	Corporate blogs and fora	Social communities (e.g., Facebook™ and Twitter™)	Virtual world (e.g., Second Life™)
	Low (collectively)	–	Content communities (e.g., YouTube™ and Flickr™)	Corporate virtual game

asynchronous communication (i.e., social presence theory). In particular, social media are more personalized compared to the mass media (e.g., radio, television, and newspaper) and allow faster interaction. Further on, social media allow providing a large amount of information in a relatively short time interval (compared to the mass media with predefined time slots), which may result in less uncertainty and more knowledge about facts (i.e., media richness theory).

On the other hand, according to theories in the field of social processes, people tend to influence what others think of them by acting as such (i.e., self-presentation theory). For instance, if you want that people see you as a creative person, you may post pictures of yourself at a museum or an art exhibition. Hence, social media can be used for reasons of image building. Besides self-presentation, you must ascertain that all personal information you (unconsciously) reveal about yourself (e.g., what you think, feel, like) is consistent with the desired image (i.e., self-disclosure theory). For instance, the image of a creative person is less compatible with a nine-to-five routine job (i.e., being possible information on LinkedIn™) or following the social media pages of a minister who decided to cut cultural incentives.

By combining these theoretical insights, social media tools can be classified according to their degree of instant contact (in the columns of Table 2.2) and image-building opportunities (in the rows of Table 2.2). To illustrate this first classification, we rely on a real-life case study in an IT organization that is highly present on social media, Cisco™. The case study focuses on an offline event for launching a new product. During this event, different social media tools were used to let participants feel more involved. Also, people who were not able to attend the event could still follow what was going on. The social media tools used in the case study are listed below:

- Blogs and fora to let participants feel more involved by sharing opinions and giving product feedback, also available for non-attendees.
- Social communities, e.g., Facebook™ and Twitter™.
- Content communities, e.g., YouTube™ and Flickr™.
- A virtual world, e.g., Second Life™, to create a conference room on an exotic beach with palm trees in order to create a more relaxed atmosphere.
- A virtual 3D game to let participants use the new product themselves.

Table 2.2 summarizes how the social media tools used in the case study relate to the theoretical classification. Only one category was not present for the case study, namely, social media tools with low instant contact and less image-building efforts, e.g., for collaborative projects (e.g., Wikipedia™).

In the columns of Table 2.2, it is specified that more immediate contact is possible when directly playing in a virtual world than posting messages on Facebook™ or Twitter™. Nonetheless, these social communities are more frequently visited than personal blogs and fora which usually cover only one individual or one topic (instead of a collection of friends/followers for diverse topics). In the rows of Table 2.2, it is specified that contributing to an encyclopedia (e.g., Wikipedia™), posting a video, or playing a game is more anonymous and reveals less information about someone's

Table 2.3 A classification of social media types and tools, based on common characteristics [adapted from Safko (2012)]

Social media types	Examples of social media tools per type
1. Social communities	1. Facebook™, LinkedIn™, Yammer™
2. Social text publishing tools	2. Blogs, Wikipedia™, SlideShare™, Quora™
3. Microblogging tools	3. Twitter™, Tumblr™
4. Social photo publishing tools	4. Pinterest™, Instagram™, Flickr™
5. Social audio publishing tools	5. Spotify™, iTunes™, Podcast.com
6. Social video publishing tools	6. YouTube™, Vimeo™, TikTok™
7. Social gaming tools	7. World of Warcraft™
8. RSS	8. RSS 2.0, Google™ FeedBurner
9. Live casting tools	9. Live365
10. Virtual worlds	10. Second Life™
11. Mobile tools	11. Foursquare™, Swarm™
12. Productivity tools	12. SurveyMonkey™, Doodle™, Google™ Workspace
13. Aggregators	13. MyYahoo!™, iGoogle™ (until November 2013)

personality, compared to personal opinions that are shared on a blog, community (which is a collection of pictures, videos, comments, interests, etc.), or the acts and talks that someone does as a virtual personality (i.e., who someone wants to be or the situation to take part in).

The second classification is based on common characteristics of social media tools to detect social media types, as proposed by Safko (2012). Table 2.3 lists some examples of specific social media tools that correspond to each social media type. The table does not intend to list all social media tools, but it gives an overview of those social media tools that are commonly used, as an illustration. An organization should not necessarily use all social media types, but it should rather focus on those types that are most important or beneficial. For instance, Safko (2012) initially used the term "social media trinity" or "social media trilogy" for showing that organizations might start with about three social media types, such as (1) social communities, (2) text publishing tools, and (3) microblogging. Focusing on three social media types can already pay off with minimal investments, before considering expanding toward other social media types.

Safko (2012) distinguishes two other social media types which are not shown in Table 2.3, namely, (1) a search social media type and (2) an interpersonal social media type.

- Regarding the "search" social media type, search engines *an sich* (e.g., Google™, Bing™, or Yahoo!™) cannot be considered as social media based on our definitions of user-generated content and social media (see Sects. 2.1.2 and 2.1.3), because they only assist in finding web pages or social media pages. Unlike the name suggests, this social media type seems to refer to search engine optimization (SEO; see Chap. 6), which increases in importance as the number of web pages, blogs, and social media pages continues to grow. Particularly, SEO investigates how a page can appear higher in the results of certain search queries. Moreover, SEO is not a tool but rather refers to tips and tricks that can also be applied to web pages (social media pages, among others). Therefore, we do not consider SEO as a social media type or tool but rather as a possible strategy (see Chap. 6).

- The interpersonal social media type refers to tools that allow interpersonal communications (e.g., with employees, customers, or prospects), such as Skype™ to organize videoconferences or tools for chatting (e.g., apps for instant messaging via private text messages or voice and video calls such as WhatsApp™ or Facebook™ Messenger). This social media type is open for discussion, as it does not comply with the conditions of user-generated content, i.e., not necessarily published or outside the professional routines and practices (see Sect. 2.1.2).

Subsequently, we have a look at each social media type, without elaborating on all social media tools.

2.2.1 Social Communities

The first social media type (social communities) is typically characterized by "wisdom of the crowd," which means that a community user can reach out to many people, listen to them, and try to get them involved. Communities can be created for external use (e.g., organizations are highly present in social communities to meet customers). But social communities can also be created for internal use (e.g., to stimulate collaboration within an organization). Social communities can be monitored and analyzed as business metrics and knowledge management tools, which reminds the reader that social media should serve a business objective (instead of just using social media because they are hip and trendy). In Chap. 5 on social customer relationship management, we will explain how social communities may act as knowledge management tools (e.g., how customer feedback can be used to improve or to design products and services).

Some examples of social communities are as follows.

- **Facebook™**:
  Including a personal timeline, news feeds, and private messages.

  Facebook™ was founded by Mark Zuckerberg and his college roommates at Harvard University in 2004, followed by the initial public offering (IPO, NASDAQ) in 2012. The name "Facebook™" is derived from the name of a book given to American students at the start of the academic year to help students get to know each other.

  Although Facebook™ remains one of the largest social media tools (see Chap. 1), Facebook™ has been frequently criticized for changing its privacy policy without clear communication to its users or for data privacy issues (see Chap. 11).

- **LinkedIn™**:
  Networking website for professionals to stay in touch or to find jobs, and for organizations to list job vacancies and to search for potential candidates.

  LinkedIn™ uses a "gated-access approach," which means that a user can only directly contact one's first-, second-, and third-degree connections. Contact with any professional in the community requires an existing relationship, a direct email address, or the intervention of a user's contact who introduces the user to other people outside one's third-degree contact network, which is intended to build trust among the LinkedIn™ users.

  More information on LinkedIn™ is given in the chapter on e-recruitment (see Chap. 9).

- **Google+™**
  Social layer that enhanced other online properties of Google™ until 2019, and showing similar features as Facebook™. Circles were used to organize and share information (e.g., friends, family, or acquaintances). Later on, Google™'s focus switched to a Google™ Workspace, showing more similarity to Yammer™ and especially emphasizing productivity tools (i.e., as being another social media type; see Sect. 2.2.9).

- **Yammer™**:
  Private social network for an organization, including productivity applications, a traditional intranet (e.g., a content management system), and an extranet. Examples of social network features are, among others, posting announcements, sharing files, creating events, swapping messages, and knowledge exchange.

For this social media type, **community management** is especially important. The following tips and tricks can be taken into account when creating a community. First, it is important to appoint a community manager (i.e., an administrator) and to identify community evangelists (i.e., who persuade other users to become active members). Different member types exist, which make or break a community, namely: (1) community members who create content and become active content contributors, (2) members who primarily comment on the content of someone else in the community, (3) members who rather share and refer content to friends or colleagues, (4) members who simply view content, and (5) members who usually ignore content. In order to compete with other communities, it is better to have a strong community with sticky content than a big community (i.e., rather a community with a few members who actively participate than a community with many members who act rather passively). For this purpose, content should be aligned with the needs of the target audience, and user-generated content should be encouraged. Organizations can follow some rules, such as:

- Enable conversations among your audience or market.
- Admit that you cannot control conversations with social media, but you can influence them.
- Influence is a basis for economically viable relationships.

2.2.2   Text Publishing Tools

The second social media type is about text publishing tools (e.g., to publish conversations or stories). Some examples of social text publishing tools are as follows:

- **Wikipedia™**:
  Free encyclopedia that anyone can edit and thus a nonacademic source of information. A revision history is saved to see track changes. Content is subject to certain terms and conditions, e.g., no promotion for commercial products, no copyright infringements, and only verifiable content.
- **Organizational wikis**:
  Easily editable web pages for internal or external secured collaboration and knowledge sharing. The use of wikis may require a cultural shift, as employees should be convinced to work with an electronic wiki rather than with local files.
- **SlideShare™**:
  Community primarily for sharing presentations, documents, and Adobe™ PDF portfolios.
- **Quora™**:
  Question-and-answer website to ask questions and get answers but also to create and follow blogs.
- **WordPress™ blog**:
  Open-source software to create and manage blogs or websites, including a content management system (e.g., to create, manage, and store content from web pages in order to organize or archive blog posts). It uses standard templates, so the user can directly start typing content without much knowledge of software development.

This social media type covers the many blogs and vlogs that exist today (e.g., on business topics, sports, fashion, traveling, music, and pets). Nowadays, **blogging** and vlogging are a real hype. Blogs are online diaries or websites about a specific subject, in which content (called posts) appears in chronological order. Vlogging is a related term, focusing more on video content.

A blogger or vlogger can keep the following tips and tricks in mind. First of all, it is important to choose a subject you are passionate about. Blogging should be fun and comparable with talking to your friends in a pub. Blog posts can be written in your own writing style. It is also advisable to create a list of topics about subjects for your inspiration and for motivating people to regularly read your blog. Furthermore, you can monitor when people are active on your site or when a post or tweet gets a lot of reactions (e.g., by using a monitoring tool such as Google™ Analytics; see also Chap. 3). Based on such monitoring information, you can decide on the number and timing of blog posts. Writing blog posts can be facilitated by templates, in which you can directly write a heading and add some visuals or videos and a short text in the sense of storytelling. To reach more readers, you may also stimulate interaction, invite guest bloggers or influencers, read other blogs about your subject, and interact with other bloggers. In sum, a blog (or vlog) can be more successful if it is characterized by (1) regular content, (2) passion, and (3) focus. Regular content means finding a balance between too few and too many blog posts. Posting once a week (i.e., 52 posts per year) may seem rather poor to inspire people. Daily posts or writing three times a week may be better to let people regularly visit your blog, and it allows you to improve your writing. Secondly, regarding passion, bloggers who are having fun are more likely to inspire others. Finally, for focus, readers must understand the aim of your blog (or subjects covered) in order to return.

2.2.3 Microblogging Tools

Microblogging tools are characterized by short text messages to avoid an information overload. Microblogging differs from social communities (e.g., Facebook™) by being publicly available (instead of being limited to the connected community members). It also differs from text publishing tools (e.g., blogs) by limiting the number of characters being published per post.

Some examples of microblogging tools are as follows:

- **Twitter™**:
  Twitter™ literally refers to "chirps from birds" or the sound that birds produce. Twitter™ posts (called tweets) are limited in characters (i.e., initially 140 but now 280) in order to be compatible with text messaging. Some typical vocabulary is used, for instance, (1) "@Username" or the "at" sign to indicate a Twitter™ user (e.g., @McDonalds), (2) "tweet" to indicate a Twitter™ post, (3) "tweep" to indicate a Twitter™ user who follows someone else's tweets, (4) RT or "retweet" to repost (and which differs from replying to a tweet), (5) "#topic" or "hashtag" to indicate the topic or keywords of the tweet and to group all tweets around the same topic which facilitates search queries for related tweets (e.g., #jobvacancy). The initial public offering (IPO, Wall Street) in November 2013 resulted in an immediate boom in Twitter™ shares, although other tools are becoming more popular nowadays.
- **Tumblr™**:
  Quick blogging platform for storytelling with multimedia (e.g., short amounts of text, photo, audio, video). For instance, Coca-Cola™ uses Tumblr™ to reach teenagers with animated picture (http://coca-cola.tumblr.com/), and Doctors Without Border™ to share short texts with stories and links to official online reports (http://doctorswithoutborders.tumblr.com/).

2.2.4 Photo Publishing Tools

The purpose of photo publishing tools is primarily sharing photos, pictures, or images. As a picture is worth a thousand words, an increasing number of social media tools are using photos to share experience or to tell stories.

Some examples of social media tools dedicated to photo publishing are as follows:

- **Pinterest™**:
  Using Pinterest™, you can share your interests with others by means of pictures or videos that you organize or "pin" on boards (i.e., one board per topic). People can also follow you (as a pinner) or one of your boards. Pinterest™ collects and organizes photos (or videos) to make a wish list, plan a trip, organize an event, start a collection, plan a project, etc. The "Pin It"—bookmarklet—allows social bookmarking, i.e., if you see a picture or video on another website or blog, you can easily pin it to one of your boards. In this case, Pinterest™ does not save the picture or video on its server or on your computer, but it only saves the link to the picture's original website.
- **Instagram™**:
  While Pinterest™ is more about sharing (existing) pictures on topics, Instagram™ enables its users to take pictures, apply digital filters, and share stories.
- **Flickr™**:
  You can also use Flickr™ for managing and sharing pictures. Flickr™ is frequently used by bloggers to make photos available to the people who matter to them, i.e., to host images (or videos) for blogs and other social media. Additionally, Flickr™ allows displaying geotagged photos on a map. For instance, photos can be added to OpenStreetMap (OSM), which is a collaborative project to create a free editable map of the world.

While explaining Pinterest™, the concept of **social bookmarking** was introduced. Social bookmarking refers to a centralized online service which enables users to add, annotate, edit, and share bookmarks (or references) of web documents and which allows tagging with keywords (metadata) to organize bookmarks (Wikipedia 2021b). Social bookmarking can be compared with website favorites that Internet users can save on their web browsers for reuse at a later moment in time, albeit now between multiple computers. Unlike file sharing, bookmarking only shares references to the original sources (e.g., the link to a website instead of the real website content). An advantage is that by adding keywords to a bookmark, you can quickly search on topics and specifically target what you want to see (e.g., recent bookmarks, popular bookmarks). Social bookmarks can give you an updated overview of social news, i.e., what many people like or what keeps them busy. We must, however, note that social bookmarking is not limited to this social media type. For instance, it is also frequently used by (micro)blogging tools (e.g., Twitter™).

2.2.5 Audio Publishing Tools

The next social media type covers tools for publishing and sharing audio fragments. Audio is frequently used in social media as they are easier to understand than text.

Some examples of social audio publishing tools are as follows:

- **Spotify™**:
  Music streaming service to listen to songs or to the radio, including a purchase service. Spotify™ has a clear business model, namely, (1) either you can use Spotify™ for free, but then you have to listen to ads between the songs and you can only use it within a limited period of time, (2) or you can pay for its service without the previously mentioned restrictions.
- **iTunes™**:
  Media player and media library application for audio and video files (e.g., music, movies, games, audiobooks, ringtones, apps, but also podcasts) from Apple Inc.™. Some radio stations have introduced an iTunes™ Top (e.g., Top 40) with an overview of the most downloaded songs on iTunes™ within a given time interval and region.
- **Podcast**:
  The term "podcast" is derived from the terms "iPod" and "broadcast." It concerns a series of episodes (and thus not a single audio recording), e.g., a series of novels, radio or television series, interviews, and music from a garage band. A podcast may cover audio or video files that users can upload and download from a website. An advantage is that podcasts allow an asynchronous use, which means on demand (i.e., chosen by an individual user, based on personal interests) and on the go (i.e., whenever and wherever one would like to use the podcast, e.g., while driving a car). New episodes in a series can be delivered automatically after subscribing to the series. The latter is done by RSS technology (see Sect. 2.2.8).

2.2.6 Video Publishing Tools

Social video publishing tools are platforms to share video fragments. Compared to text, photos, and audio fragments, videos can give information about body language that is used during communication. A common video publishing tool is YouTube™, but others exist.

- **YouTube™**:
  Website enabling users to upload, view, and share user-generated video content. It provides a forum for people to inform and inspire others and serves as a distribution platform for original content creators and advertisers. When uploading a video, YouTube™ users see a copyright message which warns them that they must have created the video content themselves or otherwise obtain permission from the copyright owner first. Controversial content (e.g., porn or criminal conduct) can be flagged as inappropriate, which is then examined by a YouTube™ employee.
- **Vimeo™**:
  To watch, upload, and share videos.

- **TikTok™**:
  To create and share short videos, focusing on genres such as dance, comedy, and education. It merged with Musical.ly™ in 2018.

2.2.7 Social Gaming Tools

Social gaming tools aim at online gaming. Organizations can (1) participate in existing online games for building brand recognition (e.g., by means of advertising), or (2) they can build a game for the corporate website to promote products or services, as well as mobile gaming apps for smartphones. World of Warcraft™ (https://worldofwarcraft.com/en-gb/) is an example for existing online games. An example developed by an organization to promote a (new) product can be found at McDonalds™. When launching the Spicy Chicken McBites™, McDonalds™ created a game in which the website visitors could make music by clicking on a McBite™, i.e., the McBites™ were used as a piano, with each McBite™ representing a piano key.

This social media type is related to the broader concept of **gamification**, in which real-life situations are turned into competition. In other words, gamification applies game thinking and techniques in real situations (thus no simulations). Users (e.g., customers or employees) are stimulated to do more of something or to do it better than others, e.g., to change behaviors, to develop skills, or to solve problems. Their efforts are quantified in order to give recognition or incentives to users who accomplish a certain action that is desired by an organization. Recognition or incentives can be obtained through different (possibly publicly available) gamification techniques, among others:

- Rewards (e.g., earned lunch, mystery box, lottery, gift, collection set).
- Challenges (e.g., linked to learning objectives).
- Levels (e.g., linked to a learning path).
- Instant feedback (e.g., a progress bar or textual feedback to aid progress).
- Scores or points (e.g., to create a sense of accomplishment).
- Badges (e.g., for significant achievements).
- Leaderboards (e.g., for analytics).
- Competition or benchmarking (e.g., to assess where the user stands against peers).
- Collaboration (e.g., when multiple teams play).

Also different gamification types exist, which can be positioned on degrees or levels. We provide one example for e-learning degrees (eLearning Industry 2020).

- Level 1 for partial gamification (e.g., a gamified quiz).
- Level 2 for game-based training (e.g., a course converted in a board game).
- Level 3 for a gamified learning path (e.g., gamified product training).
- Level 4 for a gamified portal (e.g., a complete gamified learning experience).

Gamification can stimulate engagement and return on investment (ROI), because people have the natural desire to compete with each other in order to achieve something or to strive for better. Therefore, gamification is increasingly used in social media tools but also in corporate IT tools to help organizations achieve their business objectives and to motivate users (e.g., customers or employees). Consequently, the term "corporate gamification" can be seen a method for activating the full potential of employees to support a certain strategy, and which successfully works because games can be perceived as addictive (e.g., because of a user's desire to succeed, for feeling intelligent, out of a need for association or just for having a sense of progress). In other words, using games may encourage users to do things better.

The success of gamification builds on Darwinian instincts and can be explained by traditional motivational theories. For instance, in line with McClelland's human motivation theory (1987), games primarily drive the "achievement motive" in people to meet or exceed a standard but also the "affiliation motive" and the "power motive" by, respectively, focusing on the personal relationships and influence in social media, e.g., by means of interaction and sharing expertise in communities or discussion groups. A more in-depth discussion of other (economic and psychological) theories that cope with intrinsic, extrinsic, or social motivation in the context of gamification can be found in Vassileva (2012).

Nowadays, gamification is widely used in different domains, such as in human resources, marketing, utilities, health care, and charity. Promising departments for which gamification can be relevant are, for instance, human resources (e.g., to stimulate workplace engagement or for e-learning), marketing (e.g., to stimulate customer engagement and loyalty), operations (e.g., to facilitate process improvements), and R&D (e.g., to stimulate new ideas). Gamification will also become more advanced with the help of emerging technologies. For instance, advancements in AI will result in increased tracking and analysis of user statistics, whereas AR and VR can help for developing reality-altering devices.

Some examples of gamification are listed below.

- LinkedIn™ (i.e., a social community that we discussed in Sect. 2.2.1) shows a progress bar with a percentage of profile completeness to stimulate its users to complete their profile and thus to reveal more personal information that LinkedIn™ might sell to other organizations or third parties. Other gamification examples of LinkedIn™ relate to statistics that show how many people viewed your profile, how many times your profile has shown up in search results, etc. Such statistics may stimulate LinkedIn™ users to become a more advanced user in order to get better statistics.
- The Starbucks™ coffee bars used gamification to increase customer loyalty by assigning a mayor for their stores. Per visit and per shop, a customer could collect points. The customer with the highest score per shop within a certain time interval (e.g., in the past 60 days) was crowned "mayor" of that shop. The title of "mayor" also refers to the elected leader of a town or city, which symbolizes prestige.

People were encouraged to frequently visit the same Starbucks™ shop in order to become a mayor. This kind of competition may lead to loyalty to a specific shop.

- Based on business gamification, the company Orion™ achieved a performance and process improvement, namely about 20% reduction of time to perform core activities for back-office employees. This example illustrates just one case study, but others exist with a high success rate. For other examples, see https://www. mycustomer.com/community/blogs/monicawells/top-10-best-examples-of-gamification-in-business
- For a TED talk on gamification at work, see https://www.youtube.com/watch? v=6wk4dkY-rV0.
- Similarly, gamification can work in education, as shown in the following TED talk: https://www.ted.com/talks/scott_hebert_the_power_of_gamification_in_education.
- The link between gamification and motivational theories is further explained as being the future of creativity and innovation (namely the ability to come up with new ideas). Watch this video with an anecdote about a little boy rescuing people thanks to Mario Karting: https://www.youtube.com/watch?v=ZZvRw71Slew

2.2.8 Really Simple Syndication

Really Simple Syndication (RSS) is a technology to distribute web content to subscribers. RSS is a one-click solution for website readers to subscribe to content and receive updates the moment it is published (e.g., a podcast; see Sect. 2.2.5).

RSS differs from an electronic newsletter that is regularly sent to your mailbox (e.g., every month or every week). Instead, with RSS, you will be notified about every update within your subscriptions once it is published. These RSS updates are called "feeds."

RSS also differs from alerts, which are notifications when new content about a certain topic of interest appears on the Internet. For instance, Google™ Alerts can send you an email update each time any web page communicates about a topic that you defined as interesting, without having to subscribe to all web pages separately.

RSS can be used for professional use and private use. For instance, a scholar can subscribe to the RSS of an academic journal. Every time a new issue of that journal is released, an email is sent with the table of contents of that issue, including links to the journal articles in that issue. Organizations can also release press conferences by means of RSS, which is interesting for journalists and fans, among others. As an example of private RSS use, the Apple™ website allows RSS subscriptions for the iTunes™ hit lists. This means that every time a new iTunes™ hit list is released, the RSS subscribers will be notified by email or by an RSS reader, which is an aggregator (see Sect. 2.2.9) or web page that collects all information received from all your RSS subscriptions. Further on, RSS is frequently used by news agencies. Content can be received in different ways, e.g., in an aggregator, an email, or a browser (with an automated signal that indicates new content).

```
<?xml version="1.0" encoding="utf-8"?>
<feed xmlns="http://www.w3.org/2025/Minister">
 <title>Example Feed</title>
 <link href="http://example.org/"/>
 <updated>2025-12-13T18:30:02Z</updated>
 <author>
  <name>Ashley Moore</name>
 </author>
 <id>urn:uuid:60a76c80-d399-11d9-b93C-0003939e0af6</id>

 <entry>
  <title>Minister Calls For Democracy</title>
  <link href="http://example.org/2025/12/13/minister14"/>
  <id>urn:uuid:1225c695-cfb8-4ebb-aaaa-80da344efa6a</id>
  <updated>2025-12-13T18:30:02Z</updated>
  <summary>Some news content to be added here.</summary>
 </entry>
</feed>
```

Fig. 2.3 An example of an RSS feed in XML format

An RSS subscriber will usually receive RSS updates in normal text formats. However, the feeds that are sent are lines of code, which may represent content in XML format (i.e., a computer language to mark text to be shown in computer systems). An example is shown in Fig. 2.3.

The example in Fig. 2.3 is structured according to a typical XML format to represent the content of a feed, such as the title of the feed (e.g., "Example Feed"), the authors (e.g., "Ashley Moore"), the actual content with a title (e.g., "Minister Calls For Democracy"), a summary (e.g., "Some news content to be added here."), and a timestamp (e.g., "2025-12-13 T18:30:02Z," which refers to December 13, 2025, at 18 h30 or 6.30 p.m.).

Organizations can make use of RSS for diverse purposes, for instance:

- To read industry-specific news (e.g., public relations).
- To monitor basic online issues.
- To monitor and send latest headlines, top news relevant for clients.
- To monitor competitors.
- For brand-name monitoring.
- For crisis communication.

Together with microblogging (see Sect. 2.2.3), RSS is one of the fastest ways for **crisis communication**. For instance, a small topical blog site may sleep until a crisis hits and then suddenly gets filled with "questions and answers" (Q&A), reactive statements, frequently asked questions (FAQ), data, etc. By monitoring blogs that are relevant to the organization in particular, it may become rapidly aware that something is going on in order to start releasing updates via RSS to different platforms and in different formats. For crisis communication, the advantage of RSS is that it can be launched within minutes. However, as it supplements traditional communication and classic public relations, RSS content might be managed by the MarCom department rather than the IT department.

2.2.9 Other Social Media Types

Other social media types that can be used are (1) live casting tools, (2) virtual world tools, (3) mobile social media tools, (4) productivity tools, and (5) aggregators.

- **Live casting tools**: to broadcast video in real time (e.g., reality television) and usually for free. For instance, students can make their own television show and broadcast it to fellow students. One example of a live casting tool is Live365™.
- **Virtual world tools**: to meet, talk, exchange ideas, and watch presentations in a virtual (or metaverse-based) environment. For instance, organizations can organize press conferences or hold meetings in a virtual building while customers can visit a virtual store (see the Cisco™ example of Table 2.2). One example of a social media tool with a virtual world is Second Life™.
- **Mobile social media tools**: apps for social media on mobile devices. For instance, until mid-2014, Foursquare™ users could be granted points (e.g., per check-in when entering a real venue), badges (e.g., for some place or time check-ins, for check-in frequency), the title of "mayor" or different levels of a superuser status, among others. In mid-2014, Swarm™ was introduced as a companion app to Foursquare™ for location sharing, and it limited gamification to friends instead of all users. Since then, Foursquare™ focuses on local search recommendations (see also Chap. 7 on opinion mining) instead of check-ins and gamification. For instance, it can now be used to discover and share tips on real venues. Nonetheless, Foursquare™ works together with Swarm™ to provide recommendations based on a user's profile.
- **Productivity tools**: to enhance an organization's productivity, such as supporting social event management or meetings (e.g., Doodle™), online surveys with a large audience (e.g., SurveyMonkey™), peer-to-peer downloads, alerts (e.g., Google™ Alerts), or word processing and spreadsheets if in the cloud (e.g., Google™ Docs). Other examples of productivity tools are included in Google™ Workspace, for instance.
- **Aggregators**: websites to gather information from multiple websites (e.g., webmail, news, other social media tools). They can be used as a personalized homepage, instead of starting with a search engine or corporate landing page.

Aggregators give the user a personalized overview of new content that is relevant to him or her, based on one's social media accounts (e.g., updates of blog posts, tweets, RSS feeds). The overview may also include incoming mails, a personal agenda, notes to oneself, news items, weather forecasts, etc.). Furthermore, aggregators (or RSS readers; see Sect. 2.2.8) help bloggers read hundreds of blogs per day, i.e., not by visiting each blog separately but by letting the latest blog posts of their favorite blogs come to them. One example is ACTIVATE by Impact™ (Bloglovin'™) for fashion, beauty, and lifestyle. However, before receiving those updates, it is required to subscribe to particular blogs by means of RSS.

2.3   Social Media Purposes

Although the previous section showed many different social media types and tools, organizations should not necessarily use all of them. Instead, social media types and tools should be chosen according to the social media strategy that needs to be realized. For instance, if the target group of an organization is not active on Twitter™, then the organization should not use Twitter™. More information on determining a social media strategy is discussed in Chap. 3. For an organization, it is important to know their customers, i.e., not each of them personally but rather their profiles (e.g., their interests, hobbies, and jobs) in order to provide them with more personalized communication that is relevant to them.

If you navigate to the homepage of an organization, you may already notice multiple social media initiatives that can be classified in one or another social media type and tool. For instance, website visitors may be invited to click on a link to Instagram™, Facebook™, Twitter™, LinkedIn™, RSS, or a blog. However, this chapter explained that not all initiatives to get into contact are necessarily related to social media. Examples are private (one-to-one) emails that a website visitor can send to the organization and which differ from the (social or) multi-way communication that is typical for a publicly available "questions and answers" (Q&A) web page. Also the registration for a traditional newsletter that is regularly sent to your private mailbox cannot be considered as social media and differs from an RSS subscription.

Some organizations go even one step further than merely using social media in an online context. For instance, Fig. 2.4 gives an offline example of a shop that reserved some parking lots for people that "like" the organization's Facebook™ page. These parking lots were close to the shop entry and next to the traditional parking lots for disabled people and young parents with babies. It seems that some organizations go really far (maybe too far) in promoting their social media pages (Fig. 2.4).

While social media types and tools should be chosen according to a social media strategy, the latter should serve the organization's mission and its business objectives (i.e., translated into an organizational strategy). This means that behind the social media initiatives of organizations, business models are present. A good example is LEGO™, an organization of toy building bricks, which has created a brand

Fig. 2.4 Parking lots for "likers" of an organization's social media page (2012)

community for increasing sales or brand loyalty and for product innovation, among others (https://ideas.lego.com/). Fans can share and discuss pictures of designs that they have made by using the LEGO™ bricks. A business goal behind this community is to increase sales, because other users may start building the same design after seeing the pictures. Furthermore, within this community, users can share their building experience and become more fascinated about the brand. Consequently, they may become brand advocates or enthusiasts of the brand. Alternatively, users can launch ideas for new building packages that LEGO™ can produce and sell. For this purpose, each community member can present a new design to the community (e.g., with a picture), and other community members can vote. Only those designs with many votes might be selected by LEGO™ for production. If an idea gets selected, the community member who proposed the idea gets the opportunity to explain his idea and to participate in the production process. The corresponding business goal is product innovation and to create real involvement of customers. See also Chap. 5 on social customer relationship management.

The remainder of this section turns to characteristics that are shared among the social media types and tools. Particularly, it concerns general purposes, pillars, or strategies to get the message through. Safko (2012) explains that social media can be used for four general reasons: (1) for communicating, (2) for collaborating, (3) for educating, and (4) for entertaining.

- **Social media use for communication**, e.g., to convince and to sell. Organizations should think through what they are communicating and how they measure the effectiveness of their communication and the perceptions by the audience. A popular example of social media use for communicating is the "Will it Blend" series of YouTube™ videos to promote a blender (http://www.youtube.

com/watch?v=qg1ckCkm8YI). To show the strength of the blender, a scientist tests which (household) items can be blended. Different items have already been mixed with a "smoothie button." The given example mixes an iPhone™ and became a real hit on YouTube™ in terms of "likes" and "views." This video is an example of a viral campaign (see Chap. 4), created by the organization itself in order to promote a product.

- **Social media use for collaboration**, e.g., to convince and to sell. Collaboration frequently has the same purpose of communication. However, it focuses on sharing experience between customers and prospects while using a product. The previously discussed LEGO™ community is one example of collaboration. Furthermore, a food company can collect recipes for meals that customers have made with their ingredients, in order to motivate other people to make the same meal and thus to buy the products too. Another example involves a games workshop, where gamers can meet and play.
- **Social media use for education**, e.g., to learn about an organization's products, brand, suppliers, etc. One example is "the making of" videos that show and explain how a certain product is produced, e.g., how the Prodigy's track "Smack My Bitch Up" was made. Also McDonalds™'s #MeetTheFarmers campaign is aimed at explaining the ecological nature of the ingredients in hamburgers in order to decrease the image of unhealthy food.
- **Social media use for entertainment**, e.g., trying to be funny. Organizations can use social media in order to be interesting and compelling. They can even try to experiment. Nonetheless, they should wonder whether the majority of the targeted audience will find the message funny, as people may have different types of humor. They should also be aware of cultural differences between what is considered as being funny. For instance, is a Muslim cartoon funny or rather racial? Here are some successful entertainment examples: (1) a Carlsberg™ commercial (http://www.youtube.com/watch?v=RS3iB47nQ6E) and (2) the Berlitz™ commercial "We are sinking/thinking" (http://www.youtube.com/watch?v=VSdxqIBfEAw).

Another way to focus on the different social media purposes is by looking at their degree of functionalities, such as (1) presence, (2) relationships, (3) identity, (4) sharing, (5) reputation, (6) conversations, and (7) groups. Each social media tool can be situated in one or more functionality. For instance, Foursquare™ or Swarm™ primarily focuses on "presence" or the location where users are, whereas YouTube™ focuses on "sharing" videos, LinkedIn™ mainly focuses on "identity" (i.e., work experience) and "relationships" (i.e., knowing who is connected to whom), and Facebook™ focuses on "relationships" but also on "sharing" content and revealing your personal "identity" (e.g., your hobbies). In their approach, Kietzmann et al. (2011) already explained early on that it is worthwhile to consider the implications per functionality as well. For instance, revealing your personal "identity" implies privacy concerns, while "sharing" a lot of content requires a content management system to organize and store the content in a structured way. On the other hand, gathering in "groups" (or communities) implies the need for membership rules and protocols. Other implications are network management for "relationships," reputation measurement and sentiment analysis for "reputation," conversation velocity for "conversations," and creating immediacy for "presence."

To conclude, we acknowledge that some authors give overviews with advice on which social media type can be used for which purpose or business goal (such as building a customer community, countering negative publicity, crisis management, customer conversation, exposing employee talent, generating website traffic, market research, new product ideas, product promotion, customer support, sales lead). However, such overviews reflect the opinion of an author (e.g., based on one's experience), which means that organizations can and should make their own choices for selecting one or another social media type. The next chapter elaborates on how a particular organization can define its own social media strategies.

2.4   Takeaways

This chapter has defined and demonstrated the wide variety of social media types and tools, including tips and tricks regarding community management, blogging, social bookmarking, and gamification. We conclude the chapter with some future social media trends that will be discussed in more detail in subsequent chapters regarding (1) music and influencing videos, (2) in-house community management and social media influencers, (3) big data, and (4) the business models of social media tools.

The first trend recalls that pictures and videos have become increasingly important to transmit a message and have much more power than text nowadays. When it comes to text, publishing happens more in the sense of storytelling, e.g., to share experience on how you can use a product instead of sharing sales promotions about that product (i.e., no direct sales). Also the role of influencers has increased, allowing for new branding opportunities (e.g., social media takeovers of a corporate page). Furthermore, we have seen that the amount of text remains low (e.g., limited to 280 characters for tweets on Twitter™). Also the duration of videos is preferably restricted to a few seconds or minutes. Hence, social media users and organizations should stay highly creative on social media. It is to be expected that especially music and video publishing tools (e.g., TikTok™ and YouTube™) will further gain importance during the coming decade, in addition to the power of the more traditional social media tools such as Instagram™, Facebook™, Twitter™, and LinkedIn™. This first trend may have an impact on online advertising and viral campaigns, among others (see Chap. 4).

The second trend copes with community management and explains that an increasing number of organizations try to manage their social media initiatives in-house, while also reaching out to social media influencers. The reason is that social media have become more important to organizations to reach out to customers. Gradually, more mature knowledge is available on the dos and don'ts in order to properly use social media. Furthermore, social media are often used as a complement to physical events, e.g., offline press conferences with social sharing in order to make the message stronger and to reach more people. As this trend predicts the need for more collaboration with online influencers, it relates to Chap. 4 on online advertising and viral campaigns and to Chap. 5 on social customer relationship management. Additionally, Chap. 12 will clarify lessons learned by presenting real-life bloopers of social media use by organizations.

The third trend predicts that more organizations will rely on big data to make business decisions, as will be explained in Chaps. 7 and 8. For instance, by putting all (internal and external) information about a single customer in one meaningful and unified database, organizations get to know their customers better (e.g., hobbies on Instagram™, jobs on LinkedIn™, etc.). This allows more direct marketing with personalized offers and to identify customer profiles.

Finally, the fourth trend predicts that social media will try to make more money from its audience, and this at the expense of people's privacy. This trend reminds the reader that every social media tool also has a business model itself. And similar to a commercial organization, it can try to make profit out of its users. For instance, for many social media tools, users can register for free, but in return they have to agree on the Terms of Service (see Chap. 11). Related to the previous trend, Terms of Service may allow the associated social media tool to sell profile details of users to commercial organizations or third parties as big data, albeit anonymously, as well as information about the specific pages that a user likes, one's connections, pictures, etc. (see Chap. 8 on business intelligence). Another example of how a social media tool can make money is by promoting posts and selling space for online ads (see Chap. 4).

2.5 Self-Test

- Can you define what social media are and what they are not?
- Can you explain the evolution of the Internet? What do Web 1.0, Web 2.0, Web 3.0, and Web 4.0 mean? Can you think of possible applications?
- Think of contemporary dating sites (e.g., Tinder™) or sites for renting and buying (e.g., Airbnb™). What characteristics do they have regarding Web 1.0 and Web 2.0, or even Web 3.0 and Web 4.0? Motivate why such sites can be seen (or not seen) as social media pages.
- Reflect on which phase in the Internet evolution is illustrated in the following situations.
  - The Internet will recommend new books that are of interest to you based on your earlier searches or preferences, but also reviews by other users with a similar user profile.
  - When I leave home, my smartphone alerts me when domestic appliances (e.g., heating or a television) are still on, and offers a remote to switch off the appliances.
  - The Internet helps predict which new books I would like to read next year or which people can become new friends based on similar user types.

- My smartphone warns me when it is time to go to a meeting and arrive on time, taking into account my personal agenda, real-time traffic information, and online weather forecasts.
  - The emergence of social media.
- What does the abbreviation UGC stand for? How would you define the concept? Can you give critical reflections on the meaning of UGC?
- To what extent do traditional communication models and theories apply to social media?
- What is meant by the social ripple effect in the context of social media?
- Can you apply the theoretical classification of social media tools to specific case studies or events?
- Are you able to classify social media tools in social media types? Can you explain each social media type?
- Why are the following examples not part of social media?
  - A website 1.0.
  - An email.
  - A search engine (e.g., Google™, Bing™, or Yahoo!™).
  - A browser (e.g., Firefox™, Chrome™).
  - A traditional newsletter.
- Browse to a website (e.g., of a university or organization, its competitors, or the website of a famous person) and verify to which degree it uses social media. Can you identify the social media types and tools?
- Can you give critical reflections on the typology of Safko (2012) regarding social media types and tools?
- Can you explain the social media trinity of Safko (2012)?
- What does the abbreviation RSS stand for? How would you define the concept?
- Can you give advice on community management?
- Can you give advice on blogging?
- What is social bookmarking?
- Why is gamification frequently used by organizations in software and social media tools?
- Look for two real-life examples of gamification and explain why you have chosen them (i.e., explain why you think this is a good or bad example of gamification).
- Can you apply the business gamification reasoning to specific case studies?
- Which characteristics can be used to describe social media tools?
- Which social media types would you advise for the following situations and which ones rather not? Explain why.
  - Product feedback, crisis management, exposition of employee talent, idea generation, customer service, etc.
- For the creative readers of this book: take your pencil and start drawing! Reflect on how you would re-draw the logo an existing social media tool, or create the logo for a new (self-invented) social media tool. Motivate your choice, and explain why your self-drawn representation looks like this. How does it resemble the tool characteristics?

Bibliography

Aichner, T., Grünfelder, M., Maurer, O., & Jegeni, D. (2021). Twenty-five years of social media: A review of social media applications and definitions from 1994 to 2019. *Cyberpshychology, Behavior, and Social Networking, 24*(4), 215–222.

Aghaei, S., Nematbakhsh, M. A., & Farsani, H. K. (2012). Evolution of the World Wide Web: From Web 1.0 to Web 4.0. *International Journal of Web and Semantic Technology, 3*(1), 1–10.

Benito-Osorio, D., Peris-Ortiz, M., Armengot, C. R., & Colino, A. (2013). Web 5.0: the future of emotional competences in higher education. *Global Business Perspective, 1*, 274–287.

Business2Community. (2019). *Eras of the web – Web 0.0 through 5.0*. Retrieved July 2, 2021, from https://www.business2community.com/tech-gadgets/eras-of-the-web-web-0-0-through-web-5-0-02239654

Cnet. (2018). *Inside Facebook, Twitter and Google's AI battle over your social lives*. Retrieved July 2, 2021, from https://www.cnet.com/news/inside-facebook-twitter-and-googles-ai-battle-over-your-social-lives/

Cnet. (2020). *Battle to rein in Facebook, Twitter and TikTok to heat up in 2021*. Retrieved July 2, 2021, from https://www.cnet.com/news/battle-to-rein-in-facebook-twitter-and-tiktok-to-heat-up-in-2021/

eLearning Industry. (2020). *5 killer gamification examples to enhance the impact of your corporate training*. Retrieved July 2, 2020, from https://elearningindustry.com/gamification-in-the-workplace-reshaping-corporate-training-5-killer-examples

Forbes. (2012). *Twitter has begun to cut off Instagram – Is Facebook next?* Retrieved July 2, 2014, from http://www.forbes.com/sites/ericjackson/2012/07/30/Twitter-has-begun-to-cut-off-Instagram/

Kaplan, A. M., & Haenlein, M. (2010). Users of the world, unite! The challenges and opportunities of social media. *Business Horizons, 53*, 59–68.

Kietzmann, J. H., Hermkens, K., McCarthy, I. P., & Silvestre, B. S. (2011). Social media? Get serious! Understanding the functional building blocks of social media. *Business Horizons, 54*, 241–251.

Król, K. (2020). Evolution of online mapping: From web 1.0 to web 6.0. *Geomatics, Land management and Landscape, 1*, 33–51.

McClelland, D. C. (1987). *Human motivation*. Cambridge University Press.

OECD. (2007). *Participative web: user-created content (Report)*. Retrieved August 12, 2013, from http://www.oecd.org/internet/ieconomy/38393115.pdf

Safko, L. (2012). *The social media bible: Tactics, tools, and strategies for business success* (3rd ed.). Wiley.

Santos, M.L.B.d. (2021). The "so-called" UGC: an updated definition of user-generated content in the age of social media. Online Information Review. https://doi.org/10.1108/OIR-06-2020-0258.

TechCrunch. (2012). *Instagram photos will no longer appear in Twitter streams at all*. Retrieved July 2, 2014, from http://techcrunch.com/2012/12/09/it-appears-that-Instagram-photos-arent-showing-up-in-Twitter-streams-at-all/

The Huffington Post. (2013). *Twitter's 'Vine' app users can no longer find friends via Facebook*. Retrieved July 2, 2014, from http://www.huffingtonpost.com/2013/01/25/Twitter-vine-Facebook_n_2550681.html

Vassileva, J. (2012). Motivating participation in social computing applications: A user modeling perspective. *User Modeling and User-Adapted Interaction, 22*(1–2), 177–201.

Webopedia. (2014). *UGC*. Retrieved July 2, 2014, from http://www.webopedia.com/TERM/U/UGC.html

Wikipedia. (2021a). *History of the Internet*. Retrieved July 22, 2021, from https://en.wikipedia.org/wiki/History_of_the_Internet

Wikipedia. (2021b). *Social bookmarking*. Retrieved July 22, 2021, from http://en.wikipedia.org/wiki/Social_bookmarking

Wikipedia. (2021c). *Social media*. Retrieved July 22, 2021, from http://en.wikipedia.org/wiki/Social_media

Social Media Strategy and Return on Investment

3

In this chapter, the reader will learn that organizations should not use social media as such, just to use social media as a new hype. Instead, social media initiatives should serve social media strategies, which in turn should serve the organization's strategies. Similarly, strategic business models are underlying social media tools. The chapter shows how social media strategies and corresponding tactics can be derived from the business objectives and how key performance indicators (KPIs) and tactics can be formulated in a SMART way (i.e., as concrete as possible, in order to know what to evaluate). Possible initiatives to execute a social media strategy are covered in the subsequent chapters. While executing a social media strategy, an organization should constantly monitor its initiatives, evaluate whether they pay off, and possibly redirect the strategy. Particularly, social media initiatives do not pay off by merely having a lot of "followers" or many "likes" in social media tools, but by reaching a high return on investment (ROI). Consequently, this chapter also emphasizes the importance of evaluating a social media strategy by means of social actions, business actions (e.g., sales or the number of subscriptions to a newsletter), and ultimately ROI.

Besides the MarCom department, other organizational departments are typically involved in determining and evaluating social media strategies. In particular, the CEO is globally responsible for strategy setting and communicating about policies and business objectives. The IT department can support other departments in monitoring the results (i.e., social media analytics and business outcomes) and managing tool licenses, while the finance department can support other departments in the ROI calculations and the processing of business figures (Fig. 3.1).

Nonetheless, social media management is a multidisciplinary approach that should start with a strategy to create business value. All departments in an organization can be potentially involved in strategy setting. In particular, different strategies involving different departments will be discussed in the subsequent chapters. For instance, strategies regarding online advertising and viral campaigns are primarily situated in the MarCom department (Chap. 4), while strategies on e-recruitment also focus on the human resources department (Chap. 9), crowdfunding on the finance

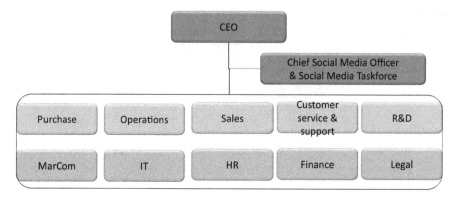

Fig. 3.1 The multidisciplinary approach of a social media strategy, monitoring, and ROI

department (Chap. 10), and social media policies on the legal department (Chap. 11). The ultimate example of social media as a multidisciplinary approach is social customer relationship management, which can affect all departments. For instance, Chap. 5 will show that social media can be used to stimulate sales (e.g., social sales), to handle complaints (e.g., social service), to gather new product ideas or new service ideas for R&D (e.g., social innovation), or to improve existing products, services, or operations (e.g., social collaboration).

> **Teaser Question**
> - Why are social media so important for organizations anyway?
> - Why is this book titled "social media management," and not just "social media"?

3.1 Introduction to a Social Media Strategy

Social media strategies are a first and essential way to look at the bigger picture of social media management by organizations. In particular, social media should only be used if they can contribute to one or more business objectives. Such examples can be internal or external (i.e., with customers, suppliers, or other stakeholders). Some examples of possible business objectives in which social media may play a role are as follows:

- To acquire new customers.
- To drive store traffic in order to increase sales or profit.
- To increase customer satisfaction and loyalty.
- To increase brand recognition or awareness.
- To increase brand engagement.

- For image building (e.g., related to social responsibility, health, environment, etc.)
- For employer branding.
- To support product and service innovation.
- To support internal communication in order to engage employees and managers.
- To support word of mouth.
- To optimize business processes (or the internal way of working) by connecting staff across different business units and locations.
- Etc.

The examples show that an organization's business goals are not necessarily linked to higher sales or profit, but that different possibilities exist. Moreover, social media do not necessarily give solutions to all business problems. For instance, if existing customers of a particular organization are rather not present on social media, then the organization should not target this audience by means of Instagram™, Twitter™, or other social media tools. An internal and/or external audit can reveal information to adopt appropriate initiatives and objectives. In other words, not all organizations should use social media, and if they do, organizations should keep specific business objectives in mind instead of an ad hoc use of social media. Such business objectives are to be derived from the organizational strategies and thus the organization's vision, values, and mission.

The importance of concrete initiatives being linked to business objectives is also expressed in general strategic management models. For instance, the balanced scorecard of Kaplan and Norton (1996) is an established framework to derive an organizational strategy from the higher vision, values, and mission and to translate that strategy into operational terms. In this framework, business objectives and corresponding initiatives are classified into four categories: (1) financial objectives related to the shareholders, (2) customer objectives, (3) objectives related to the business processes (or the internal way of working), and (4) objectives for learning and growth related to the capabilities of people, systems, and organizational procedures. Social media help realize some (but not necessarily all) business objectives across these four categories. Furthermore, as with the organizational strategy, social media strategies should be constantly monitored and evaluated by measuring the corresponding initiatives. Monitoring also allows feedback and a learning curve.

A social media strategy is an organization's plan with activities on how to develop or use social media tools, and how the contributions of these activities are expecting to support the organization's business objectives and performance. This well-thought-out plan will be monitored and evaluated to ensure successful social media efforts.

The subsequent sections deal with the different aspects for determining and evaluating a social media strategy.

3.2   Determining a Social Media Strategy

Strategy setting is crucial in any organization. This is true for organizations that apply social media as well as those that design social media tools (i.e., either as the core activity in a software development company, e.g., for Facebook™, or as a supporting corporate platform, e.g., for Lego™ or Dell™ brand communities). Both perspectives are addressed in the present section, even though the book's primary focus remains on how organizations apply social media.

Thus, besides reflecting on how organizations can strategically *use* social media (Sect. 3.2.1), we have a closer look at how business models can be formulated for organizations that *develop* social media tools (Sect. 3.2.2).

3.2.1   Strategy for Using Social Media by Organizations

Before starting to write specific social media strategies, an organization (e.g., the Chief Social Media Officer, if present) should conduct an **internal and external social media audit** to explore the initial situation, namely, by conducting surveys and in-depth interviews with employees, customers, suppliers, and other stakeholders. An audit can assess how employees communicate and collaborate, and thus whether the organizational culture needs to change while adopting social media tools or launching social media projects. For instance, a social media project may take a few years longer if the organizational culture needs to change first, e.g., before employees are willing to share knowledge or before employees are able to use social media tools.

Furthermore, Safko (2012) suggests to use a social media awareness index to assess the degree to which employees are aware of and have already used the different social media types and tools that exist nowadays (see Chap. 2). By means of a tool scorecard, employees can also be encouraged to think about future social media uses within the organization and to rank different tools per social media type that might be valuable or rather worthless for the organization.

The results of the internal and external audit may be input for a social media **SWOT analysis** (*s*trengths, *w*eaknesses, *o*pportunities, *t*hreats), which is a frequently used management method to brainstorm about the organization's current strengths and weaknesses and its future opportunities and threats. Possible questions that help fill out the SWOT table are presented by Safko (2012), e.g., about the general use of IT in the organization (as social media are social technologies), the level of creativity and collaboration among the employees, etc. Since other management books already elaborate on how to conduct a traditional SWOT analysis, this book will not go into detail.

Fig. 3.2 Deriving a social media strategic plan

Based on a SWOT analysis, it becomes easier to derive a proper social media strategy that takes into account the specific characteristics of an organization. Another proposition to remember when formulating a social media strategy is the "social media trilogy"(or trinity) of Safko (2012) (see Sect. 2.2), which reminds the reader that all social media types should not necessarily be used. Moreover, Fig. 3.2 shows that a social media strategy should be directly linked to the organizational strategy and thus be directly derived from the organization's business goals and mission statement. Fig. 3.2 visualizes a so-called social media strategic plan.

The template of a social media strategic plan, as presented in Fig. 3.2, emphasizes that each mission may have multiple business goals, and each business goal may have multiple social media strategies. Similarly, each social media strategy may have multiple social media tactics (i.e., concrete investments in social media). Each business goal and strategy is measured by a corresponding key performance indicator (KPI), while metrics are defined per tactic.

In general, an organization can consider three to five strategic realizations per organizational goal. One of the main reasons why an organization's social footprint should be in accordance with the organization's goals and mission is because social media content is rather undeletable (see Sect. 1.2).

Figure 3.3 illustrates an extract from a social media strategic plan of a particular organization. Assume that an organization has a mission to provide exceptional value to its customers. Such a mission might be realized by a business goal regarding social responsibility, among others. A corporate image of being socially responsible symbolizes that the organization is not only concerned about its profit or direct sales but also about the society in general. The corresponding KPI may refer to a minimum number of customers (i.e., a concrete and quantifiable percentage of respondents, e.g., 75%) who recognize this image in the next customer survey (e.g., to be held in the first quarter of 2024). The image of taking social responsibility can be supported by concrete social media initiatives. For instance, as shown in

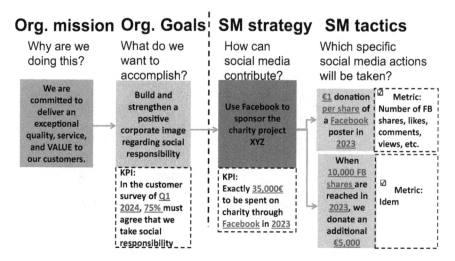

Fig. 3.3 An example of a social media strategic plan

Fig. 3.3, a social media tool such as Facebook™ can be used to sponsor a specific charity project. Such an initiative can be evaluated by a KPI that mentions an exact budget (e.g., €35,000) to be spent on charity through a specific social media tool (e.g., Facebook™) within a specific time frame (e.g., 2023). This social media initiative may involve multiple tactics (which are investments, methods, or specific actions). For instance, the organization can create a Facebook™ poster and donate a certain amount of money (e.g., €1) per Facebook™ share of that poster in the covered year (e.g., 2023). Further on, it can donate an additional amount of money (e.g., €5000) when the poster reaches a certain number of shares (e.g., 10,000 Facebook™ shares) in the same time frame (e.g., 2023) in order to stimulate more shares.

The visualization in Fig. 3.3 clearly presents a difference between business actions and social actions. In particular, the KPIs to measure an organization's business goals and social media strategies are related to business actions, whereas the metrics to monitor social media tactics are related to social actions (e.g., the number of shares, likes, comments, and views). The KPIs and metrics may refer to financial results (e.g., a targeted increase in sales) but also to nonfinancial results (e.g., a targeted increase in brand awareness or image building, newsletter subscriptions, visits of the corporate website, positive mentions, or comments in blog posts).

Alternatively, a social media strategic plan can be vertically (instead of horizontally) arranged. To illustrate a vertical visualization, Fig. 3.4 explicitly distinguishes evaluation efforts (on the left) from investment efforts (on the right). Also a feedback loop is added in case the actual results do not satisfy the defined KPIs (e.g., when having a low ROI).

Furthermore, we note that the KPIs and tactics in Fig. 3.3 have been smartly defined (i.e., with the "smart" elements being underlined). The acronym **SMART**

Fig. 3.4 An alternative way
to look at a social media
strategic plan

Table 3.1 The meaning of the acronym SMART (or SMARTER)

Acronym	Meaning
Specific	Simple
Measurable	Quantifiable
Attainable	Realistic
Relevant	Linked to organizational performance
Timely	To be realized within a specific time frame, defined in advance
Evaluate	*Ethical, ecological, excitable, enjoyable, engaging*
Reevaluate	*Rewarded, reassess*

(or rather SMARTER) means that KPIs and tactics should be formulated as SMART as possible, so they can be translated into a plan of action and unambiguously evaluated afterward (Table 3.1).

Other examples of social media strategies are shown in Table 3.2. Example A in Table 3.2 intends to acquire new customers by means of discount vouchers offered through Facebook™. The corresponding KPI explicitly mentions the expected number of new customers, the targeted social media tool, and a time stamp. In this example, the organization can count how many discount vouchers were actually used after that period of time and whether it concerns new customers or existing customers. In example B, the organization tries to increase sales by means of special offers and stimulating conversations to build stronger customer relationships (see Chap. 5 on social CRM) through Twitter™. The SMART KPI refers to a minimum increase in sales and a time stamp. However, Twitter™ as a social media tool is not included in the KPI, because higher sales do not necessarily relate to Twitter™ initiatives alone (i.e., no discount vouchers used in this example to track and trace the direct outcomes in terms of sales).

As mentioned in the previous chapter, many social media initiatives of a specific organization are visible on the corporate home page or on a dedicated corporate web page. Until now, this chapter has shown that such social media initiatives should be in line with the organization's mission statement, which is also frequently available

Table 3.2 Other social media strategy examples

	Example A	Example B
Goal:	Acquire new customers	Increase sales
Social media strategy:	Use Facebook™ to reach more prospects and a higher prospect-to-customer conversion	Use Twitter™ to stimulate customer loyalty and turn existing customers into loyal customers
KPI:	*At least 250* new customers through *Facebook™* in the *Q1, 2023*	An increase in sales of *at least 15%* in the *Q2, 2023*
Social media tactics (methods):	• *One* discount voucher valid in the organization's web shop for *every new Facebook™ connection* in Q1, 2023 • *10% reduction* on the next online purchase to *anyone who shares* one of our Facebook™ offers in *January 2023*	• Publish *daily* offers on *Twitter™* in *Q2, 2023* • As from *2023*, answer *Twitter™* questions from (prospective) customers *within 2 h* • Provide *weekly* product information on *Twitter™* to increase word of mouth in *Q2, 2023*
Metrics:	Number of new Facebook™ connections, number of Facebook™ shares	Number of new Twitter™ followers, tweets, retweets, Twitter™ comments, time to respond, time to publish

online. If desired, Internet users can make the link and check whether an organization acts in accordance with its mission statement.

Nonetheless, organizations can use social media in different ways in the sense that some organizations have a more advanced social media use than others. For this purpose, different **social media maturity models** exist with (often five) evolutionary stages through which organizations can use social media, i.e., ranging from lower to higher degrees of social media capabilities (e.g., management support, budget, resources, corporate culture, monitoring, and integration initiatives). Social media maturity models have also been translated to specific sectors, such as logistics (Jacob and Teuteberg 2019) or health care (Pour and Jafari 2019).

To give the reader an idea of how a maturity gradation can look like for social media management, we give one example for illustrative purposes only.

1. From an "ad hoc" or experimental use of social media without management support, budget, or resources.
2. Over an "engaged" use with managers aware of the power of social media and small pilots launched by volunteers or part-time resources.
3. A "structured" use with a larger social media budget and formal projects launched by full-time resources.
4. To a "managed" use with social media being part of daily management. A cross-functional task force is now created (see Sect. 1.3), and social media efforts are conducted by trained professionals.
5. And ultimately an "optimized" use of social media with social media efforts linked to the organization's goals and mission statement. Besides the task force, a Center of Excellence is created with experts in the social media methodology

(e.g., see subsequent chapters: social CRM, SEO, business intelligence, e-recruitment, crowdfunding, legal and ethical issues).

Other maturity journeys exist, such as ranging from a technological level, over operational and managed levels to a strategic level (Wang et al. 2017). Maturity models are seen as practical instruments to gradually help organizations advance in terms of their social media management, which is still considered challenging for many organizations (Michopoulou and Moisa 2019). Moreover, organizations may also have a different maturity level for their internal and external use of social media or even their B2B and B2C social media use, while all levels can meld together on the longer run.

3.2.2 Strategy for Developing Social Media Tools by Organizations

The previous section focused on how organizations can strategically use social media tools, which they either developed themselves or were designed by other (mainly software-related) companies. This means that such social media strategies depend on the broader context of digital transformations by emerging technologies (e.g., AI, IoT, VR/AR, etc.) in a digital economy, affecting the business models of underlying social media tools.

This idea is in line with Sect. 2.1, when we positioned social media tools as competing organizations that need to make profit (possibly at the expense of their users). As known from the innovation management literature, the future is in emerging technologies for enabling digital innovations that are strategically handled, and thus also requiring business model innovation (Vial 2019). The focus on developing social media tools (or apps in general) is increasingly changing toward transforming customer experience and, more specifically, providing exceptional value to end customers. For instance, the highest market capitalization is not necessarily for traditional, large, or low-cost organizations since SMEs or luxury brands can significantly transform customer experience as well. Just to give one example, think about the rising interest in electric cars even though they are still more expensive than traditional cars. The same counts for innovative social media, as illustrated when Facebook™ acquired WhatsApp™ (i.e., as a small company but with an impressive number of end users) for about $19 billion in 2014. Since business model innovation is key, we now explain how strategic business models can be formulated in the digital age.

First of all, every idea or innovation needs to pass three initial checks (Gerber 2017), also known as DFV (or desirability, feasibility, viability):

- Desirability. What is desirable to end users? Will customers use the innovation?
- Feasibility. What is feasible with technology? Is the idea technically possible with the current wisdom of IT?
- Viability. What is viable in the marketplace? Will the benefits be larger than the costs, and thus triggering a positive ROI?

DFV represents the three essential characteristics of any innovation (and thus also of digital innovations or social media innovations). If one characteristic is missing, its implementation will be riskier and more expensive. Although innovation is centered on creating value, different value types exist. For instance, values can relate to the four following needs (Almquist et al. 2016):

- Functional needs (e.g., for saving time, simplifying, making money, reducing risks or costs, integrating, providing quality, informing, connecting remotely).
- Emotional needs (e.g., for anxiety reduction, nostalgia, entertainment).
- Life-changing needs (e.g., for self-actualization, hope, motivation, affiliation).
- Social needs (e.g., for self-transcendence).

These value types illustrate that value should not necessarily be seen as value in exchange (i.e., for making money), but also as value in use. Meeting more value types will positively affect customer loyalty and revenue growth.

Until now, we explained the characteristics and values related to a digital innovation (such as a new social media tool). The next step delves deeper into the underlying digital business model. For instance, an online storage tool can offer free storage for individual users, whereas more advanced storage is to be paid by heavy users or professionals in order to make money. In this case, it is important to calculate how many professional users are needed to get a sustainable business model. Alternatively, a social media tool can offer free accounts but with third parties paying for online ads or personal data for predictive mining. And search engines can be used for free while treating end users as data (e.g., by gathering information of what a specific user searched for, what was done next, how long the search took, and what other people in the same building are searching for). Similarly, strategic questions relate to the required number of ads to become sustainable. All such assumptions will be considered in a digital business model.

Or as Mark Zuckerberg summarized when an American senator asked how he sustains Facebook™'s business model in which users do not pay for the service (Burch 2018): "*Senator, we run ads.*"

The business model canvas is one of the most popular techniques for creating a digital business model (Osterwalder and Pigneur 2013; Euchner and Osterwalder 2019). It consists of nine elements, divided among three groups. On the left, the costs are mentioned and how a new product or tool will be developed (i.e., three elements: key partners, key activities, and key resources). On the right, the revenues from the end users are listed (i.e., three elements: customer segments, relationships, channels). In the middle, the value propositions are made, making assumptions about the different value types. Finally, at the bottom are the cost structure and revenue streams, requiring more revenues than costs.

Figure 3.5 shows an example of how a business model may look like for a company that develops a new social media tool. Its revenue model focuses on a combination of free users and premium users (i.e., professionals who pay).

Any (digital) business model should be tested because its value propositions are based on assumptions or guesses. This means that a business model may look great

Key partners	Key activities	Value propositions	Customer relationships	Customer segments
• Open source development community • Content partners (influencers) • Strategic partnership with Google	• Platform design and optimization • Content management • Operations management • Analytics • Marketing	• Newness by relying on FOMO • Accessibility to an engaged community • Connect and learn to express oneself • Personalized and social experience • Customization with a continuous service • Personalization with ads • Time reduction (high-speed connection) • Simplification of a content library	• Trusted access to a community • Self-service (app) • User support and personal assistance • Recommendation system • Co-creation	• Self-serviced Internet users • Paying Internet users and professionals • Advertisers
	Key resources • Open source platform • Technology infrastructure • Algorithms • Copyrights • Human team		**Channels** • Desktop, tablet, mobile (App store) • Word of Mouth for awareness and evaluation	
Cost structure • Platform development costs, sales costs, marketing costs, distribution costs, cost for payment processing fees, other operating expenses, etc.		**Revenue streams** • Professional subscriptions with a fixed monthly charge • Advertising revenues		

Fig. 3.5 Fictive example of a business model canvas regarding a social media tool

on paper, but it needs to be adapted until the organization can prove that it works. Such testing can also include a learning phase, with first iterations between customer discovery and customer validation, and then moving up to customer creation and even company building. In this respect, innovative organizations can create a dedicated Lean Start-Up to do experimentation with quick development cycles in so-called SCRUM sprints (i.e., each with a duration of a few days or weeks). Whether digital innovation happens with or without a Lean Start-Up, the idea behind a business model canvas is that organizations should constantly try new ideas as small experiments and learn from them. For instance, Google™'s search engine also frequently tries small changes in its layout to verify if users will click more on online ads, based on data feedback. Other major innovation companies are Philips™, Amazon™, Microsoft™, and IBM™, among others.

Since digital transformations are challenging and new technologies are appearing quickly, proper change management efforts are equally needed. More specifically, an organizational culture may hinder the realization of a digital business model, for instance, due to slow decision-making, employees' fear to change, a focus on technology rather than truly rethinking work, a lack of understanding of operational issues, etc. Nonetheless, emerging technologies give ample opportunities to innovate social media tools. Some examples of expected transformations are:

• AI-driven decision-making based on voice-and-face recognition, chatbots, or self-driving cars.

- AI-driven voice searches, with SEO focusing more on long-tail keywords and detailed search phrases.
- AI combined with IoT for connecting devices in a virtual assistant.
- VR and AR for shifting social media features.
- Blockchain technology for highly secure applications to prevent fraud and ensure security during transactions with customers, partners, or other stakeholders.

3.3   Monitoring and Evaluating a Social Media Strategy

Once a social media strategy is determined, it should be constantly evaluated (i.e., during its execution as well as afterward) and redirected, if necessary, by taking corrective actions. Hence, this section deals with the performance of social media initiatives, and particularly the (new) metrics to monitor the effectiveness or the returned value of social media initiatives.

Although the SMART rule for KPIs and social media tactics facilitates this evaluation phase, many organizations and scholars do not agree on what to measure when evaluating social media initiatives (Shay and Van Der Horst 2019; Silva et al. 2020). Some have a limited interpretation and only evaluate the social actions based on web analytics (e.g., the number of "likes" or "shares"), while others also evaluate the corresponding business actions and outcomes (i.e., the actual performance in business terms).

- Examples of performance metrics based on **web analytics** are activity (i.e., how many clicks?), velocity (i.e., how many messages spread over time?), attention (i.e., how long do visitors stay on the corporate website?), participation (i.e., how many members, topics, and comments?), tone (i.e., was the message positive? See Chap. 7), qualitative analytics (i.e., what did they say?), impact (i.e., what did they do? Influencers?), etc.
- Examples of performance metrics based on **business outcomes** are frequency (i.e., how much did the number of sales transactions increase per month?), reach (i.e., how many new customers?), yield (i.e., how much did the average transaction value increase?), etc.

The present section shows that both interpretations are valid and should complement each other. For instance, people who like or follow an organization's social media pages do not necessarily visit the corporate website nor buy the organization's products or services. The performance of social media initiatives should cope with measuring both social actions (by means of web analytics, see Sect. 3.3.1) and business actions (see Sect. 3.3.2).

3.3.1 Monitoring Web Analytics and Social Media Analytics

Web analytics and social media analytics in particular focus on social actions. Some problems still exist for organizations to find appropriate social media metrics, such as:

- Different authors propose different social media metrics.
- The entire impact of social media initiatives (i.e., on-site and off-site) may be difficult to grasp, e.g., actions on other sites or other social media tools are not always accessible for monitoring purposes (i.e., which makes social media intangible to some degree).
- Qualitative metrics (e.g., the tone of social media posts or the degree of customer engagement) are more difficult to measure than pure quantitative metrics (e.g., the number of "likes," "shares," or comments).
- Some social media initiatives (e.g., SEO) rather need a long-term perspective.
- Etc.

Given these potential monitoring problems, organizations should clearly define the KPIs and tactics in their social media strategies in order to find appropriate metrics. Meanwhile, organizations can profit from the original overview of possible social media metrics by Hoffman and Fodor (2010), classified along different social media types and different business goals (albeit limited to brand awareness, brand engagement, and word of mouth).

Many monitoring tools currently exist that automatically generate statistics by collecting, analyzing, and reporting on social media data. Some tools can even be used for free. However, human beings are still needed to select those statistics that provide relevant information for a specific organization (out of a large list or a dashboard). In other words, statistical information should be customized and interpreted, because managers tend to be only interested in a summary of relevant information that is ready to be used. The IT department frequently helps other departments in monitoring social actions, because of the so-called 10–90 rule, i.e., "for every €10 or 10% of time spent on web analytics and social media monitoring tools, €90 or 90% of time is required for a human being (i.e., IT and/or business analyst) to customize and interpret the statistics, and to provide insights into the performance of social media."

For instance, Fig. 3.6 shows one monitoring output (from a larger dashboard) that distinguishes nonpaid search traffic from direct traffic for two websites (see Chap. 6 on SEO). The graph uncovers for a manager (i.e., in business terms) that website B generally has more website traffic than website A (i.e., ranging between 500 and 1000 visits for website B and between 0 and 500 visits for website A). While the nonpaid search traffic and direct traffic for website B seem to evolve equally, website A appears to profit more from nonpaid search traffic than from direct traffic. This information indicates that SEO pays off for website A, but remains lower than for website B. Website A may benefit from additional investments in SEO. Website A

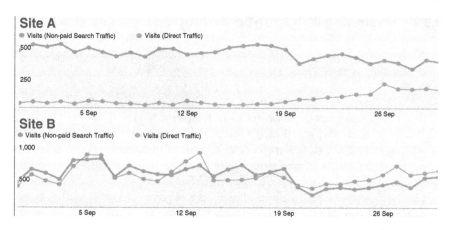

Fig. 3.6 An example of a monitoring output from a dashboard (Google™ and the Google™ logo are registered trademarks of Alphabet™ Inc., used with permission)

may also continue to stimulate direct traffic by means of online ads and viral campaigns (see Chap. 4), among others.

An example of a free monitoring tool is Google™ Analytics (http://analytics. google.com). Its dashboards give the organization insights into the way visitors use the corporate website, from which other websites they navigate to the corporate website, and whether they return. Some metrics in Google™ Analytics are the number of website visits, the number of page views, the average time on a website, the percentage of new visits, etc. In addition to the metrics shown in dashboards, Google™ Analytics allows us to generate standard reports and customized reports.

Furthermore, productivity applications such as Google™ Alerts (http://www. google.com/alerts) (see Sect. 2.2.9) can be used to monitor what is said about the organization and its products and services on the Internet and on social media. In this case, an organization will be notified by email as soon as new search results are available that mention one or more of the defined keywords (e.g., keywords such as "supply chain management" or "IT security").

Some social media tools also provide a monitoring tool with anonymous data (e.g., the number of people who shared Facebook™ posts, tweets, or YouTube™ videos). Examples of monitoring tools are Facebook™ IQ Insights tools or Twitter™ Grader.

Next, an organization can decide to use more advanced monitoring tools (which are usually to be paid). Such monitoring tools will be discussed in more detail for social CRM (Chap. 5).

3.3.2 Monitoring Business Outcomes and ROI

While monitoring tools primarily focus on social actions, an organization should not forget to monitor the outcomes of the related business actions.

Different traditional approaches exist to measure business performance in general, such as general metrics for (1) financial performance (e.g., sales growth, stock market return, ROI), (2) operational performance (e.g., market share, introduction of new products or services, and the quality of existing products or services), and (3) effectiveness performance (i.e., related to stakeholders, such as suppliers, clients, shareholders, governments, and pressure groups) (Venkatraman and Ramanujam 1986). To some degree, the general performance metrics also apply to social media investments, albeit depending on the corresponding social media strategy. Although translating social media initiatives into financial business terms is required to comprehensively evaluate the strategic results, this effort is not evident for managers (Michopoulou and Moisa 2019). Therefore, we position social media initiatives as investments in order to evaluate them similarly to typical investments.

Return on investment (ROI) is the ultimate business performance metric for an organization and therefore discussed in many management books. It can be used to evaluate the effectiveness of an investment or to compare the effectiveness of a number of different investments (such as social media investments). The standard formula of ROI is as follows (and if multiplied by 100, ROI is expressed as a percentage):

- **ROI = [(Revenue or gain from investment − costs of investment)/(Costs of investment)].**

In this formula, the revenue typically refers to the conversions (e.g., the number of Internet users who respond to an organization's call to action and convert online content or website visits into desired actions, such as actual sales, registrations for a corporate newsletter, etc.), while the costs strongly depend on the type of investment (e.g., the pricing model for an online ad; see Chap. 4).

Before making a social media investment, the expected ROI should be calculated based on the expected revenue and costs, and the organization should only invest if the ROI is positive or higher for this investment than for other, similar investments. Once a social media initiative is finalized, its ROI should be recalculated based on the actual revenue and costs in order to reevaluate its actual effectiveness. Consequently, an ROI calculation is similar to a cost-benefit analysis (i.e., a priori and a posteriori).

Organizations may experience difficulties with concretizing the revenue and costs in the ROI formula. For instance, revenue can be quantitative or qualitative (e.g., improved communication among employees, higher customer satisfaction, or brand awareness), with the latter being more difficult to measure (Khan et al. 2020; Silva et al. 2020). Some organizations use pre- and post-surveys as an alternative to ROI calculations. Nonetheless, surveys also face typical problems regarding the concretization of variables, the sample size, statistical significance, etc.

Additionally, some websites and papers report on different formulas to specifically calculate a so-called social media ROI (Khan et al. 2020; Silva et al. 2020). Such formulas add an element in the numerator of the traditional ROI formula, such as (1) plus the number of new customers (e.g., in the context of an online ad or viral campaign), (2) plus employee retention (e.g., in the context of internal social media initiatives and training), or (3) plus customer engagement or idea generation (e.g., in the context of social CRM). We must, however, note that ROI is inherently a financial metric (not a social media metric) which should express financial returns and revenue rather than the number of visitors, customers, employees, or ideas (although the latter may lead to the former). We thus strongly encourage the reader to follow the traditional way of calculating ROI. In other words, monitoring and measuring social actions (Sect. 3.3.1) differ from monitoring and measuring business actions (this section). For instance, an organization that invests a certain amount (let us say €X) in a social media initiative will be interested in the amount of money that it gets in return (€Y) rather than the amount of "likes," "followers," or website visitors. The latter do not necessarily represent prospects. Consequently, even if a "social media ROI" calculator presents a positive value, the traditional ROI can still be negative. For instance, for an initiative resulting in thousands of "likes," the organization could still experience a real negative ROI based on the costs of the full-time equivalents working on social media tools.

In sum, the metrics for social actions and business actions strongly depend on the associated social media strategy, which in turn depends on the organizational strategy. Social media initiatives can also be integrated with offline efforts. Nonetheless, whether an investment concerns online and/or offline efforts, it is paramount to monitor its ROI and to take actions on the results in order to improve.

3.4   Takeaways

An organization can apply the general principles of strategic management to social media in order to take advantage and create business value. If an organization wishes to use social media, it should first verify whether social media can contribute to the business objectives and derive particular social media strategies from the organizational strategy. For instance, similar to strategic management, an internal and external social media audit and a typical SWOT analysis can help prepare for social media strategy setting. To evaluate the social media strategies, an organization should attach more importance to business actions and ROI than to social actions, and take into account the specific problems to measure social media performance.

Thus, an organization should keep the bigger picture in mind, because a successful use of social media depends on determining, executing, and evaluating SMART social media strategies. In this chapter, the reader learned never to use social media without thinking about social media strategies that fit the organizational strategy and never to use social media without monitoring. The other chapters in this book elaborate on possible initiatives to execute a particular social media strategy. Such initiatives can be more marketing related (e.g., online ads and viral campaigns in Chap. 4) or more IT related (e.g., SEO in Chap. 6 and business intelligence with big data analytics and engineering in Chaps. 7 and 8). Other initiatives can primarily deal with human resources (Chap. 9), the organization's finances (Chap. 10), or legislation and policies (Chap. 11). Nonetheless, as social media should be used to help realize business objectives, they require a multidisciplinary approach, involving multiple organizational departments (see, e.g., Chap. 5 on social CRM).

3.5   Self-Test

- Read the following story, and reflect on what elements are good or rather bad ideas from the perspective of social media management.
  - [On a Monday morning at the coffee machine]
  - **Jane**: Hi Anna. How was your weekend? I saw some amazing pics of you on Instagram™.
  - **Anna**: Yes, it was great! I went to a bachelorette party, and it was awesome. Did you also see that picture after the "dinner in the dark"?
  - **Jane**: Hilarious! Wish I was there. Maybe we should also start using Instagram™ to promote our company products. Every serious business uses social media, so we should too.
  - **Anna**: I totally agree. This can be fun. Wait, I will quickly create an Instagram™ account. What shall we post?
- Do you think all organizations should use social media? Please motivate your choice.
- What does the abbreviation KPI stand for? Describe how and why it is important for a social media strategy.
- What does the abbreviation SMART stand for? Describe how and why it is important for a social media strategy.
- Analyze the social media strategy of a particular organization, based on the approaches explained in this chapter.
- Compare and evaluate the social media use of two organizations, based on publicly available information. Comment on the differences and similarities, and make suggestions for improvement. Also try to explicitly distinguish their social actions and business actions, and potentially reflect on their evolutionary journey from lower to higher social media maturity levels.
- Navigate to the corporate home page of an organization and try to detect which social media types and tools it uses. Have a look at its mission statement and check whether you can link some social media initiatives to it.
- Explain business model innovation.
- Explain how Start-Up organizations are linked to business model innovation.
- Think about a social media tool, and try to explain its business model by filling out the related canvas.
- What are the possibilities and problems to measure the performance of social media initiatives?
- Explain the differences and similarities between social media performance and traditional business performance?
- What does the abbreviation ROI stand for? Describe how and why ROI is important to social media.

Bibliography

Almquist, E., Senior, J., & Bloch, N. (2016). The elements of value. *Harvard Business Review, 94*(9), 46–53.

Burch, S. (2018). *Senator, we run ads: Hatch mocked for basic Facebook question to Zuckerberg.* Retrieved July 27, 2021, from https://www.thewrap.com/senator-orrin-hatch-facebook-biz-model-zuckerberg/

Euchner, J., & Osterwalder, A. (2019). Business model innovation. An interview with Alex Osterwalder. *Research Technology Management, 62*(4), 12–17.

Gerber, J. (2017). *How to prototype a new business.* Retrieved July 27, 2021, from https://www.ideou.com/blogs/inspiration/how-to-prototype-a-new-business

Hoffman, D. L., & Fodor, M. (2010). Can you measure the ROI of your social media marketing? *MIT Sloan Management Review, 52*(1), 41–49.

Jacob, A., & Teuteberg, F. (2019). Development of a social media maturity model for logistics service providers. In: Abramowicz, W., & Corchuelo, R. (Eds.). *Business information systems* (LNBIP 354), pp. 96–108, Springer, .

Khan, G., Mohaisen, M., & Trier, M. (2020). The network ROI. Concepts, metrics and measurement of social media returns (a Facebook experiment). *Internet Research, 30*(2), 631–652.

Kaplan, R. S., & Norton, D. P. (1996). *The balanced scorecard.* Harvard Business School Press.

Michopoulou, E., & Moisa, D. G. (2019). Hotel social media metrics: the ROI dilemma. *International Journal of Hospitality Management, 76*, 308–315.

Osterwalder, A., & Pigneur, Y. (2013). Designing business models and similar strategic objects: The contribution of IS. *Journal of the Association for Information Systems, 14*(5), 237–244.

Pour, M. J., & Jafari, S. M. (2019). Toward a maturity model for the application of social media in healthcare. The health 2.0 roadmap. *Online Information Review, 43*(3), 404–425.

Safko, L. (2012). *The social media bible: tactics, tools, and strategies for business success* (3rd ed.). Wiley.

Shay, R., & Van Der Horst, M. (2019). Using brand equity to model ROI for social media marketing. *International Journal on Media Management, 21*(1), 24–44.

Silva, S. C., Duarte, P. A. O., & Almeida, S. R. (2020). How companies evaluate the ROI of social media marketing programmes: Insights from B2B and B2C. *Journal of Business & Industrial Marketing, 35*(12), 2097–2110.

Venkatraman, N., & Ramanujam, V. (1986). Measurement of business performance in strategy research: A comparison of approaches. *Academy of Management Review, 11*(4), 801–814.

Vial, G. (2019). Understanding digital transformation: A review and a research agenda. *Journal of Strategic Information Systems, 28*(2), 118–144.

Wang, Y., Rod, M., Ji, S., & Deng, Q. (2017). Social media capability in B2B marketing: Toward a definition and research model. *Journal of Business & Industrial Marketing, 32*(8), 1125–1135.

Online Advertising and Viral Campaigns

4

This chapter focuses on two possible social media initiatives to execute a social media strategy, namely, online advertising and viral marketing campaigns. The chapter does not intend to elaborate on the general marketing-related aspects of ads and campaigns, but clarifies the elements typical to an online context. Regarding online ads, the chapter particularly explains the different pricing models and the bidding process. Besides tips and trips for starting and monitoring online ads, the reader learns about legislation related to online privacy and cookies for enabling personalized or targeted ads. The problem with online advertising is, however, that an abundance of ads can lead to people who try to avoid ads or who become blind for ads. Therefore, the chapter explains some alternatives as well as how viral campaigns can be a solution to ad avoidance or ad blindness by relying on mouth-to-mouth communication. Also, the rising importance of influencers is discussed. Finally, tips and tricks are given for viral marketing campaigns.

This chapter covers two topics that are primarily marketing related, namely, online advertising and viral campaigns. Both topics are subsequently discussed (Fig. 4.1).

Teaser Question
- What do cookies and social media have in common?
- How do I know what you did last night?

© The Author(s), under exclusive license to Springer Nature Switzerland AG 2022
A. Van Looy, *Social Media Management*, Springer Texts in Business and Economics, https://doi.org/10.1007/978-3-030-99094-7_4

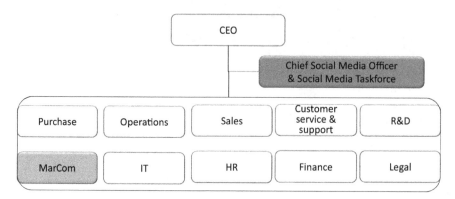

Fig. 4.1 The multidisciplinary approach of online advertising and viral campaigns

4.1   Online Advertising

4.1.1   Introduction to Online Advertising

One possibility for a social media strategy is to consider online advertising. Many online advertisements (ads) appear nowadays on websites, social media tools, or search engine results pages. The space for (paid) ads is usually indicated with a special icon or a title such as "Ads" or "Sponsored links" which is a disclosure of relationship to inform the Internet user that its content differs from regular web content and that it may influence the reader's behavior (see Chap. 11 on legal and ethical issues in social media).

Online ads can take many sizes, ranging from very small to very large. Some ads have a lot of text, while other ads are rather represented by text with a picture or a moving object and possibly with music. Some ads just appear on a website or a social media tool that the Internet user visits and still allow him or her to browse the web content. Nonetheless, an increasing number of blocking ads appear which oblige Internet users to look at their content (e.g., with a message such as "*Your video will play in 5 s*") or even to take action (e.g., with a button such as "*Go to the website*").

Ads are not only present on individual websites. Also, search engines (e.g., Google™, Bing™, or Yahoo!™) frequently sell space for ads to organizations. Chap. 6 will explain that search engine advertising (SEA) is part of search engine marketing (SEM), together with search engine optimization (SEO). Nonetheless, this chapter is broader than ads in search engines.

Ads may or may not be linked to the web page's content. Similarly, search engine results pages mostly show ads that depend on the keyword in the search query of a particular Internet user. For instance, if a user looks for information about a certain keyword (e.g., "smartphone"), then the ads are usually linked to that keyword (e.g., shops that sell smartphones). Such ads that are shown on relevant web pages or alongside relevant search results are called "personalized," "contextual," or "targeted" ads. Online advertising is able to offer a more personalized way of advertising compared to traditional (i.e., offline) ads.

Furthermore, ads can also be sponsored in a "content network." This means that web masters can collaborate and simultaneously offer their ad space to organizations. An organization's ad may then appear on multiple websites. A content network thus refers to a collection of websites or web content (e.g., an online newspaper or a blog) which frequently display targeted ads, namely, ads that are to some degree related to the content of that web page or to the interests of the website visitor. This type of advertising differs from strict search ads (i.e., ads on search engine results pages) in the sense that Internet users do not necessarily look for information by means of inserting a keyword in a search query. A content network is usually coordinated by an intermediate actor or a so-called ad server vendor (more information is available in this chapter).

Additionally, targeted ads can be considered as positive for the Internet user (i.e., including a higher probability of getting more relevant or interesting ads) and the organization (i.e., with a higher probability that people who see the ad will also click on the ad and thus reach the corporate website). Nonetheless, this chapter also discusses **privacy** drawbacks, as personal information is needed for some types of targeting (besides looking at the actual web page content), e.g., revealed by browser cookies, by collecting personal information on different social media tools through social engineering, or by profiling in social networks (see Chap. 8 on social network data).

4.1.2 Defining Online Advertising

Table 4.1 summarizes some important differences between online ads and traditional (offline) ads in the mass media.

Table 4.1 shows that social media and the Internet are characterized by a faster dissemination of information and allow more direct interaction with (potential) customers (e.g., by means of input fields in an ad which can request the home address or email address of an Internet user). Moreover, online ads always display or

Table 4.1 A comparison between online advertising and traditional advertising

Online advertising	Traditional advertising
Paid marketing initiative on the Internet or social media	Paid marketing initiative on the traditional mass media (e.g., radio, newspapers, magazines, television)
Higher efficiency expected, because of: • Fast dissemination of information possible • Interaction possible (e.g., input fields in the ad) • Niche audience possible (e.g., customized by geography, demography, hobby)	Better privacy protection

contain a direct link to the corporate website, so all information is only one click away. Further on, based on personal information (e.g., earlier search results, previous website visits, or the user's social media profiles), more personalized ads are possible (e.g., customized based on the user's hobbies, interests, location). For instance, when an Internet user lives in Ghent (i.e., to be derived from social media or an IP address), one is more likely to see ads with local offers in the neighborhood of Ghent rather than offers in Paris, New York, or Chicago. Similarly, an Internet user is likely to see more ads that are related to previously visited web shops. For instance, browser cookies can reveal that one looked for stopwatches in an online shop, resulting in a higher probability of seeing ads for stopwatches on other websites. The same applies to hobbies and personal interests. For instance, if an Internet user frequently visits websites on fishing, searches for keywords related to fishing or if the personal social media profiles reveal that one likes fishing, then this person is more likely to see ads related to fishing. This customization can result in a higher efficiency, because people are more likely to respond to ads that are relevant to them.

In general, different forms of customization or **targeting** exist for online advertising, such as:

- Targeting related to the web page that shows ads (e.g., contextual or content-related targeting, prime-time targeting).
- Targeting related to personal social media profiles or data from the computer of the Internet user who visits a web page that shows ads (e.g., sociodemographic targeting, geographic or geo targeting, behavioral targeting).

Based on the previously discussed opportunities, it is to be expected that an organization's budget for online ads will increase, while the budget for traditional ads is likely to decrease. Nonetheless, television still remains a big competitor for social media.

As an illustration, the following categories show that online advertising is broader than social media advertising:

- **Text ads**. Textual ads that are frequently based on the user's search keywords in search engines or on the content of a specific web page.
- **Display ads or banner ads**. Ads which combine text with graphical images (e.g., using pop-ups, buttons, or screen savers) and which are possibly similar to traditional ads.
- **Classified ads**. Small text ads presented by product category (e.g., classified postings in newspapers or magazines).
- **Rich media ads**. Ads that look like television commercials (e.g., with audio, video, or other animation or interaction).
- **Referrals or lead generation ads**. Ads that appear in an advertising network which serves as a lead generation device.
- **Sponsorship ads**. If an organization sponsors a third-party website, it can usually show its ads on the sponsored site too.

- **Email ads**. Ads that appear in direct electronic messages (and which inherently differ from social media ads).

Other classifications exist, for instance by focusing on static web ads (e.g., text ads or classified ads), animated web ads (e.g., display ads), and interactive web ads (e.g., rich media ads).

Independent of the categorization, the main content-related difference between online ads is whether text is accompanied by graphical elements. In the first case, the ads merely contain text without visuals or moving objects, while the second case is more graphical to attract the attention of Internet users by means of display ads or rich media ads. Those graphical elements can be static, with input fields or with rich media.

In general, Internet users tend to experience text ads as less annoying than display ads or rich media ads, because visuals typically attract more attention and thus risk disturbing more the regular browsing activities. Particularly, as Internet users are initially not looking for ads, text ads are more discrete than ads with moving objects that can catch the eye in a more disturbing way.

When taking a closer look, online ads typically contain similar elements: (1) a short and attractive title (e.g., circa 25 characters), (2) a short description (e.g., circa 35 characters), images or other animation, and (3) a direct link to the corporate website (e.g., circa 35 characters).

> An online advertisement (or online ad) is an organizational marketing message that is published on the Internet or social media tools, following a specific pricing model. It ultimately tries to manipulate the users' behaviors in favor of desired business actions.

Online ads should contain a link to the corporate website in order to stimulate a certain business action, e.g., selling a product or service and subscribing to a newsletter. However, the link should be well considered. For instance, the ad of a particular shop can directly navigate to the web shop instead of the corporate homepage, because visitors are more likely to bounce and leave the website without conducting any business action if they have to look for relevant information themselves. In the example of an ad to subscribe to a newsletter, the link may directly navigate to the subscription page instead of the homepage. Or a better alternative would be an input field for the user to subscribe in the ad itself in order to save an extra click.

4.1.3 Pricing Models for Online Advertising

As advertising should serve specific business objectives, organizations can spend a certain amount of money on online ads. The price organizations are willing to pay usually depends on their total budget and on the relevance of the corresponding business objective (e.g., which may be higher for sales than for subscriptions to a newsletter).

Although some online ads can be free, the vast majority are paid ads. It is important to know that the online advertising prices are not stable and usually depend on a bidding process (Decarolis et al. 2020; Maillé and Tuffin 2018). Similar to an auction, space for ads is rather sold to the best bidder or using an alternative auction format. More specifically, the online ad bidding market can apply different action formats, such as generalized second-price (GSP) auctions and Vickrey–Clarke–Groves (VCG) auctions. VCG is characterized by complex payments with price externalities (e.g., Facebook™ auctions), whereas GSP follows more simple rules (i.e., in which the highest bidder gets the first slot but pays the price bid by the second-highest bidder, etc., as usually followed by search engines).

In other words, organizations usually cannot buy ad space, but they can only bid. In particular, the price per ad may depend on factors such as the demand for ad space, potential reach of ad space, the keywords, and the location on a web page (among others), namely:

- **Demand for ad space**. If many organizations wish to show an ad at the same time, then the price per ad is likely to increase.
- **Reach of ad space**. The more visitors, users, or accounts a publisher has (e.g., a search engine, blog, or other social media tools), the higher the requested price for online advertising.
- **Keywords**. The price per ad can also increase if many ads are linked to the same keyword (e.g. if many competing ads use "smartphone" as a keyword). Choosing the right keywords is particularly important for targeted (e.g. contextual) ads.
- **Location on a web page**. Eye-tracking research (i.e., using an eye cam) has investigated how people generally look at a web page. It turned out that people tend to look more at the upper part of a web page and particularly the upper left corner. This most viewed area is thus the ultimate space for ads and therefore more expensive.

Given the high costs that can be linked to online advertising, an organization should decide beforehand (1) on the maximum amount of money to be spent and (2) on the pricing model (e.g., maximum 40 cents per click). Particularly, a **pricing model** determines when the organization (i.e., advertiser) needs to pay per ad (Maillé and Tuffin 2018).

Common pricing models are:

- **Pay-per-view**. An advertiser pays for each unique user view of the ad (i.e., per appearance or per impression). Alternatively, an advertiser can pay per 1000 impressions of the ad (i.e., **pay-per-mille**).
- **Pay-per-click**. An advertiser pays each time a user clicks on the ad and is redirected to the corporate website.

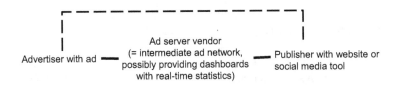

Fig. 4.2   The actors involved in online advertising

- **Pay-per-action (or pay-per-performance).** An advertiser pays each time a user clicks on the ad and completes a transaction or business action (e.g., ordering products, completing a form, registering for a newsletter).

But other pricing models also exist:

- **Fixed cost.** An advertiser pays one fixed amount of money, independent of the performance outcomes.
- **Pay-per-visitor.** An advertiser pays per visitor of the corporate website, independent of the ad.
- Etc.

Nonetheless, the concrete bidding processes vary and can depend on diverse factors. For instance, a higher ad position not only depends on the bid but can also depend on the quality of the content in the ad and the content on the landing page (i.e., the corporate web page that has a direct link in the ad). Given an online ad auction's complexity, organizations can also delegate their bids to intermediate marketing agencies specialized in online ad bidding (Decarolis et al. 2020).

Figure 4.2 shows the typical actors involved in online advertising. It concerns the organization as an advertiser (and, if applicable, its ad delegate), the web master as a publisher, and possibly an intermediate ad server vendor in case of a content network (see Sect. 4.1.1). The bidding process can be managed in a direct way (i.e., dashed line) or an indirect way (i.e., solid line).

As the prices for online ads strongly depend on a bidding process, one can also talk about a "bidding war"among organizations or advertisers. An organization's bid is the budget that it is willing to spend, which should not be higher than the maximum budget to be spent. As shown in Fig. 4.2, bidding wars can be directly organized by the publisher who sells ad space, e.g., the owner of a website, a blog, or other social media tools. Particularly, the business models of those social media tools offering free user accounts are likely to rely on advertising or selling client information to third parties instead (see also Chap. 8 on social network data). For instance, organizations can directly contact Facebook™ for advertising purposes (see https://www.facebook.com/business/). However, more frequently, an intermediate ad server vendor coordinates the bidding process (e.g., in a content network such as Google™, Yahoo!™, or AOL). As Google™ is the largest search engine worldwide (see Chap. 6), it also dominates the market of online advertising as an ad server vendor. One of the advantages of working with an intermediate actor or popular social media tool is that they frequently provide access to dashboards with real-time statistics related to the ad (e.g., how many times the ad was shown, how many clicks).

During a bidding process or bidding war, an organization can try to **negotiate** about the pricing models. Furthermore, ads in **top positions** are usually more expensive (e.g., at the top of a website or first in a list of ads). The main reason is illustrated by eye-tracking research, as previously explained. For instance, the more clicks are expected, the higher the pay-per-click will be. On the other hand, more clicks may also result in more people who conduct the desired business action. However, such business outcomes remain unsure as users also take into account the quality of the ad's content and the corporate website, besides merely the ad's position. For instance, a difference can be made between prescreening information (i.e., the ad's position) and post-screening information (i.e., the content). Consequently, one may wonder whether ads in top positions are still profitable. They can be expensive (e.g., €10 per click for ads in top positions that use popular keywords), while the business outcomes do not necessarily follow. For some organizations, it might be better to target ad space that directly comes after the top positions (Resnick and Albert 2014).

A final remark regarding the price of online advertising deals with **click fraud**, which is especially important for a pay-per-click pricing model. Click fraud refers to an abuse of clicking on a certain ad, without any interest in the corporate content or website. For instance, an unethical use of ads is clicking on ads for fun and immediately leaving the corporate website without looking at the content (i.e., deliberate bouncing; see Sect. 4.1.5). If the organization agreed to pay a certain amount per click, then the advertising costs will increase without corresponding business outcomes. Moreover, when professional clickers are hired to increase the profit for a publisher or an ad server vendor, click fraud becomes a real situation of business fraud and thus illegal.

4.1.4   Starting Online Advertising

The steps to launch an online ad are very similar to offline marketing and will not be discussed in this book. Instead, this section draws the attention to those elements specific to online advertising.

- **Determine your target audience and its needs**. Similar to offline marketing, an organization should understand its target audience. This understanding can deal with demographic and geographic questions (e.g., which types of persons are part of the target audience and where do they live) but also lifestyle (e.g., how they live), their future needs, etc.
- **Determine an online advertising strategy**. The purpose is to promote an organization and its products or services, and this by taking into account the needs of the target audience. An organization should strategically think through the content of its ad and where it will appear.

Table 4.2 Different types of keywords

Type of keywords	User's phase of purchase
Generic keywords	Many Internet users tend to look for generic keywords, but rather for raising awareness than for actually buying a specific product or service (Example: "cell phone")
Nonbrand product or service keywords	When the user is looking for a specific product or service, but not yet for a specific brand. Especially in this phase, ads may play an important role to drive website traffic (Example: "smartphone")
Branded product or service keywords	When the user is looking for a specific brand and considers buying one or another product or service of that brand (Example: "Samsung™")
Core brand keywords	When the user is aware of and considers buying a specific product or service of a specific brand (Example: "Samsung™ Galaxy S")

- **Fill out the online parameters for the ad**. A publisher or ad server vendor will probably ask the organization to fill out some parameters for the ad, depending on the determined needs and location of the ad. For instance, Google™ Ads (previously AdWords) can be used for both ads in the Google™ search engine and ads in a content network. It typically asks the advertiser about the campaign name, a location, a language, a budget (e.g., €5 per day), the targeted websites, etc.
- **Determine relevant keywords**. Keywords are relevant to characterize the ad and to allow targeting. Internet users typically choose keywords depending on their phase of purchase. Particularly, Table 4.2 shows that Internet users will rather use generic keywords for raising awareness and brand keywords for more complex searches when considering buying a specific product or service.

Furthermore, when determining relevant keywords, the following considerations can be taken into account:

- As many Internet users search for generic keywords (Table 4.2), many organizations also want to characterize their ad with such keywords (e.g., "travel" or "marketing"). As generic keywords have become expensive in the bidding process, an organization should consider whether it can **avoid using generic keywords**. For this purpose, advertisers can consult dedicated websites to know the most popular keywords, e.g., Google™ Trends.
- People usually search with **two or more keywords** or with a **sentence**. It is better to choose for a keyword such as "book airline ticket" than just "travel" or "airport." For more information on keyword statistics in search engines, see https://www.keyworddiscovery.com/keyword-stats.html.
- A distinction is usually made between **primary keywords and secondary keywords** (i.e., which support the primary keywords). For a primary keyword such as "book airline ticket," a corresponding secondary keyword can be "tips for booking airline tickets in advance in economy class for someone else."
- It is better to **avoid keywords with multiple meanings** in order to avoid confusion, leading more relevant people to the corporate website. For instance,

Table 4.3 The use of dynamic keywords

Dynamic keyword	Explanation
{keyword:}	No capitalization; all words are in lower case
{Keyword:}	Only the first word is capitalized
{KeyWord:}	Every word is capitalized
{KEYword:}	Every letter in the first word is capitalized
{KEYWord:}	Every letter in the first word and the first letter of the other word(s) are capitalized
{KEYWORD:}	Every letter is capitalized

Table 4.4 An example of an ad with dynamic keywords

Text ad with dynamic keywords	Ad shown for a search query on chocolate bars	Ad shown for a search query on lollipops
Title: {KeyWord: Candy}	Chocolate Bars	Lollipops
Description: We sell {KeyWord: Candy}! Free shipping.	We sell Chocolate Bars! Free shipping.	We sell Lollipops! Free shipping.
URL http://www.candy.eu/ {KeyWord:Candy}	http://www.candy.eu/ ChocolateBars	http://www.candy.eu/ Lollipops

it is better to avoid the keyword "bill," because that keyword can refer to a banknote, an invoice, or a proposed law.

- An organization should also **avoid using brand names** of other (competing) organizations in order to act in an ethically correct way.

- **Finalize the text of the ad**. The content of the ad can be finalized similar to traditional advertising, e.g., including an attractive title, a call to action regarding the desired business actions, and possibly with an informal writing style to identify with the user. Typical for online advertising is the use of dynamic keywords, i.e., keywords that are literally replaced by the search keyword of the Internet user. The advertiser can, however, still decide how to format the dynamic keywords in the ad (see Table 4.3).

- Table 4.4 illustrates how dynamic keywords generally work. For instance, a candy shop can use a search engine to display a text ad with dynamic keywords. If someone uses that search engine to look for information about candy (e.g., chocolate bars or lollipops), then the ad will adapt its content and refer to the exact words of the user in order to make the ad more personalized and thus more relevant to the user.

4.1.5 Monitoring Online Advertising

Chapter 3 already indicated the importance of constantly monitoring social media initiatives (e.g., online ads). It was shown that an organization does not launch social media initiatives for no reason. Instead, it tries to create value in terms of certain business actions (e.g., product selling or brand awareness). Therefore, also business actions should be monitored (besides the social actions) in order to evaluate whether the efforts pay off. This section elaborates on the way online ads can be monitored. Particularly, once an ad is launched, different (social and business) metrics can be used to evaluate its performance. Examples of metrics to be monitored are as follows:

- **Number of impressions.** First, it is important to know how many times the ad is shown, expressed as the number of impressions or appearances of the ad (e.g., based on particular keywords). This social metric is rather used to calculate other metrics.
- **Click-through rate = [(# clicks)/(# impressions)].** This social metric expresses how many times people clicked on the ad in order to reach the corporate website (thus after viewing the ad). This percentage is calculated by the number of clicks on an ad divided by the number of impressions. The average click-through rate is, however, very low.
- **Bounce rate = [(# visitors who immediately left the website after clicking on the ad)/(# total visitors who reached the website after clicking on the ad)].** Another social metric specifies the percentage of visitors who enter the corporate website and bounce (i.e., directly leave the website) rather than continue viewing other pages of the same website.
- **Conversion rate = [(# goal achievements after clicking)/(# clicks)].** The fourth metric is a business metric and refers to conducting a desired business action after clicking on the ad. It measures the relative number of visitors who convert casual content views or website visits into desired actions (e.g., sales or newsletter subscriptions), based on a subtle or direct request from marketers, advertisers, or content creators (i.e., in this case, after clicking on the ad). Also, this metric is a percentage, as it also takes into account the total number of clicks.
- **Return on investment** (ROI; see Sect. 3.3.2). ROI is the ultimate business metric to evaluate the performance of online advertising. In order to predict the ROI of different ad alternatives, a pretest can be used.

4.1.6 Legislation Related to Online Advertising

The introduction section of this chapter already referred to personalized or targeted ads, their advantages, and the risk for privacy drawbacks. The purpose of showing ads that align with the user's personal Internet history is only possible if personal data are stored to some degree (e.g., data on previous search queries or social media profiles). The question, however, remains which personal data are stored, how they are used afterward, by whom, how they can be corrected, etc. Consequently, this section looks at legal issues to protect the personal data of Internet users and social media users in particular.

Every user reveals personal information by using the Internet and social media, either intentionally or unintentionally. Some websites (e.g., http://browserspy.dk/) illustrate which data can be easily and automatically retrieved when visiting any other (i.e., regular) website. Examples are data about the user's location and time zone, computer system, browser information (e.g., whether one uses Explorer™, Chrome™, Firefox™), the fonts installed, the programs installed, etc. It is thus worth checking such dedicated websites, and the reader might be surprised of what one reveals by visiting any regular website.

Such personal information is revealed via so-called cookies. Cookies are data (i.e., in small text files) from a website that are stored in the user's browser (e.g., on computers or mobile devices) (European Commission 2021). When the user revisits the same website afterward, the cookies are reused (e.g., language settings, passwords, or content of an online shopping cart or wish list). Based on such cookies, a website can "remember" your actions and preferences. While most browsers support cookies, Internet users can also set their browsers to decline cookies or they can delete cookies manually.

Different classifications exist to distinguish cookie types, such as based on (1) duration, (2) provenance, and (3) purpose (European Commission 2021; GDPR.EU 2021).

Two cookie types are based on duration:

- **Session cookies**: temporary cookies that expire after a website visit or once the browser is closed (e.g., a shopping cart).
- **Persistent cookies**: cookies that are saved until they are erased manually or automatically after an expiration data (e.g., log-in or language settings).

Two cookie types relate to provenance:

- **First-party cookies**: cookies put on a user's computer by the website one has visited.
- **Third-party cookies**: cookies belonging to an external provider with access to the first-party website (e.g., belonging to a social media tool that is present on another website via a share button, or belonging to an advertiser or analytic system).

Finally, four cookie types are based on their purpose:

- **Strictly necessary cookies**: first-party cookies that are essential for using a website session (e.g., shopping cart details).
- **Preference cookies**: functionality cookies to let a website "remember" functional choices (e.g., language preference, username or password to authenticate, region-based information, such as for local weather reports).

- **Statistics cookies**: anonymous performance cookies about how a user visits a website in order to improve that website's functions (e.g., which pages and links are used), and which are mostly first-party cookies (or third-party cookies but with exclusive use for the website owner).
- **Marketing cookies**: persistent cookies for tracking a user's online activity for marketing purposes (e.g., targeted ads or to limit how many times a user sees the same ad), and mostly for third-party provenance.

Especially the third-party, persistent, and marketing cookies are most likely to trigger users' concerns about privacy abuse because they can contain much information about one's online activities, preferences, and locations, and for which the chain of responsibility is more complex (European Commission 2021; GDPR.EU 2021). More specifically, cookies are frequently used to determine which ads best fit the needs of an individual user and thus facilitate personalized or targeted ads by providing information on which websites the user visited before, which search queries were previously launched, etc. The following example illustrates how cookies can be used for online advertising.

A few months ago, I was looking for a stopwatch because I decided to start running (or at least to give it a try). Therefore, I looked for stopwatches in an online shop. Afterwards, other websites that I visited (i.e., which were not related to the same topic) suddenly showed ads on stopwatches of that specific online shop. This means that the other websites made use of my browser cookies and thus knew that I had visited a particular shop and looked for stopwatches.

In response, Internet users and social media users are protected by traditional (data) privacy laws that exist per country, in the European Union (EU), in the United Nations (UN), etc. (Wikipedia 2021b). Such laws usually stipulate that personal data can only be stored if necessary or with the user's permission.

Subsequently, we elaborate on EU initiatives that complement each other, namely the "e-Privacy Directive," "General Data Protection Regulation" (GDPR), and "e-Privacy Regulation."

Since 2002, the EU has a specific **"e-Privacy Directive"** concerning the processing of personal data and the protection of privacy in electronic communication (Directive 2002/58/EC) (EUR-Lex 2002). This EU Directive (2002, amended in 2009) is also called the **"cookie law,"** which stipulates how browser cookies can be used and which types of cookies require prior informed consent from the Internet user. The EU "cookie law" distinguishes nonessential cookies from essential cookies. It allows us to store cookies that are **essential or strictly necessary** for a good working of the website (e.g., order details). However, for all other (**nonessential**) cookies, prior informed consent of the Internet user is required (e.g., language settings or passwords). In order to enable this cookie use within the EU, the Internet user should approve on each particular website that it can store nonessential cookies. For instance, in order to be conform to the EU "cookie law," the websites or specific web pages can show a message such as *"This site/part of the page uses cookies to offer you a better browsing experience. Find out more on how we use cookies and how you can change your settings. (Button) I accept/refuse cookies."* Consequently, some websites also started to request permission in the sense of an acknowledgment or rather an opt-out consent (i.e., when cookies are used as long as the user does not refuse), such as *"This website uses cookies. For more information, please visit the Privacy and Cookies Policy. Click here to acknowledge and hide this message"* or *"By using our services, you agree to our use of cookies."* This directive, however, needed to be incorporated into national law by each EU Member State, and thus requiring a legally binding replacement by an EU regulation at a later moment.

Meanwhile, as more emerging technologies are entering a digital economy, the risks for privacy abuse are also growing (e.g., if sensitive customer data held by organizations are stolen or abused). Therefore, the EU has decided to further strengthen its privacy legislation for better specifying how data collecting and processing organizations should use and protect EU citizen's data by means of the **"2016/679 Regulation,"** called **"General Data Protection Regulation" (GDPR)** (EUR-Lex 2016). The European Parliament officially adopted GDPR in 2016, after which a 2-year adoption period started. As of May 25, 2018, GDPR is enforceable and applies to all organizations involved in processing EU consumer data when selling goods or services, even when the data collecting and processing organizations are located outside the EU. Such data include personal data that can identify a particular EU citizen (e.g., name, data of birth, ID number, phone number, email address, username or online identifiers, IP address, and location data). Data also cover sensitive information (e.g., sexual orientation, health data, payment data, political opinions, and one's overall social identity). GDPR applies to both online and offline data and is thus broader than the "cookie law" (i.e., with the latter remaining valid as well). This means that also organizations, website owners, and social media tools need to comply with GDPR whenever they deal with EU citizens.

Some of the GDPR restrictions are as follows, for which fines can be up to €20 million or 4% of the organization's annual global turnover (i.e., whichever is higher). For instance, in case of a data breach, organizations need to notify their customers of any risk within 72 hours. Upon request, EU customers can also obtain confirmation whether their personal data are being processed by a specific organization and they can get a free electronic copy of their personal data. Their "right to be forgotten" is also confirmed by GDPR (see Chap. 1). Organizations need to have a safe and secure administrative record, whereas large organizations (i.e., with more than 250 employees) and public authorities also need to appoint a data protection officer.

From the perspective of social media management, GDPR makes the "cookie law" more strict with two major extensions. First, GDPR confirms that **only strictly necessary** cookies can be processed without consent in order to enhance the functionality and personalization of a website, even though GDPR is stricter by requiring organizations to be more **transparent** on how cookies can be used and deleted. Secondly, for **other** cookies, organizations can only use EU personal data with the **actively expressed** consent of consumers, which means that implicit consents are no longer allowed. In this respect, GDPR is no longer accepting implied consents, pre-checked boxes, or passive notifications such as *"you accept cookies by reading this message."* Moreover, data collecting and processing organizations should write consent requests with **clear and simple** language, and it should be clear how to withdraw consent.

These GDPR restrictions will be accompanied by an upgraded "cookie law" (i.e., from an e-Privacy Directive (2002) into an intended **"e-Privacy Regulation"**) to complement GDPR for online privacy topics, such as for streamlining the use of electronic consents and browser cookies but also for guiding online tracking and electronic marketing. Although it was originally intended to come into effect in 2018 as well (i.e., together with GDPR), the "e-Privacy Regulation" is still to be expected when writing this book's edition (Cookiebot 2021; Wikipedia 2021a). You can read more details, including a chronological overview, at https://cms.law/en/deu/insight/e-privacy

Furthermore, besides granting/refusing permission or in non-EU countries, Internet users can also protect their online privacy by removing and/or blocking cookies in their browsers themselves.

While cookies can still be considered as a rather friendly way of serving the Internet users, other tracking techniques exist that can more severely damage a user's online privacy. Examples of such tracking techniques that risk privacy abuse are as follows:

- **Tracking pixels (or web beacons).** Invisible objects (of circa 1x1 pixel) on a web page or email that check whether the user has viewed that page or email, when and from which computer. They are thus typically used by organizations or other third parties for web analytics, page tagging, or email tracking. In contrast to cookies, web bugs cannot be easily blocked by the user and can be abused for sending spam or for advertising purposes.
- **Clickstream data (or a click path).** Data log of how Internet users navigate through a website (e.g., duration of a website visit, IP address of the user, the websites that lead to the current website, the sequence in which web pages are visited) based on the sequence of selected hyperlinks or "clicks through." It is typically used for analyzing web activity, software testing, market research, or even employee productivity when performing a specific task. Legislation is generally more unclear for this tracking technique.
- **Malware** (i.e., malicious software, also called spyware, adware, or viruses of hackers). Programs that pretend performing a simple service in a pop-up or an ad (e.g., weather forecasting), but are intentionally designed as Trojan horses to dupe the user. These applications are difficult to remove or to uninstall and remain illegal. So be careful when an unexpected pop-up suddenly appears and never click on its content (because it might be a virus).

More legal and ethical issues on social media can be found in Chap. 11.

4.1.7 Challenges for Online Advertising

The problem with online advertising is that numerous ads appear online. One of the greatest challenges for online advertising is called "ad blindness" or "ad avoidance." This means that Internet users tend to avoid ads, independent of the ads' content or quality.

According to the original study of Cho and Cheon (2004), three types of ad blindness exist:

- **Affective avoidance**. People who intensively dislike something are more likely to increase that negative feeling. Similarly, if Internet users detest ads, then this negative feeling will only increase by seeing more ads. Consequently, they do not pay attention to the content of ads anymore.
- **Cognitive avoidance**. People may intentionally ignore ads due to negative beliefs associated with ads. For instance, if you think spiders are creepy animals and you know that spiders are frequently present in the corner of a certain room, then you might just walk through that room without looking at the corner (and possibly see a spider). The same applies to online ads. Users know that ads are present on a certain web page, but they do not pay attention to the ads and just browse the visited page. In contrast to affective and behavioral avoidance, the feelings or behavior of people will not change, but users do not pay attention to ads and focus on the web content instead.
- **Behavioral avoidance**. This type involves avoidance actions which differ from a lack of attention. For instance, if you know that a certain web page always shows ads on top of its page, then you might automatically scroll down the page to avoid the ads. This action of scrolling down refers to a behavior in order to avoid the content of ads.

The study of Cho and Cheon (2004) also showed three main reasons to explain ad avoidance or ad blindness:

- **Perceived goal impediment**. Because ads interrupt a goal-directed use of the Internet. For instance, if you are reading an online newspaper, then your goal is to know what is going on in the world and not to buy something (e.g., a watch, shoes, clothes).
- **Perceived ad clutter**. Because the excessive number of ads is irritating. People might just get annoyed by an abundance of ads and particularly if many ads appear on the same web page.
- **Prior negative experience**. Because of a perceived lack of utility or lack of incentive to click on ads. For instance, if you already clicked on ads which did not add any value to you or which seemed to abuse your privacy, it is likely that you will not click anymore on other ads (based on this negative experience).

Meanwhile, these types and reasons are still mentioned in recent literature (Bang et al. 2018; Youn and Kim 2019). Additionally, the psychological reactance theory

(Brehm and Brehm 1981) helps explain this "experience reactance" when users' freedom is limited once they recognize the manipulative intent of online ads, resulting in skepticism and negative feelings or attitudes toward online ads (Youn and Kim 2019). In addition, similar determinants were investigated in other studies, such as perceived personalization, ad irritation, and privacy concerns. Nonetheless, privacy concerns are not necessarily linked to prior experience and can also include a preventive way of handling. Furthermore, ad avoidance can be caused by ads irrelevant to the user, skepticism toward the ad or the advertiser, the expectation of a negative experience, etc.

Besides these causes of ad blindness, other explanatory factors might exist (e.g., age, gender, income, privacy concerns) (Lu et al. 2018). For instance, maybe more men than women avoid ads, or older people and with a higher income? Consequently, more research is needed to fully explain the broad concept of ad blindness and to verify the extent to which the factors for avoiding traditional ads also apply to online advertising.

4.1.8 Alternatives to Online Advertising

In response to the challenges for online advertising, both Internet users and organizations can choose for some alternatives or solutions.

First, an Internet user can take some actions to block online ads. If IT savvy, one can adapt the hosts file of one's operating system (i.e., a file that maps hostnames to IP addresses). Otherwise, browser extensions or plug-ins have been developed that help block online ads by free open-source or commercial software (e.g., https:// adblockplus.org/ or http://www.admuncher.com/).

Another solution (but from the perspective of organizations or publishers of advertisements) is to make online ads more personalized (i.e., more targeted) and with more interaction.

Other views on online ads relate to sponsored geolocation alternatives, such as 360-degree virtual tours in cities and indoor maps. A 360-degree virtual tour is based on a series of pictures that look similar to a video. This way, an Internet user can look inside hotels, restaurants, and other organizations. Such organizations, however, pay for having their interior being shown on Google™ Maps or consult specialized IT organizations (e.g., Poppr: https://www.poppr.be/). For an impression of a virtual tour, see https://www.poppr.be/virtualtour/mechelen360/index.html?startscene=0& startactions=lookat($-48.12,23.99,108.66,0,0$).

On the other hand, indoor maps can be used for online advertising. Based on magnetic fields, a supermarket or shop can improve its targeted ads and mobile ads. So when a customer actually walks in a physical building, one will receive product promotions on one's mobile phone just by walking along the different products. For instance, if you walk along pasta dishes, you will receive online ads for promoting those pasta dishes. Ads kindled by indoor mapping are also increasingly used in airport stores. Similarly, based on turbocharged predictive analysis, organizations become able to better predict someone's geographical route to send targeted ads.

Another application based on geolocation is weather-based geolocation advertising (e.g., to receive ads for cold drinks on a hot day but ads for raincoats on a rainy day).

Finally, the literature presents viral campaigns as a possible solution to ad blindness or ad avoidance. For this purpose, the next part of this chapter elaborates on viral marketing campaigns.

4.2   Viral Campaigns

4.2.1   Introduction to Viral Campaigns

Besides online ads, social media strategies may consider the creation of viral marketing campaigns. A viral campaign can be seen as a possible solution to an abundance of advertisements because it relies more on personal communication. Particularly, people are unable to process an excessive number of ads, resulting in a higher probability of ad avoidance or ad blindness (see Sect. 4.1.7). In such situations, personal communication and recommendations of relatives or peers tend to prevail. For instance, in Sect. 1.1.1, this book described the evolution from "*word* of mouth" toward "*world* of mouth," given the impact of social media on offline relationships and businesses. It was told that people tend to believe their acquaintances more than an organization that tries to sell its products or services. Nowadays, people can talk to, make referrals to, and influence others around the globe. Consequently, when seeing viral campaigns as a solution to ad avoidance or ad blindness, viral campaigns can be described as "word-of-mouth advertising."

4.2.2   Defining Viral Campaigns

In contrast to traditional mouth-to-mouth communication, a viral campaign is inherently created by an organization to promote itself as an employer (e.g., for e-recruitment), its brand (e.g., for brand recognition), or its products and services (e.g., for product awareness, higher sales). Particularly, a viral campaign can help create awareness, trigger interest, and generate sales or product/service adoption.

> A viral campaign is an organizational marketing message that heavily relies on unsolicited (i.e., not upon request) mouth-to-mouth communication through the Internet and social media tools. After creation, the message goes viral by spreading exponentially out of the organization's control.

Once a viral campaign is launched, the receivers become new senders, and the message continues to spread, independent of the organization (e.g., mouth-to-mouth communication). In other words, while the original source of a marketing campaign is inherently an organization, people can start sharing the campaign. The literature

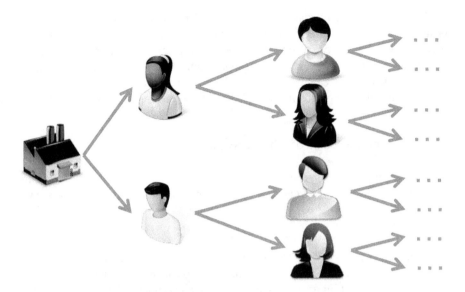

Fig. 4.3 Defining viral campaigns

compares the intention of a viral campaign with an "echo," a "virus," or a "viral infection" that can spread exponentially and create a buzz or contagious talk (Arjona-Martín et al. 2020). The term "viral" is the adjective of the noun "virus" (i.e., derived from the Latin, where the word refers to "poison"), but has been adopted for online content that rapidly becomes popular or well known. Kaplan and Haenlein (2011) correctly defined a viral marking campaign as "electronic word-of-mouth whereby some form of marketing message related to a company, brand, or product is transmitted in an exponentially growing way—often through the use of social media applications" (p. 253). Dadwal (2020) adds that it is an electronic extension of word of mouth (eWOM), as well as a strategy and a process for encouraging Internet users to let a message's exposure and influence exponentially grow.

The way a successful viral campaign works is an illustration of the "social ripple effect"(see Sect. 2.1.1). Figure 4.3 illustrates how a viral campaign typically works. As shown on the left, it starts with an organization (otherwise it would concern customer conversations or criticism instead of a campaign; see Chap. 5 on social CRM). When people receive the message, they can share it in their network. As such, the receivers become new senders. When those people also start sharing the content, a social ripple effect is created. Similar to an "echo," a "virus," or a "viral infection," the message can reach an increasing number of people as it exponentially moves to the right of Fig. 4.3. This characteristic implies that the success of a viral campaign strongly depends on how many times the corporate message is shared (i.e., and which defines at which level Fig. 4.3 actually stops).

Another implication for a viral campaign is that the message (once launched by an organization) continues to spread, independent of the original source. The latter implies that people may change the content before sharing. Such changes can be positive, e.g., to make the content more funny (resulting in even more shares). Nevertheless, changes can also be negative, e.g., if pressure groups turn the content into criticism with drawbacks for the organization. Before launching a viral campaign, an organization should be aware of the fact that it cannot control its corporate message once the campaign is launched (i.e., in contrast to online advertising).

4.2.3   Success Stories of Viral Campaigns

This section illustrates some successful viral marketing campaigns. We remind the reader that success not only depends on social metrics (e.g., the number of views, likes, comments, shares) but also on the realization of business objectives (e.g., conversions, ROI, branding).

- **Hotmail™ launch (1996)**. One of the first viral campaigns was launched by the electronic mail service of Hotmail™ in the 1990s, namely, during the upcoming use of the Internet. In order to obtain more email accounts, Hotmail™ automatically added a short message at the bottom of every outgoing mail: "*PS: Get your private, free email from Hotmail™ at http://www.hotmail.com.*" The message was an invitation for the mail recipient to join Hotmail™ too. The campaign can be called a success as 12 million users signed in within 18 months. Only recently, in 2013, Hotmail™ stopped existing and sold its mail service to Microsoft™'s outlook.com.
- **Blendtec™ (2006)**. The famous "Will it blend" campaign was launched by an organization that sells blenders. In order to show the power of the blenders, the organization recorded a series of videos in which household items (instead of food) are being blended, e.g., an iPhone™, an iPad™, a skeleton, super glue, and glow sticks. The YouTube™ videos are still available on a corporate website: http://www.willitblend.com/. The website also suggests some blending experiments that customers can try at home (i.e., by distinguishing the category "Try this at home" from "Don't try this at home"). For a direct link to a popular video that shows how an iPhone™ is being blended, see https://www.youtube.com/watch?v=qg1ckCkm8YI. Although a scientist seems to test the blender, the videos are part of a viral campaign created by the organization itself.
- **Mentos™ and Diet Coke™ (2007)**. Another notable YouTube™ video that refers to an experiment of scientists was launched to promote Mentos™ mints and Diet Coke™. In contrast to the "Will it blend" video, this experiment was initially not meant as a commercial campaign. Instead, the Discovery Channel program "MythBusters" (http://www.youtube.com/watch?v=LjbJELjLgZg) broadcasted an experiment for children that created large eruptions or geysers by dropping Mentos™ chewy mints in bottles of soda (e.g., Perrier™, Sprite™, classic Coke™, Diet Coke™). The scientists also explained the phenomenon by stipulating that a fountain of spray and foam comes out of the bottles based on an acid-based chemical reaction (i.e., as soda beverages are acidic). Although Coca-

Cola™ and Mentos™ had no part in creating the original video, their sales significantly increased. Afterward, viral campaigns were launched with the same scientists, among others (e.g., http://www.youtube.com/watch?v=hKoB0 MHVBvM&gl=BE), but now sponsored by the organizations involved.

- **#IceBucketChallenge (2014).** The ALS association created a successful viral campaign to raise awareness of the ALS disease and to encourage donations to research on ALS (https://www.als.org/stories-news/ice-bucket-challenge-dramati cally-accelerated-fight-against-als). The campaign challenged people to dump a bucket of ice-cold water on one's head and to nominate others for the challenge by means of social media and/or to donate money. In 2014, this charity campaign went international, many celebrities participated in the challenge (e.g., actors, politicians, football players, CEOs), and millions of dollars were donated to the association. In some countries (e.g., India), an alternative "rice bucket challenge" was introduced to give a bucket of rice to someone in need.

- **Gillette™ (2019).** This company for men's razors and shaving products initially launched a controversial #MeToo-related video to combat toxic masculinity, asking men to take responsibility in addressing sexual harassment and bullying issues by changing its traditional slogan from #TheBestMenCanGet to #TheBestMenCanBe (https://twitter.com/i/status/1084850521196900352). The brand also made a 3-year commitment to fundraising and donations to men's organizations. Although the campaign was meant to support the brand's value of corporate social responsibility in order to build trust and to support social change, the video received a lot of mixed reactions, including a wave of YouTube ™ downvotes, a potential brand boycott, and (above all) a heavy public debate. More specifically, this example of so-called outrage marketing triggered many people to talk about the brand, even celebrities, politicians, and human rights organizations. Consequently, a few months later, Gillette™ launched its #MyBestSelf video of a transgender man's first shaving, resulting in overall praise. This story can be seen as a success in terms of brand awareness, generating conversation, and positively replying to feedback.

- **e.l.f.™ (2019).** This cosmetics organization created a TikTok™ video for brand recognition with a call for users to post videos of their eyes, lips, and face with #eyeslipsface (https://www.youtube.com/watch?v=OAj9B2OvJwM). Also celebrities joined (unpaid), and the campaign organically spread to other social media tools (e.g., Instagram™, YouTube™, Twitter™). This was one of the first and most successful campaign on TikTok™, triggering more than 7 billion views, five million user TikTok™ videos, and 30 million music streams (outside of TikTok™) for the original music track used in the campaign (Movers+Shakers 2020). This company truly understood what young people like and share, and how it can take advantage of TikTok™.

- **Heineken™ (2020–2021).** This brewing company initially launched its #BetterTogether campaign for promoting celebrations with friends when spon- soring the UEFA Champions League and Formula1 in 2019. However, when the COVID-19 pandemic required international lockdowns in 2020–2021, Heineken™ changed its campaign to #SocialiseResponsibly in order to put health and safety first, including virtual events for safely gathering (e.g., a live-streamed concert, a "we'll meet again" film, and #BackTheBars local initiatives to safely reopen bars). Additionally, the brand donated €15 euro to the International Federation of Red Cross and Red Crescent Societies to help the most vulnerable people and countries during this pandemic. This example illustrates some alternative contents to be included in a viral campaign, combining online and offline results.

4.2.4 Tips and Tricks for Viral Campaigns

Before a viral campaign can become successful and thus an alternative to online advertising, it should be voluntarily shared and spread exponentially (i.e., similar to an echo, a viral infection, or a virus). The following goals can help satisfy this condition:

- Goal 1. Create content that people are eager to share (e.g., video clips, interactive games, e-books, images, text messages).
- Goal 2. Focus on trendsetters, namely, people who can influence others and who can start the sharing process.

The first goal implied by viral campaigns is related to the content of the corporate message. A message is more likely to be shared when it applies some factors to engage people, for instance:

- The message teases emotions (e.g., surprise, joy, sadness, anger, fear, disgust), such as being extremely funny or extremely sad (e.g., in the Mentos™ and Diet Coke™ example or the #IceBucketChallenge example).
- The message gives away free products (e.g., in the Hotmail™ example).
- The message gives advice that encourages ease of use (e.g., in the Blendtec™ example).
- The message is well targeted and contains highly relevant information to people (e.g., in the Hotmail™ example).

If such factors are absent, other factors can still stimulate sharing, such as:

- People already have a long-term relationship with the organization (e.g., with a bank).
- The message is about innovative products that make people curious (i.e., with curiosity being a type of emotion; see previous factor).
- People have less knowledge about the product or service themselves and are thus more likely to rely on word-of-mouth recommendations (i.e., shares).

These factors illustrate which content can be more engaging or more sensitive for sharing and can be kept in mind when creating a viral message.

Table 4.5 The main advantages and disadvantages of viral campaigns

Advantages	Disadvantages
Higher efficiency expected, because of: • Lower costs than (online) advertising as people (customers) voluntarily spread the message • Many people can be reached in a short period of time • Possible integration with other campaigns • Viral campaigns never stop • ROI can be monitored online	• Low control over content and timing • Sharing strongly depends on the goodwill of people • Possible miscommunication between cultures (e.g., humor)

Besides content that is more likely to be shared, some types of people are more likely to share. The second goal implied by viral campaigns is to reach those people who are generally more willing to share the corporate message. For this purpose, an organization can start by targeting groups of people who are considered as credible sources and able to influence others in order to start the sharing process. In particular, trendsetters or opinion leaders typically (1) have many people in their network to spread the message and (2) have such an impact on their network that other network members are more likely to share the message too (because people tend to listen to trendsetter). In terms of the theory on the diffusion of innovations (Rogers 2003), as discussed in Chap. 1, viral campaigns can be boosted by the "innovators," the "early adopters," and (to a lower extent) even the "early majority." An organization can try to reach these groups in order to indirectly reach the "late majority" and the "laggards" too. Synonyms for trendsetters are, among others (Kaplan and Haenlein 2011), (1) salesperson, i.e., who are very convincing for others to act; (2) mavens or evangelists, i.e., who are recognized as experts and like to share information; or (3) connectors, i.e., who have many people in their network and thus know many people to spread the message.

This chapter particularly described the advantages of viral campaigns, for instance, in response to ad avoidance or ad blindness. Nonetheless, Table 4.5 summarizes the main disadvantages or concerns that are linked to viral campaigns.

A first important disadvantage reminds the reader that an organization cannot control its content anymore once the message is spread. This means that people may change the corporate content before sharing, which can either be positive (e.g., more funny) or negative (e.g., when pressure groups or vocal minorities are active). Secondly, as viral campaigns are characterized by voluntary sharing, they strongly depend on the people's goodwill to share. For instance, as shown in Sect. 2.2.1 on community management, not all types of community members are active in sharing. Thirdly, the message of viral campaigns can be misunderstood due to cultural differences. For instance, humor or the notion of "funny" strongly differs between groups of people (e.g., a Muslim cartoon can be considered as funny or rather racist). Consequently, an organization should also consider such concerns when creating a viral campaign.

4.2.5   Alternatives to Viral Campaigns

Sect. 4.2.3 showed that viral campaigns are not limited to YouTube™ videos, and should be seen from the perspective of their business outcomes. Although viral campaigns are an ultimate solution to ad blindness (Sect. 4.1.7), they also face disadvantages (Sect. 4.2.4). Since especially starting a social ripple effect remains challenging, a sharing process can also be triggered by alternatives that are increasing in popularity. Following the alternatives to online ads (Sect. 4.1.8), we now explain alternatives to viral campaigns and which also heavily rely on "word of mouth," namely unboxing videos, influencers, and social media takeovers.

Unboxing videos are a first alternative to viral campaigns. It concerns videos showing how customers unpack items for the first time in order to see their reactions or to know their product reviews, either voluntarily or sponsored (e.g., testimonial advertising) (Evans et al. 2018). For instance, unboxing videos are frequently made for toys and electronic devices, but they can exist for almost all product categories (e.g., food, fashion, games). In terms of tips and tricks, successful unboxing videos can be creative and fun, but provide useful product information, explain different product features, and ideally be relevant year-round (i.e., in order not to limit the sharing period to, for instance, Christmas only).

Furthermore, influencers are gaining popularity on social media, leading to a significant increase in influencer marketing (Vrontis et al. 2021; Ye et al. 2021). Influencers are often celebrities, key opinion leaders (e.g., journalists, industry experts, academics), or self-made personalities, who can target any organizational sector. In line with Sect. 4.2.4, influencers are the trendsetters, innovators, or early adopters. They can work as bloggers, podcasters, and/or rely on regular social posts (e.g., Instagram™, YouTube™, TikTok™). Since most influencers are paid by the brands they are promoting (e.g., by fees or free products and services), they should also have a strategic business model in order to become the manager of their own company (Chap. 3). However, compensations can depend on multiple factors such as the social network (i.e., how many users can be reached), the extent to which they endorse a product or service, the success of their past endorsements, etc. Different influencer types exist, depending on their follower numbers, such as (Campbell and Farrell 2020):

- Celebrity influencers or "*the rich and famous*" (e.g., more than one million followers on a single social media tool).
- Mega-influencers or "*the everyday celebrities*" (e.g., more than one million followers on a single social media tool).
- Macro-influencers or "*the sweet spots*" (e.g., between 100,000 and one million followers on a single social media tool).
- Micro-influencers or "*the rising stars*" (e.g., between 10,000 and 100,000 followers on a single social media tool).
- Nano-influencers or "*the newcomers*" (e.g., fewer than 10,000 followers on a single social media tool).

Thus, the relevance of social media monitoring and evaluation for influencer marketing is confirmed (Chap. 3), as well as the link to an influencer's social network data (Chap. 8). Furthermore, one may think of different initiatives for influencer marketing. For instance, more recently, organizations start relying on social media takeovers (i.e., when someone temporarily takes over another account to create and share content, usually on behalf of a brand). Takeovers can be done by influencers, but also by customers for product awareness and social engagement, regular employees for the sake of employer branding, or students to promote a university. While takeovers can trigger a new and inspiring angle for community engagement with possibly an increased followers count due to cross promotion, such initiatives should also fit into a social media strategy, which is to be monitored and evaluated based on social actions and business actions (Chap. 3).

The abovementioned alternatives can still be sponsored by an organization for marketing purposes or they can be independent and based on users' initiatives. The latter should be closely monitored in terms of social CRM (Chap. 5) and opinion mining for assessing peer recommendations (Chap. 7). Otherwise, if any sponsoring is involved, this relationship needs to be disclosed (e.g., by using a hashtag such as #sponsored) (Chap. 11). Moreover, extra legal and ethical concerns arise when minors are targeted (as kids are an audience that needs extra protection against persuasive attempts) or engaged (as influencers, e.g., in terms of child labor conditions and compensation) (De Veirman et al. 2019). Anyway, such alternatives can perform well as people tend to believe peers more than organizations, resulting in a higher perception of neutrality, approachability, and credibility than typical viral campaigns or online ads.

4.3 Takeaways

To some degree, the general marketing principles of advertising and campaigns can be applied to an online context. Similar to traditional marketing and mass media communication, an organization takes the initiative to create online ads and viral campaigns (i.e., not customers, prospects, or Internet users). The content should also be attractive and relevant to effectively reach the target audience in order to satisfy the related business objectives and strategies, and to address ad avoidance or blindness.

Nonetheless, this chapter discussed some additional considerations concerning the specific context of the Internet and social media. For online ads, the target audience is not necessarily the mass of the people, but a more personalized approach is possible. As a result, online marketing faces more specific legislation, for instance, to protect a user's online privacy. Furthermore, an organization should reconsider how its online initiatives are monitored and how conversions can be encouraged, for instance, by using dynamic keywords, by adding input fields in the ad, or by strategically choosing the landing page (i.e., the corporate web page that has a direct link in the ad). Moreover, the bidding process of online advertising differs from traditional advertising and especially includes alternative pricing models. With regard to viral campaigns, the main challenge is to create online content that users are eager to share and to start targeting those users who can influence others to share (e.g., trendsetters) in order to stimulate the sharing process.

The subsequent chapter on social CRM (Chap. 5) differs from this chapter in the sense that communication is more solicited (i.e., on the initiative of Internet users, who can be customers but also prospects or anyone else) and/or more proactive (i.e., without a direct link to sales or profit). Hence, social CRM gives more opportunities to organizations to contrast with traditional marketing and mass media communication.

4.4   Self-Test

- How do you see the future of traditional ads versus online ads? Please motivate your choice.
- What is meant by "targeted marketing"in the context of online ads? Can you give examples?
- Can you distinguish text ads from banner ads? Can you give examples?
- Can you explain the pricing models for online ads? Which ones are most common and why?
- What is meant by a "bidding war"in the context of online ads? And how is a bid determined?
- Can you give examples of keywords that are typically more expensive in bidding wars for online ads? Why?
- What is meant by click fraud?
- What is meant by cookies? Why are they important in the context of online ads?
- To which degree is the privacy of Internet users protected from harm?
- Which metrics are frequently used to monitor online ads? Can you explain and calculate each metric?
- Why should organizations reflect on ad blindness? How can they tackle this problem?
- Do you also apply some type of ad avoidance yourself? Do you understand why other people are sometimes blind for online ads?
- Several authors have explained ad avoidance by means of multiple factors. In response, the literature proposes different solutions to address ad blindness. Elaborate on possible solutions to ad blindness, and explain how and why they can work.
- How can viral campaigns be a solution to ad avoidance?
- A current social media trend covers unboxing videos in which products are unpacked by customers. One example are Kinder Surprise egg unboxing videos, which are particularly loved by children. When can unboxing videos be considered as a viral marketing and when not? Explain the conditions for viral campaigns.
- Do you know the important elements that encourage a successful viral marketing campaign?

- Can you explain the success of alternatives to online ads and viral campaigns?
- Explain why social media takeovers can be successful. Compare this initiative to the advantages and disadvantages of online advertising and viral campaigns.

Bibliography

Arjona-Martín, J.-B., Méndiz-Noguero, A., & Victoria-Mas, J.-S. (2020). Virality as a paradigm of digital communication. Review of the concept and update of the theoretical framework (e290607). *Profesional de la información, 29*(6), 1–9.

Bang, H., Kim, J., & Choi, D. (2018). Exploring the effects of ad-task relevance and ad salience on ad avoidance: The moderating role of internet use motivation. *Computers in Human Behavior, 89*, 70–78.

Brehm, S. S., & Brehm, S. S. (1981). *Psychological reactance: A theory of freedom and control.* Academic Press.

Campbell, C., & Farrell, J. R. (2020). More than meets the eye: The functional components underlying influencer marketing. *Business Horizons, 63*(4), 469–479.

Cho, C.-H., & Cheon, H. J. (2004). Why people avoid advertising on the internet. *Journal of Advertising, 33*(4), 89–97.

Cookiebot. (2021). *EU cookie law – A right to privacy.* Retrieved July 31, 2021, from https://www.cookiebot.com/en/cookie-law/

Dadwal, S. S. (2020). *Handbook of research on innovations in technology and marketing for the connected consumer.* IGI Global.

De Veirman, M., Hudders, L., & Nelson, M. R. (2019). What is influencer marketing and how does it target children? A review and direction for future research. *Frontiers in Psychology, 10*, 1–16.

Decarolis, F., Goldmanis, M., & Penta, A. (2020). Marketing agencies and collusive bidding in online ad auctions. *Management Science, 66*(10), 4433–4454.

EUR-Lex. (2002). *Directive 2002/58/EC of the European Parliament and of the Council.* Retrieved August 18, 2021, from https://eur-lex.europa.eu/legal-content/EN/TXT/PDF/?uri=CELEX:32002L0058&qid=1627736553687&from=EN

EUR-Lex. (2016). *Regulation (EU) 2016/679 of the European Parliament and of the Council.* Retrieved August 18, 2021, from https://eur-lex.europa.eu/legal-content/EN/TXT/HTML/?uri=CELEX:32016R0679&from=EN

European Commission. (2021). *Cookies policy.* Retrieved July 31, 2021, from https://ec.europa.eu/info/cookies_en

Evans, N. J., Hoy, M. G., & Childers, C. C. (2018). Parenting "YouTube natives": The impact of pre-roll advertising and text disclosures on parental responses to sponsored child influencer videos. *Journal of Advertising, 47*(4), 326–346.

GDPR.EU. (2021). *Cookies, the GDPR, and the ePrivacy Directive.* Retrieved July 31, 2021, from https://gdpr.eu/cookies/

Kaplan, A. M., & Haenlein, M. (2011). Two hearts in three-quarter time: How to waltz the social media/viral marketing dance. *Business Horizons, 54*(3), 253–263.

Lu, Y., Qi, W., & Qin, J. (2018). Research on the memory of online advertising based on eye-tracking technology. *ICEB Proceedings*, 324–328, IEEE.

Maillé, P., & Tuffin, B. (2018). Auctions for online ad space among advertisers sensitive to both views and clicks. *Electronic Commerce Research, 18*, 485–506.

Movers+Shakers. (2020). *E.l.f. Cosmetics – TikTok.* Retrieved July 26, 2021, from https://moversshakers.co/elf-tiktok-challenge

Resnick, M., & Albert, W. (2014). The impact of advertising location and user task on the emergence of banner ad blindness: An eye-tracking study. *International Journal of Human-Computer Interaction, 30*, 206–219.

Rogers, E. M. (2003). *The diffusion of innovations* (5th ed.). Free Press.

Vrontis, D., Makrides, A., Christofi, M., & Thrassou, A. (2021). Social media influencer marketing: A systematic review, integrative framework and future research agenda. *International Journal of Consumer Studies, 45*(4), 617–644.

Wikipedia. (2021a). *ePrivacy regulation*. Retrieved August 2, 2021, from https://en.wikipedia.org/wiki/EPrivacy_Regulation

Wikipedia. (2021b). *Privacy law*. Retrieved August 2, 2021, from http://en.wikipedia.org/wiki/Privacy_law

Ye, G., Hudders, L., De Jans, S., & De Veirman, M. (2021). The value of influencer marketing for business: A bibliometric analysis and managerial implications. *Journal of Advertising, 50*(2), 160–178.

Youn, S., & Kim, S. (2019). Newsfeed native advertising on Facebook: Young millennials' knowledge, pet peeves, reactance and ad avoidance. *International Journal of Advertising, 38*(5), 651–683.

Social Customer Relationship Management

This chapter gives the reader a broader perspective on social media by discussing social customer relationship management (social CRM). Social CRM is the best example of a multidisciplinary social media approach, as it involves almost all departments in the organization. Instead of only contacting people with sales offers, the aim of social CRM is to build strong relationships with Internet users by giving them a positive experience of the organization's brand, products, and services. Ultimately, social CRM tries to turn an organization's social media connections into loyal customers and particularly brand advocates who influence others to like the organization (and only indirectly to buy the organization's products and services). This chapter discusses the use of social CRM and how it can generate business value. As a continuation of the previous chapters, some more advanced monitoring tools are presented for organizations to monitor and evaluate social media actions.

In contrast to other topics or chapters in this book, social CRM covers almost all departments in the organization. The typical departments that are directly linked to or have direct contact with customers are the MarCom (i.e., presales), the sales department, and the department for customer service and support (i.e., after-sales). Particularly, (1) the MarCom or the presales department organizes marketing initiatives, (2) the sales department actually sells products or services (possibly after marketing ads or campaigns), and (3) the after-sales department or a helpdesk answers customer questions, handles their requests or complaints, etc. (Fig. 5.1).

Besides these three departments, the chapter elaborates on other departments that can be involved in social CRM in order to illustrate that social CRM is the ultimate example of social media management as a multidisciplinary approach (see Sect. 5.4).

Teaser Question
- How can customers gain more power, even if this is sometimes to the detriment of businesses?

A. Van Looy, *Social Media Management*, Springer Texts in Business and Economics, https://doi.org/10.1007/978-3-030-99094-7_5

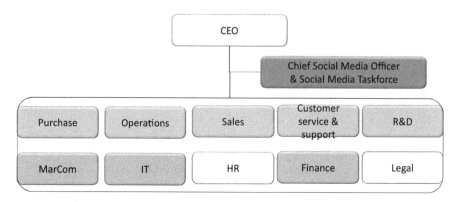

Fig. 5.1 The multidisciplinary approach of social CRM

5.1   Introduction to Social CRM

The term "social CRM "consists of two parts, namely, "social" and "customer relationship management" (CRM). Regarding the latter, some examples of traditional CRM deal with follow-up conversations by coupling information of the sales departments to the department of after-sales or customer service and support (e.g., example 1) and to the MarCom department (e.g., example 2).

- **CRM example 1.** After buying a product or service in an online shop (e.g., books or cinema tickets), the customer receives an email with a satisfaction survey.
- **CRM example 2.** After buying a product or service (e.g., clothes or a stopwatch), the customer receives an email with sales promotions for other related products or services of the same organization (e.g., shoes or jogging outfits).

The traditional view on CRM tries to combine all information about a specific customer into a single database in order to better serve customers in a more personalized way (although customers may dislike spam mails).

Additionally, possible triggers for social CRM are linked to online content. Some examples are as follows.

- **Social CRM trigger 1.** A customer is complaining about an organization and its products or services on a public social media tool.
- **Social CRM trigger 2.** People are publicly criticizing an organization's industry on social media.
- **Social CRM trigger 3.** An Internet user publicly posts a forum question related to the products or services of an organization.
- **Social CRM trigger 4.** An independent blogger posts a positive message about an organization and its products or services.

In contrast to Chap. 4 on online ads and viral campaigns, the direct triggers for social CRM are not necessarily initiated by an organization itself. Instead, the examples describe situations in which Internet users post online content that can highly affect a business or a brand and is thus worthwhile to monitor. Particularly, the first two triggers may have a negative impact on the organization involved, while the other triggers create new opportunities for that organization. Regarding the negative triggers, the organization can try to avoid crisis communication by listening to such negative messages in an attempt to better understand the customer needs. For instance, for an organization, it is important to know whether an angry customer also contacted the organization's helpdesk and whether the helpdesk responded properly (and if not, take actions). In sum, social CRM can help an organization identify and properly respond to (negative or positive) triggers on the Internet and social media and try to take advantage of them. It implies truly listening to customers and prospects, whenever and wherever they are, as well as responding, anticipating, and making commitments to improve products and services. In sum, social CRM is rather user driven than organization driven.

> Social customer relationship management (social CRM) is a multidisciplinary and user-driven approach to acquire but also retain customers, and to turn them into loyal and engaging customers. It focuses on collaboration rather than marketing or selling efforts. Social media tools help create mutually beneficial relationships between an organization and its (prospective) customers to stimulate positive customer experiences and ultimately brand advocacy.

A well-known example of social CRM is titled "United breaks guitars" (Wikipedia 2021b). In 2009, a customer of United Airlines™ made a video with a protest song to complain that the organization had broken his guitar without compensation. He posted the protest video online, which became a direct hit on YouTube™ and iTunes™ (see http://www.youtube.com/watch?v=5YGc4zOqozo). However, the song does not mention that the organization acted in accordance with its customer service policy. The customer's complaint was rejected because it did not comply with the stipulations (e.g., the complaint was not filed within 24 h). Still, the customer negotiated several months with the organization, resulting in two follow-up videos that went viral and a negative stock price effect for the organization. In response, the organization decided to apologize, to use the protest videos for internal training, and to change its customer service policy. The organization also donated a compensation to the music industry in an attempt to save its corporate image. On the other hand, the guitar manufacturer decided to offer the customer some free products in order to get even more publicity for the guitar's brand. In the end, both customers and organizations can learn from this example. First, the videos show customers how they can affect organizations in a rather respectful (instead of aggressive) way. Secondly, the videos confirm that organizations are currently facing another type of customers, i.e., who may easily raise their voice by means of social media. Thus, the "United breaks guitars" example shows that social CRM has become increasingly important given the rising impact of social media worldwide. Even today, the importance of social CRM is still frequently illustrated with this notable example. Moreover, from time to time, the related hashtag (#unitedbreaksguitar) becomes trending again for describing similar issues.

Alternatively, an airline company can also track passengers who check in through social media (e.g., Foursquare™/Swarm™) or who positively tweet about their flight. As an experiment, a company can check the publicly available social media profiles of passengers in order to know them better and to offer them a personalized gift (e.g., a voucher or a gadget related to their hobbies or interests). As a result, such passengers tend to post an additional positive message about the gift. In this example of social CRM, the promoters or fans of the organization can be identified, activated by a personalized gift, and turned into brand advocates (i.e., "super promoters" or "super fans").

The examples show that social CRM is about putting the individual customers first by converting (1) online **content** into (2) **conversations**, extending those conversations into (3) **collaborative experiences**, and then transforming those experiences into (4) **meaningful relationships**. In other words, social CRM tries to turn social media connections (e.g., fans and followers) into real customers and even brand advocates who make recommendations to others. Possible synonyms for social CRM would be "customer experience management," "customer-centric management," "fan relationship management," or "community relationship management."

This chapter on social CRM differs from the other chapters in this book by focusing more on direct and personalized communication with customers on a more individual basis, i.e., based on their actual behavior. While a chapter or book dedicated to traditional CRM would rather focus on a single database that centrally stores all customer information (instead of different databases per department), this chapter takes a broader perspective by adding social media conversations and customer collaboration to traditional CRM. Furthermore, social CRM reminds the reader that organizations should not use social media for marketing purposes alone but also to focus on better customer experiences by means of better or more innovative products and services, better business processes (i.e., internal way of working), better internal communication, etc. For this purpose, an organization should try to gain insight into the public conversations on social media and take advantage of the gained insight to continuously improve. Social CRM can contribute to a social or collaborative business (or an "enterprise 2.0"), namely, an organization that deeply integrates social media tools and related strategies in order to create business value.

5.2   Defining Social CRM

This section first elaborates on the meaning of customer relationship management (CRM), before turning to a definition for social CRM.

5.2.1 Traditional CRM

Traditional customer relationship management (CRM) is all about an organization's customers. Particularly, it takes a 360-degree view on customers to generate value for both the customers and the organization. The main goals of CRM are (1) finding and acquiring new customers, (2) retaining existing customers (and decreasing customer churn or attrition), and (3) turning customers into loyal or lifelong customers. These three goals are linked to a customer pyramid, as shown in Fig. 5.2. The top of the pyramid refers to emotional loyalty of (lifelong) customers toward an organization or brand (e.g., by offering them incentives for repeated purchases).

Moreover, traditional CRM is all about managing the organization's relationship with those customers. Relationship building is an important factor to explain why organizations win or lose customers and deals, which indicates that strong relationships are needed for doing business. Nonetheless, relationships should also be challenged, e.g., by teaching the customers about new opportunities or by tailoring the message to the customer needs. In general, the main reasons why Internet users participate in brand communities or corporate social media pages are for information, self-discovery, social integration, social enhancement, and entertainment purposes (Madupu and Cooley 2010). As relationships can be created for different purposes, organizations may also misinterpret the reasons why certain customers interact with them. For instance, customers can interact with organizations for sales offers that directly affect them, while organizations rather think those customers connect with them on social media for keeping up to date about products and services or for feeling connected in a community.

Customer relationships can be managed by aligning different departments in the organization and particularly those that are directly related to customers (i.e., MarCom, sales, customer service, and support). CRM is about creating a single database that comprises all customer information, instead of maintaining different

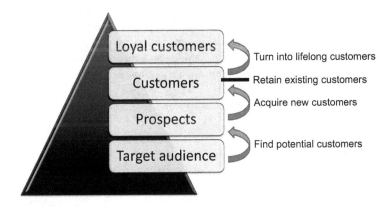

Fig. 5.2 The customer pyramid

Fig. 5.3 The traditional view
on CRM

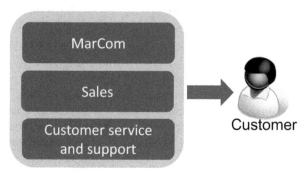

databases across departments with possibly inconsistent information. Such unique customer database can be used for diverse applications, such as:

- For contact management (i.e., saving the name, address, and phone number of customers only once in order to avoid inconsistencies between departments, e.g., when a customer moves or changes contact details).
- For managing transactions and money (i.e., centrally storing information about orders, invoices, warranty, inquiries, etc.)
- For managing potential customers (i.e., centrally storing information about prospects, leads, opportunities, etc.)

It follows that the original definitions of CRM (Marolt et al. 2015), for instance, refer to "a philosophy and a business **strategy**, supported by a system and a **technology**, designed to improve human **interactions** in a business environment" (Greenberg 2004, 2009, 2010: p. 414). The central constructs in this illustrative definition are indicated in bold, which emphasize that CRM is a strategy that is often supported by various tools and technologies (although, in theory, it can also be done manually, i.e., on paper if not using big data). The strategy is based on customer engagement and interactions, with transactions or sales being of secondary importance. However, many CRM definitions only implicitly focus on creating a mutually beneficial relationship between buyers and sellers, i.e., between an organization and its customers. Based on the literal meaning of the acronym "CRM," the traditional view on CRM seems to focus on managing customer relationships rather than engaging customers and providing them with a positive brand experience.

In sum, CRM in the strict sense is an integrated and customer-centric strategic approach for better understanding customers by focusing on the development and retention of customer relationships, for which social CRM can add important extensions (Arora et al. 2021; Marolt et al. 2015). As shown in Fig. 5.3, this traditional view on CRM rather emphasizes one-way communication between an organization and a particular customer. Such (personalized) communication primarily involves collecting data and information about particular customers in a single database (i.e., a CRM system) in order to better target individual customers through the pipeline of presales, sales, and after-sales.

5.2.2 Social CRM

When entering a digital economy, conventional CRM is increasingly modernizing into the notion of social CRM (or CRM 2.0) by also focusing on social customer engagement (Arora et al. 2021). The need for social CRM can be explained by today's information society. Particularly, the evolution from an "information asymmetry" to an "information democracy" has resulted in more empowered and well-informed customers who dislike one-way communication. For instance, customers can educate themselves by means of the Internet and social media connections worldwide. In addition, prospects can talk to existing customers, which may affect traditional presales, sales, and after-sales (e.g., requiring "connect-and-collaborate" marketing rather than "command-and-control" marketing). While Chap. 2 discussed the traditional marketing funnel in the context of social media, social CRM will extend AIDA with the necessity to turn customers into loyal customers (i.e., AIDAL or Awareness, Interest, Desire, Action, Loyalty). Further on, social CRM is needed as traditional CRM does not fully recognize the impact of influencers (e.g., contributors of user-generated content related to the organization's brand, products, or services, such as recommendations, peer reviews, product ratings, or competitive alternatives). The new social customer can use social media for communicating with acquaintances and strangers, for connecting with peers, for online purchasing, for reading and creating reviews or rankings of purchases, for online support, etc. Social CRM is relevant as customers also choose between competitors, products, and services based on personal experience, corporate brands, and recommendations from others (instead of only direct marketing ads or campaigns).

When looking at the meaning of "social CRM," the term "social" literally refers to social media as communication tools and social technologies in general (i.e., CRM 2.0; see Chap. 2 on Web 2.0). Social CRM thus concerns an extension of CRM that uses social media to capture customer information and to engage with customers (Al-Omoush et al. 2021). It integrates CRM with social media feeds and data and enhances online collaboration for the same goals, namely, (1) acquiring new customers, (2) retaining existing customers, and (3) turning customers into loyal or ideally lifelong customers. For instance, social CRM involves tracking user requests, checking social media feeds from CRM contacts, and posting supporting questions online, among others. Compared to CRM, social CRM also allows acquiring more emotional and behavioral insights about customers in order to facilitate more effective and efficient interactions (Al-Omoush et al. 2021). The ultimate goal is to foster customer relationships, better understand the customer needs, and create customer experiences that lead to repeated purchases.

However, a possible drawback of more personalized communication with Internet users is that some customers might risk feeling less important than other (more empowered) customers might. For instance, in the airline company example of the Introduction section in this chapter, other passengers may wonder why they did not get a gift (namely, because they did not post a message about that particular flight, even though they can be a fan or follower of the company too). In other words, not all customers are necessarily of equal value, which may, for instance, depend on the

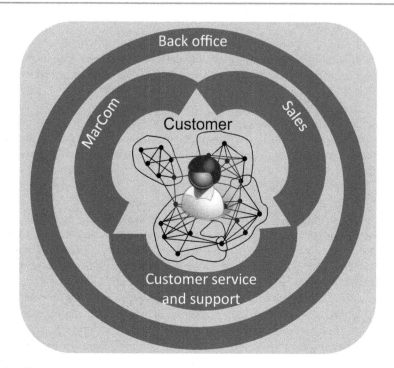

Fig. 5.4   The recent view on social CRM

budget a customer spends on average, on the number of one's social media connections and posts, etc. This issue of inequality will be further discussed in Sect. 5.6.

A generally accepted definition for "social CRM" is (Gamage et al. 2021; Marolt et al. 2015): "a philosophy and a business **strategy**, supported by a **technology** platform, business rules, processes and social characteristics, designed to engage the customer in a <u>collaborative</u> **conversation** in order to provide <u>mutually beneficial</u> value in a trusted and transparent business environment. It is the <u>company's response</u> to the <u>customer's ownership</u> of the conversation" (Greenberg 2004, 2009, 2010: p. 413).

As indicated in bold, this definition contains similar constructs as the CRM definition, namely, "strategy," "technology" (although, in theory, social CRM can also be done with a large physical social network, if not using big data), and "conversation" (or "interaction" in the traditional CRM definition). Mutual benefits can relate to building and strengthening trust, customer satisfaction, retention and loyalty, collaboration (e.g., ideation or co-creation for new product or service development), customer lifetime value and reputation management, but also lowering the cost of service, etc. (Arora et al. 2021; Marolt et al. 2015). The underlined constructs indicate some important refinements, emphasizing a stronger focus on the customers and their initiatives rather than a focus on the organization. Consequently, Fig. 5.3 is adapted by Fig. 5.4.

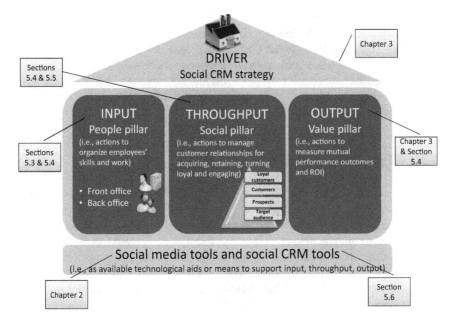

Fig. 5.5 A social CRM framework (partly based on the "social CRM house" of Malthouse et al. 2013)

In contrast to Fig. 5.3, Fig. 5.4 focuses more on positive customer experiences and brand advocacy (i.e., people influencing others to buy the organization's products and services), instead of pushing information to customers. While a particular customer was not part of the CRM system in Fig. 5.3, a stronger customer relationship and collaboration is visualized in Fig. 5.4 by putting the customer at the center of the organization. Social CRM takes advantage of the social media opportunities to create personal interactions with customers and prospects based on their needs instead of based on the organization's rules and business hours (i.e., social CRM occurs whenever and however the customers or prospects feel the need to interact). For instance, with social media, Internet users can set the hours themselves and choose their preferred communication channels. Given the central role of the customer in the organization and the interdependence between the organization and its (potential) customers, the social CRM system of Fig. 5.4 can also be called a social CRM "ecosystem," including the customer's network (i.e., the customer ecosystem) and the organization's front office and back office (i.e., the corporate ecosystem).

As an alternative view, Malthouse et al. (2013) present a so-called social CRM house to demonstrate the ultimate goal of an organization in terms of strategically applying social media tools and other tools (e.g., monitoring tools or more dedicated social CRM tools) to create mutual value. This metaphor emphasizes that social CRM is multidisciplinary, and thus a matter of everyone involved in the organization. In the middle of Fig. 5.5, we put social engagement as an addition to the traditional CRM goals. Tools serve as a foundation underlying those efforts.

As this metaphor of a "social CRM house" visually links this chapter to the strategic view taken in this book, we share a refined version to motivate the chapter's remaining structure. In addition, we organize Fig. 5.5 along the idea of driver-input-throughput-output to illustrate the typical way of working for defining, executing, and evaluating strategies (Fangfang et al. 2021).

5.3   Types of Social CRM

Although social CRM promotes a multidisciplinary approach, the typical CRM departments (i.e., MarCom, sales, and customer service and support) are closely linked to the customers. Therefore, they can act as a bridge between the organization on the one hand and the market on the other hand. In other words, these front-office departments interact with the market and should pass relevant information on to the back-office departments. Different types of social CRM can be distinguished, depending on which typical CRM (front-office) department is primarily involved, namely, (1) social marketing, (2) social sales, and (3) social service.

- Type 1. Social marketing if the MarCom is primarily involved.
  This social CRM type mainly aims at social marketing insight, rapid marketing response, and tracking online campaigns or events. For instance, deal-of-the-day websites (e.g., Groupon™) can successfully combine social marketing with social sales by regularly mailing local offers to their subscribers (e.g., deals at restaurants, retailers, or service providers). If these websites work with quantity discounts instead of direct sales offers, a deal will only become available if a certain number of people sign in for that specific offer in order to reduce the risks of investment. Such business models can be a social CRM success for the different parties involved: (1) the website owner keeps a certain amount of money that the customers pay for the voucher; (2) customers get a reduced price and can save money; and (3) the local partner organizations can attract new customers or use the offers for brand awareness. The latter is particularly interesting for SMEs or start-ups to spread the word. We mainly classify this example as social marketing since the deals generally emphasize a high reduction rate with low profit for the local partner organizations in order to convince people and create future sales opportunities.
- Type 2. Social sales if the sales department is primarily involved.
  This social CRM type mainly aims at social sales insight, rapid sales response, and proactive lead generation to find more prospects. For instance, online shops can successfully combine social sales with social service by creating a helpdesk or support group on social media tools. Besides answering questions, a social media-based helpdesk can show customer reviews or post links with information to their products or services that solved the problems encountered by the market, resulting in higher sales and extra support for the customers.

- Type 3. <u>Social service</u> if the department for customer service and support is primarily involved.
  This social CRM type mainly aims at social support insight, rapid service response, and stimulating brand advocates. For instance, an organization can decide to create and manage a focused social media tool itself (e.g., a branded social community) to enhance customer engagement. This initiative is particularly interesting if the organization is characterized by customers who are familiar with social media and IT in general and who like participating in communities (e.g., an IT-related company). For such organizations, a focused community as a social service can be a success with value for both customers and the organization. If the community is linked to a helpdesk ticketing system, support cases can be tracked and accessed at any time. Closed tickets of customers can also be documented within the community in order to give customers an incentive to use that specific community (instead of an external one). Finally, besides customers and helpdesk staff, back-office employees and subject matter experts can participate in the community as a way to strongly commit to the market and to the organization.
  Nonetheless, social CRM can also involve other (i.e., back-office) departments and go beyond marketing, sales, or service (i.e., front-office) initiatives. To emphasize the multidisciplinary approach of social CRM, additional social CRM types can help obtain social customer insight. For instance:
- Type 4. <u>Social innovation</u> if the R&D department is primarily involved.
  This social CRM type mainly aims at innovative insight or crowdsourced R&D (see also Chap. 10 on crowdfunding). For instance, Sect. 2.3 already talked about LEGO™'s brand community (https://ideas.lego.com/), in which users can launch ideas for product innovation through co-creation and ideation. Similarly, a brand community can invite Internet users for crowdsourcing, for instance, to submit ideas about product/service features, to brainstorm about or rate the submitted ideas, or to design products/services in collaboration with its customers via fora, contests, and polls. Another social innovation example is a "hackathon" (or hack marathon), i.e., an exploratory event or ideation contest in which people related to software development (e.g., computer developers, graphic designers, project managers) collaborate intensively on a short-time project to generate a solution to a predetermined problem, e.g., to build a proof of concept (Wikipedia 2021a). Also IT organizations (e.g., Google™, Yahoo!™, or Facebook™) regularly make use of external or internal hackathons for new product development or for solving security issues. For instance, for more information about Google™'s initiatives, see https://codingcompetitions.withgoogle.com/.
- Type 5–6. <u>Social collaboration</u> and <u>social customer experience</u>, which may also involve other departments (e.g., purchase or operations).
  On the one hand, external collaboration and customer experience can be facilitated by the typical CRM departments (i.e., by means of social marketing, social sales, and social service) or may have different business goals (e.g., social innovation, which is another social CRM type; see supra). On the other hand, social collaboration can also be internal (i.e., social media use within and across

the departments) or B2B (i.e., social media use with partnering organizations), with an improved internal way of working leading to better customer experience.

The refined typology suggests that social CRM types can be intertwined and rather serve as labels to name or classify social CRM initiatives. Therefore, the next section elaborates on the multidisciplinary approach of social media and clarifies in more detail the extent to which social CRM can create business value in the different departments of an organization.

5.4   Value Creation by Social CRM

The benefits of social CRM are primarily focused on increasing customer insight and engagement in order to drive business performance. Therefore, this section looks at value creation by social CRM and presents two value creation perspectives, namely, (1) based on interaction types and (2) department based.

Regarding the first perspective, Fig. 5.6 shows that social CRM intends to create value for both the market (e.g., customers and prospects) and the organization (i.e., with a front office and a back office). In particular, interaction generally happens between the market and the front office on the one hand and between the front office and the back office on the other hand (Harrigan et al. 2020).

The first interaction type in Fig. 5.6 is between the market and an organization's front office. Customers and prospects can get involved in social CRM by means of initiatives explained in Sect. 5.3 (e.g., social marketing, social sales, or social service). Such initiatives can be launched by the organization itself, but individual customers or prospects can also react to online or post messages that affect the organization or its industry (e.g., blog posts, reviews, ratings, questions, or complaints). As such, customers can get value from spontaneous reactions of social media connections and peers, as well as from gathering additional information about an organization and its products or services from the market in a minimum of time. Customers and prospects can save time and money by browsing the Internet and using social media in order to educate themselves or to raise their voice. For instance, before buying a product or service (e.g., a smartphone), prospects can compare prices of different shops online and read customer reviews.

Fig. 5.6 Value creation by social CRM

An organization's front office refers to all employees who have direct contact with the market and especially includes the typical CRM departments (e.g., marketers, salesperson, or helpdesk members). The front office can make use of existing social media tools (e.g., Instagram™, Facebook™, or Twitter™), but the organization can also decide to create its own social media tools (e.g., a corporate blog or a branded community). As front-office employees directly contribute to a customer's experience, they should try to detect the market's needs. Besides personalized or targeted ads and viral campaigns (see Chap. 4), social media can also be used for other topics discussed in this book (e.g., e-recruitment in Chap. 9, crowdfunding in Chap. 10, etc.). Particularly, social CRM can create value for the front office as follows.

- Better understanding of customer needs.
- More responsive to customer needs and improved customer experience.
- More information for targeted marketing (e.g., personalized ads, adapted to someone's interests).
- Reach more prospects due to the social ripple effect (see Chap. 2).
- Attract new talent from the market through communities (e.g., to help e-recruitment, Chap. 9).
- Detect new revenue opportunities on the market (e.g., to facilitate crowdfunding, Chap. 10).

The second interaction type in Fig. 5.6 is between an organization's front office and back office. If necessary, the front office can ask questions to back-office employees through internal social media tools (e.g., internal blogs, wikis, or social communities; see Chap. 2). In addition, back-office employees can facilitate internal collaboration by means of social media. Social CRM creates value for the back office as follows:

- More efficient knowledge management (e.g., better and faster knowledge sharing).
- Better recognition of internal experts (e.g., by actively looking for internal talent and expertise to respond to market inquiries).
- Improved way of working with better internal collaboration and B2B collaboration.
- More committed employees who are less likely to resign by feeling more connected.

Another way to look at value creation by social CRM is department based. This second perspective is closely linked to the multidisciplinary approach of social media and considers the entire value chain within an organization. In particular, social CRM can create value for the typical CRM departments as follows.

- **MarCom.** Social CRM can give insights, among others, to evaluate and refine an organization's marketing efforts, to proactively build relationships with (potential) customers, and to avoid a crisis. For instance, based on real-time listening and monitoring online conversations, MarCom can learn about the effectiveness of their initiatives and the related behavior and sentiment of the market. Alternatively, prospects can be identified when they are actually considering a purchase and target them by more personalized marketing.

- **Sales**. The sales department can profit from the presence of one integrated customer database to get more information about the organization's customers and prospects (see Sect. 5.2.1). For instance, salesperson can have an integrated view on their customers and prospects based on the traditional CRM activity history (e.g., contact details and transaction history), supplemented by personal information obtained from monitoring the Internet and social media in particular (e.g., online profiles and conversations). Because of social engineering, the sales department becomes able to better understand the needs of particular customers or prospects and find sales opportunities to turn prospects into existing customers and to turn customers into loyal customers in order to sell more products and services.
- **Customer service and support**. By means of a social media-based helpdesk (i.e., a contact center or support group on social media), the customer service and support department can try to proactively build relationships with customers. For instance, the department can provide better services by proactively responding to customers. Furthermore, a social CRM tool can offer this department an integrated view on the conversation history per customer and per customer inquiry (see Sect. 5.6).

Additionally, other departments are likely to profit from social CRM, namely:

- **Chief social media officer and social media task force**. The business value of social CRM for a specific multidisciplinary task force is similar to the value described for the other departments. Particularly, it can get more context for its customer engagement efforts.
- **R&D**. As discussed in Sect. 5.3 on social innovation, the R&D department can profit from social CRM for innovating its products and services by encouraging and facilitating new ideas from its customers, prospects, and social media connections (e.g., LEGO™: https://ideas.lego.com/). A direct collaboration with the market from idea generation to idea realization may result in more advocacies and a positive word of mouth. Moreover, the users engaged in the R&D project are also more likely to buy the resulting product or service afterward.
- **Operations**. Regarding the operations department, social media may stimulate and improve internal collaboration (e.g., by means of an internal social media tool such as Yammer™; see Chap. 2). Further on, customer feedback (e.g., received by the department for customer service and support) can be used to adjust the internal way of working and thus to improve the organization's business rules, procedures, and processes.

- **Purchase**. The purchase department can use social media to strengthen its B2B relationships, i.e., as being a customer of the organization's suppliers. Social CRM may result in better internal collaboration but also in better collaboration with the partnering organizations. Further on, social CRM can affect an organization's suppliers by improving the demand forecasts.

Additionally, Fig. 5.1 indicated the involvement of the IT department and the finance department in the multidisciplinary approach of social CRM. Both departments rather have a supporting role for monitoring social actions and business actions (i.e., for the IT department, see Sect. 5.6) and to evaluate the corresponding strategy in financial terms (i.e., for the finance department, e.g., to calculate and evaluate the ROI of social CRM initiatives, see Chap. 3).

5.5 Tips and Tricks for Social CRM

While the previous section specified which business value can be created by social CRM, this section provides the reader with some tips and tricks that may facilitate value creation.

Social CRM strongly depends on the needs of an organization's market (i.e., customers, prospects, but also social media connections, e.g., Facebook™ fans or Twitter™ followers who are not necessarily a customer yet). Therefore, the following advice can help an organization identify when and where Internet users wish to get value.

- **Multichanneling**. Organizations should offer both offline and online channels to communicate with the market, so customers and prospects can choose how they wish to contact an organization (e.g., by phone, postal mail, email, social media tools). Clearly mention all contact details, so people know about the different channels (e.g., phone number, postal address, email address, link to social media tools). However, an organization should not necessarily be present on all social media tools (see Chaps. 2 and 3).
- **Test**. Organizations should test in advance whether the offered online channels and the social CRM system (e.g., with a helpdesk) actually operate in a user-friendly way and without technical problems. For instance, if an organization develops its own social media tool (instead of using an existing tool), the tool should be carefully tested from an end user's point of view before getting launched.
- **Monitor** (see Sect. 5.6). Organizations should monitor web content that is related to the organization and its industry in general, as well as social media messages. For instance, an organization can set up alerts to be notified whenever its brand is mentioned online and pay specific attention to review sites (see also Chap. 7).
- **Listen**. Organizations should analyze the monitored web content and social media messages in an open and emphatic way to truly understand the needs, problems, or frustrations of Internet users.

- **Respond**. Based on the monitored content, organizations should respond to Internet users in a user-friendly, timely, and relevant way. They should also regularly respond to direct inquiries from customers or prospects, e.g., by checking emails and social media at least once a day or more regularly.
- **Informal and personalized**. On social media, organizations can approach Internet users in a more personalized and informal (although respectful) way (e.g., on first-name terms and by means of targeting based on their interests, location).
- **Content**. Organizations should encourage online discussions and give solutions which stay in the mind of customers and prospects and which let them talk about the organization and its products and services to others (see the Introduction section for the example of an airline company that gave its customers a personalized gift). Such content can also be supported by a content calendar, which gives an overview of an organization's social media use within the past year and the current year as well as the planned actions for the coming year.

The advice above aims at creating **meaningful conversations** between an organization and its market, i.e., conversations that are not directly related to sales offers. On the one hand, conversations should be meaningful for the market, which means that they serve the customers (i.e., the users of an organization's products or services) beyond the context of direct sales offers. But ultimately, social CRM intends to create meaningful conversations for the organization, which means that they drive business value and have a purpose to fulfill that goes beyond marketing or sales. For this purpose, just being present on social media (e.g., by having a Facebook™ page or a Twitter™ account) does not suffice. Instead, the following methods illustrate how an organization can create meaningful conversations, among others.

- **Encourage Internet users to ask questions and respond with advice to show an organization's expertise (Q&A)**. For instance, an organization can create an online forum or community for people to ask questions (possibly part of the corporate home page). This method is also helpful to detect what customers are concerned about. If the forum is publicly available, other website visitors can read the answers and even participate in the conversations.
- **Ask questions to Internet users to encourage lightweight interaction (instead of traditional content)**. A good example to stimulate interaction is storytelling. For instance, an organization can post short stories with pictures and videos about events that they sponsor (e.g., Nike™ frequently posts images and videos about athletes wearing Nike™ products). Furthermore, an organization can show a sentence that social media connections can complete by filling out the blank, e.g., "The best shop of organization XYZ I have ever been to, was in. . . ." In this example, people who comment by replying with a city name contribute to brand recognition and customer loyalty regarding a certain shop of the organization. A similar example is a survey with predefined answer options instead of an open question, such as "The best product of organization XYZ is: product A, product B, or product C." This example focuses more on product awareness

and higher sales, because the survey may stimulate users to buy a certain product (e.g., the one with the highest percentage). In both examples, the name of the organization or its products and services is explicitly mentioned to guide the responses to some extent and to avoid that Internet users turn the conversation in favor of the organization's competitors (e.g., by mentioning that a certain product of a competitor is better). Possibly, a general question can be formulated in such an open way that does not directly relate to a certain brand but just intends to interact (e.g., "Which Christmas present did you get for Christmas" instead of merely wishing "Merry Christmas" to social media connections).

- **Help Internet users when needed to turn them into brand advocates.** This method particularly tries to turn a negative customer experience into a positive one (i.e., with "customer experience management" being a synonym of CRM). For instance, if a customer publicly complains about an organization on social media (e.g., Twitter™), the organization can quickly respond and try to find a solution. Monitoring allows an organization to detect brand-related questions and complaints in an early phase and to manage them properly in order to encourage a positive customer experience (see Sect. 5.6).
- **Encourage ideas for product innovation or service innovation.** This method relates to the social CRM type of social innovation (see Sect. 5.3). For instance, a brand community can use the concept of "gamification"(see Sect. 2.2.7) to stimulate social innovation. Its header can indicate how many ideas have been submitted and realized, how many votes have been received, how many comments, etc. Depending on one's contributions, a user can also earn points. The community's home page can also list the top recent contributors, ranged according to their number of points, ideas, and votes.
- **Link online messages to build longer conversations.** A good example to link online messages of different users is by using the same "hashtag" to interact about a brand, product, or service (e.g., on Twitter™; see Chap. 2). For instance, an organization can launch a contest for which users post comments or videos with the same hashtag. As such, Internet users can see how many users participate (e.g., as an indication of how "popular" an organization is) and more users can be reached by means of the social ripple effect (see Chaps. 2 and 4).

As the relevance of social CRM continues to evolve, organizations also increasingly profit from a closer integration with emerging technologies. For instance, AI-powered automated workflows (i.e., personalized automation of work processes through AI platforms) can enhance virtual customer support, data analysis and predictions, and social media monitoring. AI evolutions are also transforming service desks into automated chatbots, allowing for self-service. Additionally, a tighter integration with external tools is increasing (e.g., for combining mobile and web-based information into meaningful relationship intelligence). Similarly, based on an IoT integration, different devices can connect with each other more easily. In sum, the future of social CRM continues to create an omnichannel approach with more personalization by benefiting from technological advancements that help identify attention-grabbing information (e.g., for sending the right message at the right time).

5.6   Monitoring Social CRM

Chapters 3 and 4 already discussed the importance of monitoring social media actions, as well as making the ultimate link to business actions and ROI. For instance, for an online ad ór a viral campaign, an organization can monitor whether Internet users click on the ad or share the campaign, and whether this marketing initiative results in the desired business outcomes (e.g., higher sales or brand awareness). The present section elaborates on social media monitoring in the context of social CRM and is thus broader than initiatives launched by the organization itself. For instance, a specific organization may decide to track the number of social media connections and posts per customer in order to define a customer's social media presence. Customers with a higher social media presence can potentially reach more Internet users and may possibly have more influence on others (e.g., their complaints are more likely to go viral). Consequently, based on the social media presence of customers, an organization may decide to prioritize complaints or telephone calls. This example suggests different (or even unequal) treatments among customers, as customers with more social media connections or posts may be helped faster than others may.

As already known for years within the marketing discipline (Hallberg 2004), the efficiency and effectiveness of engaging with customers in loyalty programs (and thus also social CRM initiatives) need critical considerations. In other words, organizations should not necessarily treat all customers equally. Advocacy is key for social CRM, with loyal customers making or breaking a brand. Consequently, not only sales count, but also emotional loyalty matters a lot for bonding and brand leadership. The most loyal customers are not necessarily the most valuable customers because the degree of loyalty is not the same as the degree of business value (e.g., the amount of money a customer can spend). Social CRM can focus on customers with high loyalty and high business value via social engagement and collaboration with the brand. Simultaneously, organizations should also try to connect with customers characterized by high loyalty but lower value in order to let them convince other customers. On the other hand, it is less profitable for organizations to spend much money on customers with low loyalty and low business value.

In general, different reasons exist for monitoring social media actions in the broad sense (i.e., not limited to the social media initiatives of the organization itself), namely:

- To measure the impact of online ads and viral marketing campaigns (see Chap. 4).
- To understand what people say about the organization and its products and services.
- To support customer care.

- To identify needs and questions in the organization's market.
- To interact one to one with customers.
- To find trends per region and/or globally in order to make more informed decisions.
- To identify and react fast against rumor and crises.
- To monitor competitors and their activities.
- Etc.

Most monitoring reasons aim at understanding and responding to customers in a more personalized way. It is also worthwhile to monitor competitors and to take advantage of general trends. Moreover, social media monitoring can notify an organization when a crisis hits in order to take actions in a timely manner or to anticipate rumors that grow on social media. However, as previously discussed in Chap. 3, organizations should also monitor and evaluate the related business actions.

More specifically, social CRM monitoring integrates different types of metrics, namely (Marolt et al. 2015):

- Web analytics (i.e., digital analytics, e.g., metrics about web activity, emails, mobile applications, search queries, videos).
- Social media analytics (i.e., conversational analytics; see also Chap. 7 on sentiment analysis or opinion mining, also for measuring the emotional tone and influence of conversations).
- Business performance analytics (e.g., ROI).
- Traditional CRM analytics (e.g., about orders, invoices, inquiries).

In addition to Chap. 3, social CRM can use specific analytics related to traditional CRM in order to gain customer insight. For instance, social CRM can help an organization gain insight into which social media types and tools work best to generate positive word of mouth, into the direct effect between brand advocacy and the desired business actions, into customer loyalty, and (above all) into ROI. Social CRM information can also be used as input for social network analytics or big data analytics, e.g., for targeted marketing, churn prediction, credit scoring, fraud detection (see Chap. 8 on business intelligence).

Different metrics can be used for social CRM, depending on what the organization intends to measure (e.g., user involvement, interaction, intimacy, or influence).

- User involvement (e.g., web analytics: how many people visited a corporate website, for how long, which web pages did they see, etc.)
- User interaction (e.g., UGC: the number and frequency of blog posts, comments, etc.)
- User intimacy (e.g., opinions about a brand, product, or service on third-party review sites, in a corporate survey or customer inquiries received by the corporate helpdesk).

- User influence (e.g., the number of messages shared or posted on high-profile blogs, product/service satisfaction rates, or brand affinity measured in a corporate survey).

Afterward, the technique of "correlation mapping" can be used to link social media actions to business actions (e.g., which can be visualized in a scatterplot). For instance, shortly after the iPhone™ 4 was launched in 2010, Apple Inc.™ faced an immense crisis (called "Antennagate"), because the mobile device experienced some problems with the new antenna system (Forbes 2010). As a result, the negative messages on social media rapidly increased, while the value of the company's market shares significantly decreased (i.e., a negative correlation between social actions and business actions). As a reaction, the company's founder Steve Jobs held a legendary press conference to explain the problem and propose a solution. Shortly afterward, the negative buzz drastically decreased, while the value of market shares started to increase again (i.e., a negative correlation in the opposite direction). By also monitoring social actions initiated by Internet users (instead of the organization), the impact of a crisis such as "Antennagate" could be estimated in order for the organization to react in a timely and relevant way.

5.6.1 Social Media-Based Helpdesks, Contact Centers, or Support Groups

Besides monitoring social actions and business actions, helpdesks (i.e., contact centers or support groups) play a central role in social CRM. A helpdesk is usually part of the department for customer service and support by means of a ticketing system. The latter converts (positive, neutral, or negative) customer inquiries (e.g., problems, complaints, or questions) from different channels (e.g., postal mail, email, phone, or social media) into support tickets for reasons of track and trace (i.e., one ticket with a unique ID per inquiry). Nonetheless, a helpdesk can also assist the MarCom (e.g., for lead generation to find prospects and stimulate their interest or inquiries into the organization's products or services) or the sales department (e.g., for direct selling). Generally, a distinction can be made between inbound calls (i.e., initiated by the customer) and outbound calls (i.e., initiated by the organization, such as sales, telemarketing, fund-raising, surveys).

Although it takes time to handle customer inquiries, an organization may lower its costs and get more satisfied customers by investing in the efficiency and effectiveness of a helpdesk. The work of a helpdesk can also be facilitated by IT tools (e.g., a ticketing system and a corresponding reporting system). Particularly, for every incoming call, a contact center can create a digital ticket (i.e., an inquiry or case to be solved) in its ticketing system (e.g., Table 5.1). The tool helps an organization manage all tickets, without forgetting one. It also typically provides different ticket views by filtering the conversations (e.g., to give an overview of all unsolved tickets, all recently updated tickets, the unsolved tickets in a certain helpdesk team). For instance, a helpdesk manager can request all tickets with the status "new" and assign

Table 5.1 An example of a ticketing system

ID	Satisfaction	Subject	Requester	Date	Assigned to agent
596	Unassigned	How do I return my camera?	Andy James	Sept. 3	–
597	New	I love your store!	Christian Walls	Sept. 3	Andrew Spring
598	Pending	Changing resolution	Kelly Chang	Sept. 1	Julia Reynolds
599	Solved	Help with camera	Jacob Meltzer	Aug. 31	Julia Reynolds
600	Solved	How can I change the lens of my camera?	Andrea Roseann	Aug. 28	Andrew Spring
601	Unoffered	Camera speed	James Gory	Aug. 27	Andrew Spring
602	Unoffered	Camera battery	Cori Oliver	Aug. 27	Julia Reynolds

them to a helpdesk member or agent. Alternatively, one can request all tickets related to the same subject, e.g., related to shipping and returns. By assigning metadata to each ticket by means of specific fields and tags, tickets can be classified for tracking and archiving purposes. For instance, a complaint about a camera's battery might get a tag such as "camera battery" (i.e., a keyword to summarize or characterize the content of the ticket). Afterward, tags allow filtering related tickets, e.g., to verify how many battery-related complaints the organization received or how similar complaints have been handled.

Besides a ticketing system, a helpdesk frequently uses a corresponding reporting system to create management reports. For instance, a report can be generated based on agent metrics (e.g., to know the average time each helpdesk member needs to provide the customers with a first response, the average resolution time, etc.). By conducting (descriptive) statistics, an organization can also verify when peaks arrive in customer care. A helpdesk reporting system is actually a management tool to quantify how a helpdesk works and, above all, how the organization works. For instance, in case of a problem with a certain product or service (e.g., in the "Antennagate" example), the organization's helpdesk will suddenly receive many complaints. Helpdesk statistics can also be used for marketing reasons.

Moreover, based on monitoring social media and incoming inquiries, a helpdesk gives input for a more detailed analysis in the following domains, among others:

- **Text mining** (see the "Antennagate" example or Chap. 7 on business intelligence). A content analysis of the received inquiries may uncover when inquiries peak, the polarity of the content (i.e., generally positive, neutral, or negative), and a possible correlation with events (e.g., press releases, rumors, technical problems). For instance, when a crisis hits, the organization should decide when and how to react. An organization should also decide on thresholds (e.g.,

Post date :   2021-07-20 21:07:03
Wanted to check brothers ice watch, see that the battery is working ok. And I couldn t even get into the Lego money box case! #Seriously

url : http://twitter.com/ladykrw/statuses/93767394526380032
Language : en
User : ladykrw (id: 3947352)
User link : http://twitter.com/ladykrw
User GEO :

Post date :   2021-07-21 12:07:59
Want a purple ice watch!!

url : http://twitter.com/Beck_Milnes/statuses/93986321588170752
Language : en
User : Beck_Milnes (id: 261105355)
User link : http://twitter.com/Beck_Milnes
User GEO :

Post date :   2021-07-26 16:07:29
ripcurl watches.. buy now.. get discount if you buy more :)
Want those cool watches.? get yours now for only Php 200 each. Lacoste watches for Php 250 additional Php 20 if you want it with box Happy Shopping :)
url : http://www.facebook.com/profile.php?id=1253627213&v=wall&story_fbid=222430281132993
Language :
User : Mitch Mikimiki (id: 1253627213)
User link : http://www.facebook.com/profile.php?id=1253627213
User GEO :

Post date :   2021-07-30 03:07:38
Ice watch for sale.. buy now :)
Want those cool watches.? get yours now for only Php 200 each. Lacoste watches for Php 250 additional Php 20 if you want it with box Happy Shopping :)
url : http://www.facebook.com/profile.php?id=1253627213&v=wall&story_fbid=139245282827622
Language :
User : Mitch Mikimiki (id: 1253627213)
User link : http://www.facebook.com/profile.php?id=1253627213
User GEO :

Post date :   2021-07-30 18:07:06
wants an ICE watch =)

url : http://twitter.com/chispunks/statuses/97340696293421057
Language : en
User : chispunks (id: 25864998)
User link : http://twitter.com/chispunks
User GEO : 12.879721#121.774017

Fig. 5.7 An example of social media lead generation by Royer (2012), printed with permission

the maximum number of negative inquiries before reacting). Further on, Google™ Alerts (http://www.google.com/alerts) can be helpful in a crisis situation (see Chap. 2 on RSS and Chap. 3 on monitoring).

- **Predictive mining.** The social CRM database can be used for big data analytics (i.e., profiling) in order to predict trends (see Chap. 8 on business intelligence).
- **Competitive monitoring**. Inquiries and monitoring social media in the broad sense may uncover whether Internet users are talking more about the organization or about its competitors and through which channels. Such information can be used to derive KPIs for new campaigns, among others.
- **Identification of influencers**. An in-depth analysis can reveal the persons who (frequently) post negative or positive messages about the organization and how many followers those persons have. This analysis is important due to the social ripple effect (see Chaps. 2 and 4).
- **Lead generation**. If an organization knows which topics are discussed through which channels, it can more easily start conversations about a certain topic related to the organization. As such, social media have become important sources of leads. For instance, Fig. 5.7 gives an example of social media lead generation for a brand of watches.

5.6.2 Social CRM Tools

As a continuation of Chaps. 3 and 4, this section discusses more advanced tools for organizations to monitor and evaluate social media actions (i.e., without intending to be comprehensive or to promote one or another tool). In general, many social CRM tools exist. Some of them can be used for free, while others are more advanced and payable. Examples of frequently used social CRM tools are Salesforce™, Hootsuite™, Nimble™, Oracle™, HubSpot™, Pipedrive™, Monday.com™, Freshsales™, and Zoho™, among others.

The monitoring tools for social CRM can be divided into four categories or groups (Bonde 2013), which are subsequently discussed:

- **Social listening, monitoring, and analytics tools** (i.e., as a traditional helpdesk, either reactive or proactive).
- **Fan marketing and profile management tools** (i.e., as a fan database).
- **Social sales and marketing automation tools** (i.e., to automatically send and manage deals).
- **Community and collaboration tools** (i.e., to collect innovative ideas and create knowledge articles).

In line with Sect. 5.3 on social CRM types, the first three groups of tools refer to social service, social marketing, and social sales, while the fourth group rather refers to other social CRM types (i.e., social innovation, social collaboration, and social customer experience). All these tools contribute to social customer insight by recognizing that an organization should not only communicate on a one-to-one basis with its customers or prospects but also listen to online interactions between individuals or peers.

First, social CRM tools can focus on social listening, monitoring, and analytics. As these are the basic functions of social CRM, an organization can start with this group of social CRM tools. Social media monitoring can be done reactively or proactively. Reactive monitoring refers to helpdesk ticketing, whereas an organization can also proactively monitor online content (e.g., tweets, blog posts) in order to create leads. Examples of tools for social listening, monitoring, and analytics range from free social search grader tools to more advanced analytical tools. Since monitoring is more than just looking for hashtags, this group of social CRM tools allows an organization to monitor social media conversations that deal with organization-relevant keywords (e.g., "smartphone case and recommend" to find online inquiries and recommendations about a certain product, i.e., smartphones). Once a question of an Internet user is found, the organization (e.g., a sales representative or a helpdesk member) can create a lead by means of a ticket in the ticketing system to track and manage the lead. The system will also record additional personal information (i.e., as background information) about the user by means of social engineering (e.g., the user's profile on other social media, e.g., Twitter™, Instagram™, LinkedIn™). Nonetheless, it should be clear that responses to inquiries are on behalf of the organization (see Chap. 11 on legal and ethical issues in social media).

Secondly, fan marketing and profile management tools intend to (1) acquire and (2) engage fans or social media connections, before (3) letting them act. Therefore, they first build an active and engaged "fan database" to acquire social media connections. Then, they typically try to engage their social media connections by discovering popular content or trends in their social media messages, which they organize into categories. Afterward, this fan database can be used to unlock social data and to convert social media connections into actual customers and brand advocates (e.g., by means of viral campaigns). The latter may also benefit from predictive mining techniques for profiling users (see Chap. 8 on business intelligence). Possible tools to illustrate this group are campaign-centric tools or more integrated social management tools. For instance, they can assist in launching interactive contests (e.g., photo or video contests, quizzes, or polls) and sales offers on websites and social media in order to create customer-driven marketing campaigns. Alternatively, they help schedule targeted messages in the same dashboard, among others. An organization can also adopt its social media content to what fans like at a certain moment in time. For instance, a food shop can search for themes driving online conversations by means of latent sentiment analysis (see also Chap. 7 on business intelligence). As such, the food shop learns about the most favorable product-related topics and activity moments of its social media connections. Consequently, the food shop can post images or offers accordingly in order to resonate well with its fan database (e.g., a Facebook™ poster of chicken with aubergine at noon).

Thirdly, social sales and marketing automation tools combine CRM database management with campaign management to automatically send and manage deals (i.e., sales offers or contracts), among others (e.g., deal-of-the-day websites; see Sect. 5.3). To acquire a better look and feel, organizations are offered an overview of all open deals or contracts through this type of social CRM tools.

Fourthly, community and collaboration tools constitute a benefit compared to the traditional view on CRM. This group of tools focuses on innovative ideas in collaboration with social media connections (i.e., fans) to leverage a customer network. For instance, with these tools, people in general (i.e., not necessarily limited to customers or prospects) can submit suggestions, while other community members can discuss and vote on them. Furthermore, these tools also give the organization an opportunity to create a knowledge base and to share articles based on previous inquiries (Q&A). All community members may profit from the collective wisdom that is created within the community. To create such a knowledge base, the organization's helpdesk can contact other (back-office) employees when more inside information is needed to respond to an inquiry. In addition, user content from discussion fora can be copied into a knowledge article, so users feel appreciated and continue to contribute. This way of working creates new opportunities to build a stronger relationship with the market. As such, a corporate community can drive innovation faster and create knowledge articles that are approved by the organization. For instance, possible tools of this group of social CRM tools are offered by enterprise vendors for support communities.

5.7 Takeaways

Social CRM is highly important for contemporary organizations to create business value by means of social media. It gives organizations the opportunity to use social media in a broader perspective than marketing-related initiatives, e.g., to supplement online ads or viral campaigns. Nonetheless, before social CRM can create business value, an organization should consider the following issues. Most of these issues can be linked to Chap. 3 on social media strategies and ROI and to Chap. 11 on legal and ethical issues in social media.

- Integrate all social media initiatives in a CRM system, and link them to broader organizational strategies.
- Assess the degree to which employees are aware of and use social media tools, and train them accordingly.
- Possibly change the internal way of working (e.g., the organization's business processes, procedures, and rules) and encourage social behavior within daily work. If necessary, increase the productivity of front-office employees, i.e., who directly communicate with the market.
- Properly reflect on how and which (social and business) metrics are monitored and how to calculate ROI within the organization.
- Think about the privacy and security issues related to any IT system in general and, above all, to the social media use within an organization.

5.8 Self-Test

- What does the abbreviation social CRM stand for? How would you define the concept?
- What are possible synonyms for describing social CRM? Which alternatives can serve as antonyms? Explain.
- Can you compare the traditional view on CRM with social CRM?
- Do you understand why a social CRM system can also be called an "ecosystem"?
- Are you able to explain real-life examples of social CRM initiatives, and classify them in a social CRM type?
- Can you explain the multidisciplinary approach of social CRM and the degree to which it can create business value?
- Do you know the reasons why organizations should monitor their social media use?
- Do you know why social CRM risks treating customers in a different way (or even an unequal way)?
  - What is your opinion about prioritizing customers?
  - What can organizations do to prevent an inferior customer experience?
- What does correlation mapping mean in the context of monitoring social and business actions? Can you give an example?

- What is the role of a helpdesk (i.e., contact center or support group) for social CRM?
- Which type of monitoring tools would you advise to an organization? Motivate your choice. On which factors does your advice depend?
- Reflect on potential situations for which social CRM can be useful, and give advice on which social CRM tool category is best suited per situation.
- Look for the corporate website or a tutorial video of a concrete social CRM tool and classify its features along the different tool categories.
- Can you uncover the related social CRM tool type of the following demonstration videos? For instance:
  - https://www.youtube.com/watch?v=295brS23_4I
  - https://www.youtube.com/watch?v=vntyBvrRFTY
  - https://www.youtube.com/watch?v=ugmgifAy_ZM
  - http://www.youtube.com/watch?v=j1ozGiXSpI0

Bibliography

Al-Omoush, K. S., Simón-Moya, V., Al-ma'aitah, M. A., & Sendra-García, J. (2021). The determinants of social CRM entrepreneurship: An institutional perspective. *Journal of Business Research, 132*, 21–31.

Arora, L., Singh, P., Bhatt, V., & Sharma, B. (2021). Understanding and managing customer engagement through social customer relationship management. *Journal of Decision Systems*, 1–21.

Bonde, A. (2013). *In search of real, practical social CRM*. Retrieved September 5, 2014, from http://www.digitalclaritygroup.com/search-real-practical-social-crm/

Fangfang, L., Larimo, J., & Leonidou, L. C. (2021). Social media marketing strategy: Definition, conceptualization, taxonomy, validation, and future agenda. *Journal of the Academy of Marketing Science, 49*, 51–70.

Forbes. (2010). *Lessons from Apple's 'Antennagate'*. Retrieved September 2, 2021, from http://www.forbes.com/2010/07/20/apple-antennagate-steve-jobs-technology-iphone4.html

Gamage, T. C., Gnanapala, A., & Ashill, N. J. (2021). Understanding social customer relationship management adoption: Qualitative insights. *Journal of Strategic Marketing*, 1–25.

Greenberg, P. (2004). *CRM at the speed of light* (3th ed.). McGraw-Hill.

Greenberg, P. (2009). *Time to put a stake in the ground on social CRM*. Retrieved March 12, 2014, from http://the56group.typepad.com/pgreenblog/2009/07/time-to-put-a-stake-in-the-ground-on-social-crm.html/

Greenberg, P. (2010). The impact of CRM 2.0 on customer insight. *Journal of Business and Industrial Marketing, 25*(6), 410–419.

Hallberg, G. (2004). Is your loyalty programme really building loyalty? Why increasing emotional attachment, not just repeating buying, is key to maximizing programme success. *Journal of Targeting, Measurement and Analysis for Marketing, 12*(3), 231–241.

Harrigan, P., Miles, M. P., Fang, Y., & Roy, S. K. (2020). The role of social media in the engagement and information processes of social CRM. *International Journal of Information Management, 54*(102151), 1–19.

Madupu, V., & Cooley, D. O. (2010). Antecedents and consequences of online brand community participation: A conceptual framework. *Journal of Internet Commerce, 9*(2), 127–147.

Malthouse, E. C., Haenlein, M., Skiera, B., Wege, E., & Zhang, M. (2013). Managing customer relationships in the social media era: Introducing the social CRM house. *Journal of Interactive Marketing, 27*(4), 270–280.

Marolt, M., Pucihar, A., & Zimmerman, H.-D. (2015). Social CRM adoption and its impact on performance outcomes: A literature review. *The Organ, 48*(4), 260–271.

Royer, C. (2012). Guest lecture of Cédric Royer in the course Creating Value Using Social media at Ghent University, December 2012.

Wikipedia. (2021a). *Hackathon.* Retrieved September 15, 2021, from http://en.wikipedia.org/wiki/Hackathon

Wikipedia. (2021b). *United breaks guitars.* Retrieved August 27, 2021, from http://en.wikipedia.org/wiki/United_Breaks_Guitars

Search Engine Optimization

6

This chapter discusses how an organization can get its website, blog, or other social media pages higher on the (natural or organic) results page of search engines. This topic is highly relevant as Internet users are more likely to visit search results that are at the top of a results page. In order to decide which web pages appear higher on a results page, search engines typically evaluate which web pages are more relevant after applying an indexation mechanism. Such an indexation mechanism will rank web pages by means of so-called spiders. In response, web page owners can try to obtain higher ranks in search engines by applying search engine optimization (SEO) for internal improvements (e.g., on-page or on-site) and external improvements (e.g., link related). Alternatively, the importance of user experience optimization is increasing. This chapter offers the reader some tips and tricks to apply SEO and to evaluate which websites, blogs, or social media pages are more SEO friendly than others are.

This chapter particularly takes the perspective of the IT department and engineers to support other departments in the organization (Fig. 6.1).

> **Teaser Question**
> - What do spiders and hats have in common with social media?

6.1 Introduction to SEO (or SEM = SEO + SEA)

Today, search engines (e.g., Google™, Bing™, or Yahoo!™) help people browse the Internet to avoid an information overload. Although a search engine emphasizes the verb "search," its aim is to let people "find" information on the Internet. Hence, the term "find engine" might be more appropriate than "search engine" in order to describe search engines as applications to help find information on the Internet (Barbar and Ismail 2019). In sum, Internet users can use search engines for

© The Author(s), under exclusive license to Springer Nature Switzerland AG 2022   125
A. Van Looy, *Social Media Management*, Springer Texts in Business and
Economics, https://doi.org/10.1007/978-3-030-99094-7_6

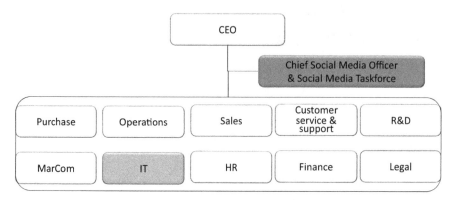

Fig. 6.1 The multidisciplinary approach of SEO

Fig. 6.2 SEO being part of
search engine marketing
(SEM = SEO + SEA)

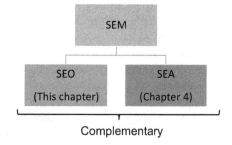

navigating to textual content, but also to images, videos, applications, social media
content, etc.

As search engines are frequently used to find commercial information, most
traffic to a corporate website, blog, or other social media page tends to come from
search results (i.e., even rather from natural or organic search results than from
sponsored or paid ads in search engines; see also Chap. 4). Moreover, the higher a
web page appears on a search engine results page, the higher the probability that
people will click on the link and visit that page. The topic of this chapter deals with
search engine optimization (SEO) in order to get higher page rankings in natural or
organic listings. Four SEO-related stakeholder types are involved (Schultheiß and
Lewandowski 2021): (1) search engine providers (e.g., Google™, Bing™, or
Yahoo!™), (2) Internet users, (3) organizations or website owners as content
providers, and (4) search engine optimizers (i.e., experts who are internal or external
to the content providers).

SEO is encompassed in a broader concept called "search engine marketing"
(SEM) (Matošević et al. 2021; Schultheiß and Lewandowski 2021). Being part of
the umbrella term "e-marketing"or "Internet marketing," SEM covers two parts
(Fig. 6.2): (1) SEA or search engine advertising, as discussed in Chap. 4, and
(2) SEO, which is the topic of this chapter. Both parts (i.e., SEA and SEO) are
complementary and can be simultaneously applied by organizations. Looking at this
broader perspective of SEM counts as stimulating (relevant) traffic to a website,

Table 6.1 The old and new way to find customers

The old way	The new way (SEM)
Customers must find the organization's contact details in a paper-based telephone directory (e.g., Yellow Pages)	Customers must find the URL to the organization's website, blog, or social media pages
Geographical location is crucial	Top 10 search results are crucial

blog, or social media profile should also involve some benefits for the organization, such as reputation management, increasing brand awareness, direct marketing, and more desired business actions (e.g., sales or subscriptions to a newsletter).

SEM combines SEO with SEA to help an organization acquire customers when they are looking for the brand and its products or services. For instance, when a customer launches a search query for a keyword (e.g., "smartphone") in a search engine, one is likely to get an overload of search results that deal with the keyword. Therefore, an organization can (1) apply SEO and try to get its web pages higher in the organic or natural listings of search results that are linked to keywords relevant to that organization (e.g., in the top 10) or (2) apply SEA and try to reach higher visibility by means of online ads.

As Table 6.1 explains, customers must first find the door to the organization (e.g., the address of a physical store or the link to the organization's website), before actually visiting the organization and buying its products or services. Figuratively speaking, SEM helps customers find the organization's (physical or electronic) door.

SEO thus focuses on the organic or natural listings on a search engine results page (SERP), while SEA deals with paid ads in search engines. This chapter elaborates on SEO, which has the potential to pay off because of the following reasons (Dimalanta and Escober 2018).

- When people look for information in a search engine, most of them will visit those links that appear on top of their screen (i.e., which are considered to be trusted and more relevant), without scrolling down or visiting a page that appears rather at the bottom.
- The vast majority of clicks in search engines tend to come from organic listings, whereas a minority of the clicks come from online ads.
- Some easy-to-use SEO tips and tricks with a relatively low cost of ownership can be applied to potentially obtain more clicks.
- SEO makes a website easier to understand and more user friendly, resulting in more targeted traffic, increased brand visibility, cost-effective sales and marketing efforts, and thus a relatively high ROI.

The literature describes SEO as a "multi-billion-dollar industry" because it is a widely used (and even necessary) Internet service to ensure that online content is visible through search engine results pages or SERPs (Schultheiß and Lewandowski 2021). Nonetheless, SEO is not always perceived as easy to realize because the requirements (i.e., ranking factors) differ among search engines, change from time to time, and are rather based on guesses instead of publicly known requirements. Consequently, SEO requires continuous improvements with trial and error.

6.2 Defining SEO

Search engine optimization (SEO) can be briefly defined as "the art and the science of getting a website to appear prominently in organic search engine results when a search submits a query relevant to that website" (Lieb 2009: p. xiii). It covers all required actions "to produce a high volume of referral hits from search engines, web directories and other websites, with the ultimate goal of making the website popular" (Jerkovic 2010: p. 1). In other words, the ultimate aim of SEO is to enhance the quality and ranking of a website in order to optimize user experience (Palanisamy and Liu 2018).

> Search engine optimization (SEO) involves tips and tricks to improve an organization's website or social media pages in order to make them more visible (i.e., with a higher ranking) on the organic SERPs when Internet users launch relevant search queries. It aims at stimulating the number of website visitors and optimizing their user experience (i.e., the quantity and quality of unpaid website traffic).

Table 6.2 further clarifies SEO's focus, as opposed to SEA. This chapter gives tips and tricks that are relatively easy to use and may possibly result in a higher ROI than the more expensive pricing models for online ads (e.g., pay-per-view or pay-per-click; see Chap. 4). In particular, for applying SEO, an organization is not involved in a bidding process (or bidding war; see Chap. 4). Nonetheless, in order to profit from SEO, an organization should continuously improve its website, blog, or other social media pages in order to keep them up to date. Finally, in strong contrast to online ads, SEO has a long-term impact without being limited to the duration of a marketing campaign. This implies that an organization also needs to wait longer

Table 6.2 The difference between SEO and SEA

Search engine optimization (SEO)	Search engine advertising (SEA)
Organic (or natural) search results	Sponsored, paid online ads
Universal search (e.g., web pages, social pages, images, video, news, and books)	Bidding process based on keywords
Continuous website improvements (e.g., architecture, content, links)	During a marketing campaign
Long-term impact	Short-term impact
Long - term strategy ⇒ patience	Quick setup ⇒ immediate results
Higher ROI and lower cost of ownership	Expensive pricing models (e.g., pay-per-view, pay-per-click, and pay-per-action)

before seeing its SEO results (while some managers may not have the patience to wait for the results of SEO).

6.3   Search Engine Results Page

Although different search engines exist (e.g., Google™, Yahoo!™, Bing™), some early search engines have already disappeared such as AltaVista™, Ask Jeeves™, or MSN™ Search. For more information about the history of search engines in the 1990s, see http://www.thehistoryofseo.com/The-Industry/Short_History_of_Early_Search_Engines.aspx.

The choice for one or another search engine can depend on the targeted region as well. For exact statistics about search engines and browsers per region and worldwide, see http://gs.statcounter.com/. For instance, the statistics show that Google™ remains the dominating search engine worldwide (with almost 90%). On the other hand, a country such as China does not frequently use Google™ (but rather Baidu™ or Sogou™).

When looking at a regular search engine results page (SERP), a clear distinction should be visible between the online ads and the organic search results. For instance, the reserved space for online ads is frequently indicated in another color and with a title such as "Ads" or "Sponsored links" in order to inform the Internet user that it concerns paid search results. Particularly, as will be explained in Chap. 11 on social media ethics, disclosure of relationship is relevant to the Internet user who might get influenced to purchase the product or service in the ad.

As shown in Fig. 6.3, the paid ads are followed by the natural or organic search results. The reason why paid ads appear first is because research has shown that the upper left corner of a website is typically the most viewed area and thus the best eye catcher for positioning paid ads (albeit more expensive; see Chap. 4). As an example, Fig. 6.4 illustrates how a search engine results page is typically arranged in conformance with eye-tracking research (Chap. 4) (Marks and Le 2017).

In sum, an SERP typically consists of the following elements:

- **Search area**. An input field to insert one or more keywords (e.g., "smartphone") and a button to launch the search query.
- **Online ads**. The search area is directly followed by the sponsored search ads, which must catch the eye (see Fig. 6.3). The ads that appear are likely to be directly or indirectly linked to the keywords of the search query. For instance, in the example of the keyword "smartphone," targeted ads may promote particular shops to buy a smartphone or websites to review or to compare the price and features of smartphones.
- **Natural or organic search results**. The organic listings that follow the online ads may refer to similar websites as in the online ads but also to other sources of information (e.g., books, encyclopedias, or dictionaries). Organic search results may also cover images or videos that relate to the search query, as well as news items (e.g., articles that report on the keyword "smartphone") or local search

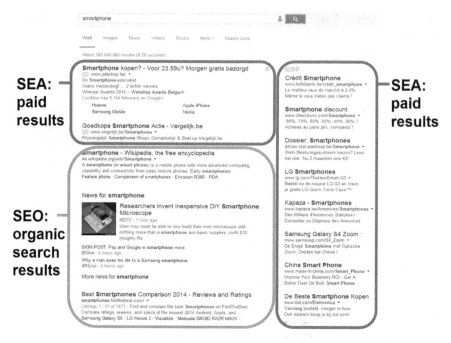

SEA:
paid
results

SEA:
paid
results

SEO:
organic
search
results

Fig. 6.3 Typical areas for SEO and SEA on a search engine results page. (Google™ and the Google™ logo are registered trademarks of Alphabet™ Inc., used with permission)

Fig. 6.4 The most viewed area on a web page

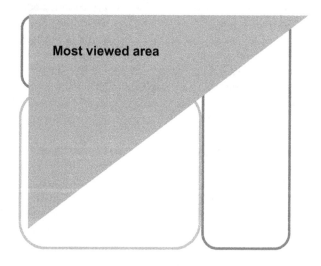

Most viewed area

results (e.g., a geographical map with local shops). Additionally, Google™ works with answer boxes to predict which questions Internet user might have for certain search terms in order to propose quick answers by means of indexed content (i.e., on top of the listed search results, or "Position 0," e.g., based on the indexed websites' FAQ pages or step-by-step advice).

6.4   Indexation Mechanism

Each search engine has its own business model for selling space for online ads (i.e., related to SEA; see Sect. 4.1.3 on pricing models), as well as for their natural search queries (i.e., related to SEO). To facilitate the natural or organic search process, a search engine will assign a ranking to web pages by following a specific indexation mechanism. This ranking process can be influenced by SEO, i.e., by adapting web pages to the assumed requirements of one or more indexation mechanisms in order to obtain higher page rankings.

However, the indexation mechanisms of specific search engines are not fully known, differ from search engine to search engine, and may regularly change for the same search engine. An organization can try to focus on the indexation mechanism of one or only a few search engines and this with continuous efforts. For instance, given Google™'s dominating role (see Sect. 6.3), an organization can decide to focus on the indexation mechanism of this search engine (which also comprises requirements of other search engines to some degree) and rather buy ads on other search engines. Section 6.5 illustrates some general tips and tricks to start with.

The indexation mechanisms of search engines are a strong motivation in favor of SEO because organic or natural website traffic is significantly higher for websites with higher rankings. For instance, SMEs with relatively unknown brands can generally profit from SEO's lower cost of ownership (i.e., compared to online ads), albeit only in the long term.

Different types of search indexes exist (Barbar and Ismail 2019), such as web directories, crawler-based search engines, or hybrid (i.e., combining both). Directories can be seen as categorized lists of links to other websites, which are manually maintained (i.e., with manual submissions by website owners and manual reviews or approvals by editors). On the other hand, crawler-based search engines use sophisticated algorithms to automatically locate and index online content.

The following steps illustrate how a crawler-based search engine typically works, namely based on dedicated steps for crawling (i.e., for collecting information related to the search parameters) and for building an index (i.e., for evaluating the collected information and assigning an index) (Dimalanta and Escober 2018). A search engine considers the Internet as a web of links, i.e., with web pages linked to each other as a spider's web. At regular times, the so-called spiders of search engines crawl over the web (i.e., WWW). For instance, when a new web page is created or an existing page modified, a "spider" should first find it and crawl over that page. Particularly, it will skim the page's text, image descriptions, metadata, page titles, and URL. It will also follow links and count the incoming and outgoing links. Next, the keywords linked to that page will be indexed (i.e., added to a database), and the frequency of words will be analyzed. Afterward, based on this information, the web page will be weighed and ranked in comparison with other web pages. Thus, a "spider" is a simplified term, referring to "a program or automated script that (. . .) navigates from URL to URL by following links on the pages of the websites that they visit" (Lieb 2009: p. 2). By doing so, it applies the indexation mechanism of a specific search engine and browses the Internet to look for the most popular web pages, resulting in a page ranking (i.e., similar to a score out of 10). Metaphorically speaking, a "spider" crawls over the web in search for content and can also be called a "robot," "bot," or "crawler" (Barbar and Ismail 2019). Finally, when a particular search query is launched, the search engine will only rely on the identified index (i.e., similar to a database with information of all web pages that have been visited by its "spiders") in order to show relevant organic search results in a faster (and thus rather asynchronous) way.

More than 200 ranking factors or parameters exist (Dean 2020), and which are mostly related to expertise/relevance, authority/links, and trust/security (or E-A-T). Ranking factors thus determine the ranking in a search engine's natural search algorithm and typically refer to trust of the host domain, link popularity, on-page keyword usage, click-through data or traffic, registration and hosting data, etc. Additionally, Google™ uses the abbreviation YMYL ("Your Money or Your Life") to refer to online content that could have a direct and negative impact on one's life or financial situation if presented incorrectly, and which should better be written by subject matter experts (e.g., about news, politics, law, science, and health safety). Consequently, Google™ applies very high-quality rating standards for YMYL pages. In response, SEO tries to consider these parameters in order to obtain a higher organic page ranking (i.e., a score out of 10).

Nonetheless, a search engine can also "punish" websites that are too optimized in terms of SEO (e.g., which have an extensive use of keywords or which have incoming links of low quality, such as links from gambling sites or adult-oriented sites). The latter is called an "over-optimization penalty," and the SEO efforts will not result in a higher page ranking. Instead, web pages can even get a worse placement on SERPs or be banned from SERPs for a period. SEO penalties can also be used to "punish" the use of "black hat" SEO techniques (or "search engine index spamming"), if discovered. "Black hat" SEO techniques are unethical attempts to get a higher page ranking or manipulations that violate the search engine requirements (Zhang and Cabage 2017). Particularly, they contrast with the ethical "white hat" SEO techniques (Killoran 2013). Examples of "black hat" SEO techniques are:

- Hidden content on web pages.
- Duplicating content (i.e., canonicalization).
- Stuffing pages with keywords irrelevant to the page's content.
- Selling or buying incoming links (i.e., link farming).
- Page hijacks redirecting to malicious websites.
- Cloaking (i.e., showing different contents to search engines than to humans).
- Bowling (i.e., manipulating the competitors' search engine results, e.g., by manipulating the quality of their incoming links).
- Etc.

On the contrary, Sect. 6.5 focuses on "white hat" SEO techniques.

An advantage of search engines is that they are characterized by a high coverage (i.e., reaching many people, similar to mass communication) and a high precision (i.e., reaching people fast and in a personalized way, similar to niche communication and direct marketing). On the other hand, an implication and possible critique on the business model of search engines relates to the real power they have nowadays. Particularly, many people browse the Internet by primarily using search engines and tend to browse only the highly ranked web pages. Consequently, organizations are seemingly forced to follow what search engines find important (in terms of ranking factors in the indexation mechanisms), in order to get higher page rankings and thus to appear higher in those search queries that are related to the keywords of an organization's website, blog, or other social media pages. Moreover, the power of search engines is not limited to SEO and covers SEM as a whole. The more Internet users launch search queries, the more power search engines also have during the bidding process of SEA.

6.5 Tips and Tricks for SEO

The chapter continues with tips and tricks on how a website, blog, or other social media pages can potentially reach a higher ranking in search engines and this with a relatively low cost of ownership (i.e., compared to online ads). Different lists with suggestions exist (Matošević et al. 2021). For instance, Marks and Le (2017) refer to the four Cs of SEO to indicate which best practices are most essential, namely (1) create effective titles, abstracts, and metadata, (2) cross-discipline posting, (3) cross-post on multiple locations, and (4) convert PDFs in searchable PDFs. A variety of (free or payable) webmaster tools and SEO consultancy services help organizations in this endeavor. For instance, based on SEO software, one can predict the degree of adjustment of web pages to certain SEO recommendations (Matošević et al. 2021). A common way is running a website or specific page in an SEO tool for analysis, resulting in specific recommendations for changing the online content (Dimalanta and Escober 2018). Such SEO tools follow the findings of prior research (including several online experiments and AI-based predictions), allowing organizations to start applying SEO with a relatively small budget.

More generally, the SEO literature typically classifies SEO tips and tricks in different categories or pillars (Das 2021; Jerkovic 2010) (Fig. 6.5):

- Internal (off-page but on-site) improvements relate to the architecture of a website, blog, or social media page.
- Internal (on-page) improvements relate to the online content of a website, blog, or social media page.
- External (off-site) improvements relate to the external links to a website, blog, or social media page.
- Improvements can also relate to how Internet users experience a website, blog, or social media page.

Please note that we deliberately present four dedicated pillars, although the literature sometimes only differentiates between internal and external improvements. For instance, authors then respectively refer to on-page versus off-page SEO (Barbar

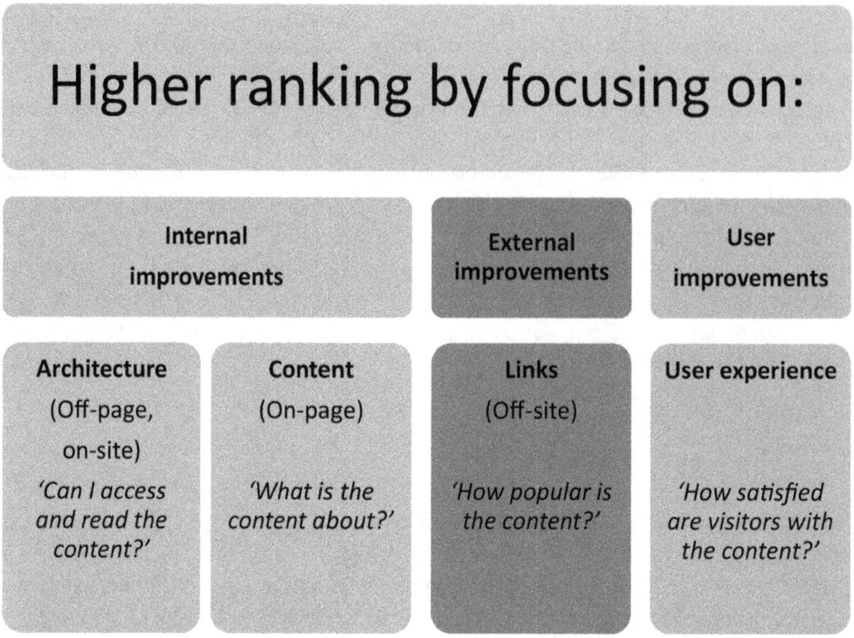

Fig. 6.5 Tips and tricks for SEO

and Ismail 2019; Lopezosa et al. 2018; Matošević et al. 2021), whereas our suggested typology is more refined. More specifically, we gradually extend the scope from individual web pages to the overall website, and beyond (i.e., from on-page, over off-page but on-site, to off-page and off-site, and ultimately adding the user perspective).

Subsequently, a selection of tips and tricks is illustrated per SEO category, without intending to be comprehensive.

6.5.1   Internal Off-Page but On-Site SEO Improvements

The first category of SEO tips and tricks deals with the architecture of a website and determines who can access and read the content, as summarized in Fig. 6.6.

- **Tip 1—Readable URLs with keywords.** URLs (i.e., website addresses) should have a meaningful understanding for humans. Particularly, URLs should:
    - **Tip 1.1 Contain meaningful keywords that are understandable for humans instead of computer language.**
    - **Tip 1.2 Contain hyphens (rather than underscores) between the keywords to increase readability.**
    - **Tip 1.3 Be translated into different languages**
      With regard to this factor, an SEO-unfriendly example would be a URL such as   http://www.**title**.com/**article/SB10014241278530518069748**.html,

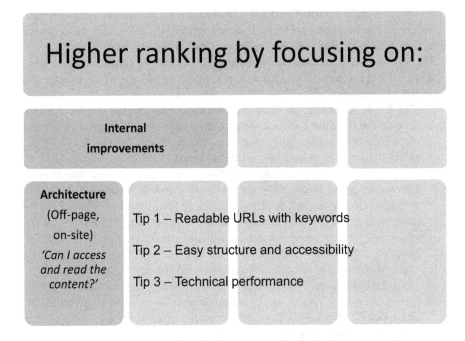

Fig. 6.6 Tips and tricks for off-page or on-site SEO improvements

because it contains computer language that remains unreadable for humans. On the other hand, a better example would be http://www.**title**.com/**article/ article-title-is-shown-here**.html, which uses meaningful keywords with hyphens in between. Some examples are:

- http://www.feb.ugent.be/**nl/subtopics.asp?mainID=30&catID=304**   This example concerns a Dutch web page (indicated by "nl") with Dutch acronyms (e.g., "feb" and "ugent"). However, since the link contains English keywords (e.g., "subtopic") and computer language (e.g., "asp? mainID = 30&catID = 304"), it is rather SEO unfriendly. It would be better to have keywords with hyphens in between, which are translated into the language of the web content, for example: http://www.feb.ugent.be/**nl/ informatie-over-doctoraten**.
- http://www.ugent.be/**en/teaching/studying/languageofinstruction** The next example concerns an English web page (indicated by "en") and with keywords being translated into the language of the web content (e.g., "teaching" and "studying"). The URL is free of computer language, which is also positive. Nevertheless, the keyword "languageofinstruction" is presented as a single word without hyphens, which is more difficult to read than "language-of-instruction."
- http://www.uct.ugent.be/**en/open-program/continuing-education-language- teachers**

This final example is SEO friendly in the sense that it shows no computer language. The keywords are in the same language as the web content and contain hyphens. As such, this URL is a better example of the first SEO tip.

- **Tip 2—Easy structure and accessibility**. The second tip emphasizes that when spiders crawl the web, they usually do not fill out forms or wait for the possible results. Hence:

  - **Tip 2.1 It is better to have simple page constructions (i.e., without dropdowns or input fields).** Instead of dropdowns or input fields, an alternative would be to list all options with links, radio buttons, or checkboxes (or to mention all options somewhere on the website).

  - **Tip 2.2 Use words with internal links (i.e., internal link building as alternative paths to the different pages of a website and an overview of web pages in a sitemap).** Spiders can click on links to other web pages of the same website. This technique is frequently used by Wikipedia™ and is one reason why this online encyclopedia usually appears very high on an SERP (see, e.g., http://en.wikipedia.org/wiki/Smartphone). Other reasons why Wikipedia™ is SEO friendly will follow in the subsequent tips and tricks.

  - **Tip 2.3 Adopt mobile technologies.** The need for an easy structure with high accessibility also counts for websites on mobile devices (e.g., tablets or smartphones). It is advisable to offer a mobile alternative, e.g., with a larger letter size, easiness of navigating by means of finger gestures, etc.

- **Tip 3—Technical performance**. An organization should pay attention to the technical performance of its website, blog, or other social media pages because of two main reasons. First, when SEO spiders visit a website (e.g., once a week), the links must work. Secondly, people dislike "slow" websites, i.e., which take a lot of time to load. If a corporate website or web page fails to load or if the load time is too long, potential buyers tend to switch to a competitor's website and search engines will not find the web pages. Particularly, website visits are usually short (e.g., a few minutes per website and even a few seconds per page), while visitors who stay longer are potential buyers. Therefore:

  - **Tip 3.1 Remove old links** (i.e., links that are missing, lost, or broken) after modifying or updating the web content.

  - **Tip 3.2 Skip (large) pictures to speed up slow websites.**

  - **Tip 3.3 Regularly measure the speed and popularity of a website**, e.g., by using rank websites such as the Alexa Rank (http://www.alexa.com/). For instance, to check the speed and popularity of Wikipedia™, see: http://www.alexa.com/siteinfo/wikipedia.org. Such rank websites can give information about the rank of other websites, their bounce rate, daily page views per visitor, daily time on site, audience demographics and geography, top keywords from search engines, etc. This information gives relevant input to the organization's SEO efforts and alarms the organization when action is needed.

  - **Tip 3.4 Enhance website security.** A website on HTTPS is more secure than a website on HTTP.

6.5.2   Internal On-Page SEO Improvements

Figure 6.7 illustrates the second category of SEO tips and tricks, which relates to the content or what a particular website is about, and highly emphasizes keyword optimization.

- **Tip 1—Unique and relevant browser titles**. This SEO factor emphasizes the need for meaningful website names and keywords. Hence:
  - **Tip 1.1. Use the keywords of Internet users in the URL and repeat them in the content of the web page and in the meta-description (see next tip).** This tip continues to explain why Wikipedia™ is a top search result for many keywords. For instance, Fig. 6.8 starts by showing the most relevant keyword (e.g., "smartphone") and frequently repeats that word in the content.
  - **Tip 1.2. It is good to start with content-specific terms as "head" keywords (e.g., "Samsung™ Galaxy") and end with generic terms as "tail" keywords" (e.g., "smartphone").** For instance, if an Internet user searches for a specific term, one will rather be interested in content-specific websites than websites with only generic keywords. However, in an example such as "Smartphones: Samsung™, Blackberry™, and Palm™ smartphone reviews," the generic keyword precedes the specific brand names as this web page rather provides an overview of brands instead of being limited to one specific brand.
  - **Tip 1.3. Give PDF files unique and relevant titles.**

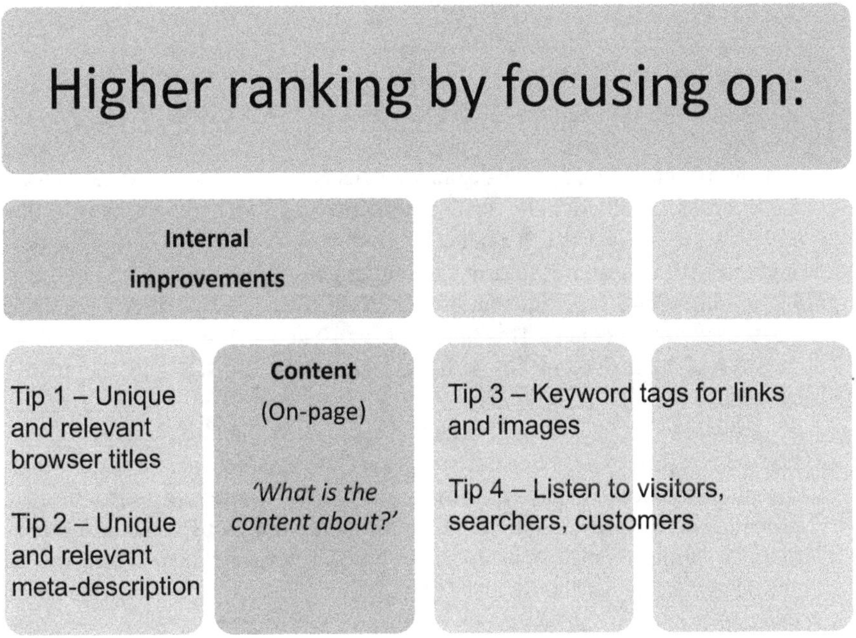

Higher ranking by focusing on:

Internal improvements

Tip 1 – Unique and relevant browser titles

Tip 2 – Unique and relevant meta-description

Content

(On-page)

'What is the content about?'

Tip 3 – Keyword tags for links and images

Tip 4 – Listen to visitors, searchers, customers

Fig. 6.7 Tips and tricks for on-page SEO improvements

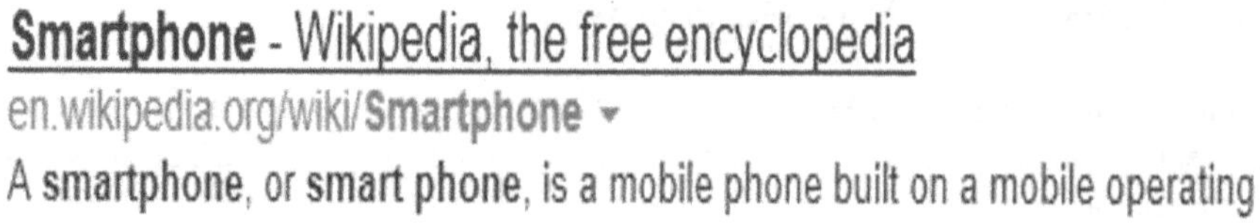

Smartphone - Wikipedia, the free encyclopedia

en.wikipedia.org/wiki/**Smartphone** ▾

A **smartphone**, or **smart phone**, is a mobile phone built on a mobile operating

Fig. 6.8 An example of a unique and relevant browser title. (Google™ and the Google™ logo are registered trademarks of Alphabet™ Inc., used with permission)

Table 6.3 An example of a meta-description in HTML format

```
<html>
<head>
<title>Smartphones: Samsung™, Blackberry™, and iPhone™
smartphone reviews</title>
<meta name="description" content="Interested in the latest
smartphones such as the Blackberry™, iPhone™, Palm™ Pre or
HTC™ Touch? Our smartphone coverage includes software
downloads, news, ..."/>
<meta name="keywords" content="smartphone, Samsung™,
Blackberry™, iPhone™, Palm™, HTC™, review, cell phone,
PDA, organizer, email, hybrid"/>
</head>
</html>
```

- **Tip 1.4. Use short titles (e.g., maximum eight words).** Otherwise, titles might become too long to be fully shown on an SERP. Consider, for instance, a rather SEO-unfriendly example such as "An information-flow tracking system for real-time . . . ." The example does not seem to start with a relevant keyword (e.g., "smartphone") and the Internet user will probably not see the full browser title in a search engine. Such a browser title is less likely to appear in the top 10 of search results in a search engine.
- **Tip 2—Unique and relevant meta-description.** Besides the browser title, also the meta-description counts. This tip can be translated as follows.
  - **Tip 2.1. Add a description to be shown under the URL in the search results.**
    As shown in Fig. 6.8, an SERP usually supplements the URL and the browser title with a short description (or snippet). This meta-description differs from the first sentences of the actual web content, as it aims to get traffic to a particular web page and thus needs to be short, well-thought-out, and attractive. As an illustration, Table 6.3 shows how a header with a meta-description and keywords looks like in an HTML format (i.e., a computer language to mark text so that it can be seen on the Internet). It concerns a line of code with specific areas for the browser title, meta-description, and meta-keywords.

- **Tip 2.2. Find ideal keywords.** An organization should find keywords with (1) high volume (i.e., used in many search queries), (2) low competition (i.e., used less by other websites), and (3) high value (i.e., leading to a high number of conversions). (1) The volume of keywords can be derived from the bidding process of online ads (see Chap. 4), which is available by ad server vendors (e.g., by Google™ Ads, https://ads.google.com/home/). (2) Unfortunately, other websites are also likely to use high-volume keywords, resulting in more competition among websites. Therefore, a balance should be found between the so-called popular keywords and keywords that are used less by other websites. For instance, an organization can choose for less-competitive "tail" keywords. To get information about competition, an organization can verify which websites in its domain are highly ranked on different SERPs or it can use a keyword difficulty tool. Thus, low competition means that the web pages in the top 10 of SERPs are weaker in terms of SEO than the corporate web pages and this for particular keywords. (3) Finally, high-value keywords can lead to website visitors who are more likely to make conversions to business actions (e.g., actually buying a product or service or subscribing to a newsletter). This can be monitored, as discussed in Chaps. 3, 4, and 5 (e.g., by Google™ Analytics, http://analytics.google.com/).
- **Tip 3—Keyword tags for links and images.**
  - **Tip 3.1. Add an alternative text or keywords to be shown when a website visitor scrolls over links and images.** For instance, an image with a graph related to smartphones may display the keywords "*smartphone-comparison*" as ALT attribute (i.e., short image description). For a link, the brand name or a keyword can be used as the descriptive anchor text (e.g., "*smartphone*").
- **Tip 4—H tags for headings and body tags for main content.**
  - **Tip 4.1. Add HTML tags to mark heading titles, ranging from $<h1>$ (i.e., the most important headings where keywords are applied, along the title tag) to $<h6>$ (i.e., the least important).** Since section titles are highly descriptive, they help to get an idea about a page's content. As a result, explicitly H tagging those headings helps to structure a page. If multiple sections are equally important, their headings can have the same tag number.
  - **Tip 4.2. Add HTML tags to the body or content of different sections.** As a first paragraph is most important for SEO, it should be brief (e.g., not more than 100 words) and contain the essential keywords.
- **Tip 5—Listen to visitors, searchers, and customers.**
  - **Tip 5.1. Ask open questions to derive keywords and feedback.** It is important to regularly ask open questions in order to gain more information about the customers and this without making assumptions (e.g., "Why do you visit this website?").
  - **Tip 5.2. Reuse keywords in trends.** Monitoring tools are another way to listen to people in order to find keywords. For instance, Google™ Trends (http://trends.google.com/) may show the search interest over time for a specific search term (e.g., "smartphone") in order to indicate the degree to which people are using a particular keyword in a search engine. It may also

show regional interests in order to refine keywords depending on the targeted region. For instance, a keyword such as "smartphone" might be more frequently used in Europe and America than in Asia, or it might be frequently combined with other keywords, such as "Samsung™," "Android," or "Nokia™."

We remind the reader that SEO tips and tricks may change over time. For instance, in the early 2010s, it was still worthwhile to consider misspellings in keywords. For instance, if an Internet user tends to write the organization's brand or product names incorrectly, then one will probably write the same spelling mistakes when searching for information in a search engine (e.g., "bluetooth" versus "bleutooth" versus "bluethoot"). An organization could add those spelling mistakes as keywords for the website to be found when spelling mistakes are made in a search query. However, nowadays, optimizing a website for misspellings will rather have a negative impact on its ranking.

Another example concerns the use of keywords in the meta-description. While meta-keywords initially had a large and direct impact on web ranking, they now have a more indirect role to play (see, e.g., Sect. 6.5.4 on user experience). One of the main reasons was misuse, e.g., an abundant use of irrelevant meta-keywords or copying meta-keywords of competitors.

6.5.3 External Off-Site SEO Improvements

Figure 6.9 gives an overview of the third category of SEO tips and tricks, which determines how popular the content of a website is based on links from other external websites (i.e., external link building, with external links being known as backlinks, inbound links, or referral links).

In general, link building can be done in various ways, such as social media presence, social bookmarking, forum posting, blogging, blog commenting, guest blogging, wikis, article submissions, or content aggregators. It is not only important to have a large number of backlinks, but also to have strong backlinks (i.e., when the sites from which the links originate are also highly linked).

Nevertheless, a distinction should be made between normal links (i.e., "dofollow" links that combine related themes) and "nofollow"links (Lopezosa et al. 2018). The latter are links that will not be followed by SEO spiders because of a specific attribute or tag in their source code. Consequently, they have no impact on a website's ranking (i.e., not on the site that shows the link nor on the linked site). The concept of "nofollow" links is especially introduced for potentially untrusted content, paid links, and crawl prioritization (i.e., as SEO spiders cannot register as a member). For instance, a webmaster who cannot control the trustworthiness or relevance of links added to their website may consider using "nofollow" links, which is often the case in social media comments or blog comments made by other users (and thus to prevent that those websites will be punished by a search engine). For instance, Wikipedia™ uses "nofollow" for its external links.

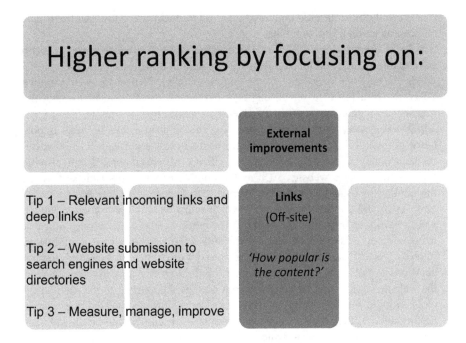

Fig. 6.9 Tips and tricks for off-site or external SEO improvements

- **Tip 1—Relevant incoming links and deep links**. External links matter to search engines, because what other trusted web pages tell about an organization is considered more important than what the organization tells about itself.
  - **Tip 1.1. Referring websites**. An organization can attempt to attract incoming links from other related websites. As discussed in Sect. 6.5.1 on off-page or on-site SEO improvements, the reputation and rank of specific websites can be verified on rank websites, e.g., http://www.alexa.com/. Such websites also mention how many other websites have links to a particular website. For instance, millions of external websites have links to Wikipedia™.
  - **Tip 1.2. Use social media to link to your website**. Also social media profiles can be used to include links to an organization's website. As such, an organization can benefit from the fact that social media are easy to share and can easily contain external links to websites. For instance, the URL to the corporate website can be mentioned on the organization's Facebook™ page or its LinkedIn™ page. Links to a web page can also be mentioned in a blog post or in a certain topic on a forum. Further on, the organization can share relevant Pinterest™ pictures with links to the corporate website for more information. Other tips for "social media optimization" are regularly posting new content and stimulating links to other social media pages (e.g., posting slides on Slideshare™ or a video on YouTube™ and then sharing, tweeting, or blogging about it). Nonetheless, we remind the reader that links on social media (and

especially those in blog comments) are often made "nofollow" and will thus not impact on a site's ranking.

- **Tip 2—Website submission to search engines and website directories**. This tip advises an organization to submit its web content to directories (e.g., Google™), which can help optimize the website, blog, or social media pages (e.g., to submit a URL for inclusion in a search engine's indexation mechanism or to label the structured web content in order to increase its visibility).
- **Tip 3—Measure, manage, and improve**. The final tip recalls the high importance of monitoring tools (e.g., Google™ Analytics; see Chap. 3 on a social media strategy and Chap. 5 on social CRM). Monitoring tools can provide information about a website, such as the number of site visits and page visits, the number of pages per visit, the average duration per visit, the percentage of new visits, and the bounce rate (i.e., which refers to how many people leave a website without browsing the content). In other words, a monitoring tool can uncover some weaknesses about a website that the website owner should try to improve. As an example, a high bounce rate may reveal that the keywords are not appropriately determined, while a high click-through rate may give evidence of the website's relevance for certain search queries. In addition to the monitoring tools, Google™ offers search console help for webmasters to check the organic performance of their websites (https://search.google.com/search-console/about). For instance, if critical website problems arise, Google™ will notify the corresponding webmaster by means of this tool.

6.5.4 SEO Improvements Related to User Experience

Besides the three traditional SEO categories, a rising fourth category focuses on user experience (Fig. 6.10) (Palanisamy and Liu 2018). The tips and tricks in this fourth SEO category are less easy to use (compared to the other categories) because user experience can only be manipulated to a minor extent. In particular, search engines are likely to rank pages higher if visitors are satisfied with the content. User experience or satisfaction is hard to measure, but search engines can rely on their own data. For instance, data may concern user metrics as previously discussed (e.g., the bounce rate, the average time spent per visitor, the click-through rate; see also Chaps. 3 and 4). Also other data can be tracked by a search engine. One example is called "search pogo sticking," i.e., the degree to which an Internet user reaches a website by using a search query and returns to the search results in order to visit another website in the same search query or to refine the search query and try again. Pogo sticking thus measures the (dis)satisfaction of users after visiting a particular website (i.e., based on "mining" log files; see also Chap. 8 on predictive mining). This also relates to measuring the dwell time, or how long Internet users stay on a certain website after a search engine query. In other words, are Internet users generally satisfied with the information found on a website, or do they still require other websites to find the information relevant to them?

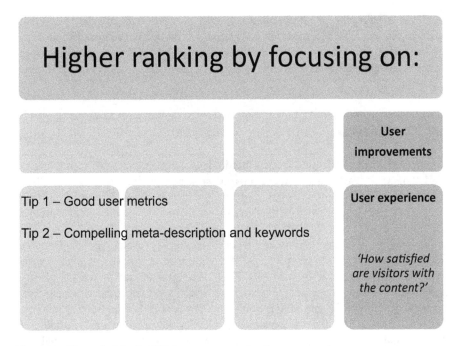

Fig. 6.10 Tips and tricks for SEO improvements related to user experience

- **Tip 1—Good user metrics**. Even if a website is optimized internally and externally (i.e., the previous SEO categories), it will not obtain a high ranking if its user metrics are poor. We remind the reader that monitoring is of paramount importance. Also some proactive initiatives can be taken, such as:
  - **Tip 1.1. Conduct user satisfaction surveys**. Ask website visitors how satisfied they are with the website, and look for suggestions for improvement. This best practice also helps create a better match between the users' search intent and online content.
  - **Tip 1.2. Empathy.** Answer the questions that website visitors might have, use intuitive layouts, link to relevant sources, update regularly so website visitors will return, etc.
- **Tip 2—Compelling meta-description and keywords.** As explained for on-page SEO improvements (Sect. 6.5.2), search engines frequently reuse the meta-description as the search result snippet. Well-defined meta-descriptions help increase the click-through rate (and possibly the conversion rate) from search results to a website, which can indirectly result in a better ranking.
- **Tip 3—Add an "About us" section.** In order to increase the E-A-T score, it is better to provide some information about one's background, skills, certifications, etc.

Finally, it is worthwhile to emphasize that SEO is constantly evolving, including changing best practices. Therefore, we end this section with some of the expected

SEO trends along the pillars. Particularly, more research is conducted to let SEO advance (among others by means of AI) (Jenkins et al. 2020). For instance, scholars are heavily interested in natural language annotations related to pictures, voice searches using mobile or smart devices, video-based SEO, users' intent, highly secure links, etc.

6.6   Takeaways

To conclude the chapter, this section first looks at the takeaways for search engine marketing (SEM) in general and zooms in on search engine optimization (SEO) afterwards.

SEM is frequently used by organizations to acquire customers online during a certain period of time. Still, it is a never-ending story that requires continuous improvements. On the one hand, it can operate by means of paid online advertisements (SEA; see Chap. 4). On the other hand, it tries to stimulate natural or organic website traffic by means of SEO. Through paid and/or organic efforts, SEM intends to bring more people to an organization's website, blog, or other social media pages. Both SEA and SEO are thus important to SEM, namely, SEO rather in the long run (i.e., similar to investments affecting an organization's sustainable growth) and SEA in the short run (i.e., allowing personalized or contextual ads within the duration of a campaign). Since SEM aims at reaching an organization's business objectives, the results and ROI of SEM efforts should by carefully monitored and measured.

Regarding SEO, this chapter provided the reader with an overview of tips and tricks that an organization can apply relatively easily to get its website, blog, or other social media pages higher in a search engine's listing of free search results (e.g., in search engines such as Google™, Bing™, or Yahoo!™).

As explained in Fig. 6.11, SEO inherently starts with good and relevant content online that is regularly updated. This means that the success of SEO strongly depends on content that people are likely to share or to follow. When supplementing good and relevant content with SEO tips and tricks, higher rankings in search engines are more likely to be reached, resulting in more readers, followers, and

Fig. 6.11 The value-enabling effect of SEO

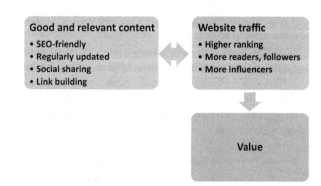

influencers. In turn, more website traffic may stimulate an organization to provide even better content. In sum, the value-enabling effect of SEO is about creating such a virtuous cycle.

In terms of SEO, social media pages can be treated similar to other web pages, even though they are especially useful for stimulating potential links (e.g., by sharing, liking, using hashtags). In this respect, social media help build an audience, stimulate branded searches, and help promote a brand.

6.7   Self-Test

- What does the abbreviation SEO stand for?
    - How would you define the concept?
    - How does it relate to SEM and SEA?
- Do you think SEO and SEA can pay off in terms of ROI?
- What does the abbreviation SERP stand for? How would you define the concept?
- How would you describe the advantages and disadvantages of search engines?
- What do you think is the real power of search engines today?
- Do you know what is meant by an SEO spider?
- Can you explain why some SEO techniques can be considered as ethically incorrect? Do you know the difference between "white hat"and "black hat"SEO? Can you give examples?
- Can you explain the different tips and tricks for SEO?
- Look for URLs of websites that you frequently visit, and evaluate them in terms of SEO. Which ones are most SEO friendly?
- Can you explain why Wikipedia™ is frequently a top search result on SERPs?
- Do you know the difference between "dofollow" and "nofollow"links? Why is it useful?
- Can you explain pogo sticking?
- Are you able to conduct an SEO audit of an existing website?
- How does SEO relate to the previous chapters?
- If an organization asks your advice about e-marketing, what would you suggest? SEA or SEO? Which circumstances you consider in your advice (e.g., organization size, organization sector, and budget)?

Bibliography

Barbar, A., & Ismail, A. (2019). Search engine optimization (SEO) for websites. *ICCTA Proceedings, 51–55*, ACM Digital Library.

Das, S. (2021). *Search engine optimization and marketing.* CRC Press.

Dean, B. (2020). *Google's 200 ranking factors: The complete list (2021).* Retrieved August 16, 2021, from https://backlinko.com/google-ranking-factors

Dimalanta, V. A. R., & Escober, R. E. (2018). Smart editor: A webpage enhancer tool for Seo on page recommendations with page view stats. *ICCIS Proceedings*, 253–258, IEEE.

Jenkins, P., Zhao, J., Vinicombe, H., Subramanian, A., Prasad, A., Dobi, A., Li, E., & Guo, Y. (2020). Natural language annotations for search engine optimization. *WWW '20 Proceedings*, 2856–2562, ACM Digital Library.

Jerkovic, J. I. (2010). *SEO warrior*. O'Reilly Media.

Killoran, J. B. (2013). How to use search engine optimization techniques to increase website visibility. *IEEE Transactions on Professional Communication, 56*(1), 50–66.

Lieb, R. (2009). *The truth about search engine optimization*. Pearson Education.

Lopezosa, C., Codina, L., & Gonzalo-Penela, C. (2018). Off-page SEO and link building: General strategies and authority transfer in the digital news media (article e280107). *El profesional de la información, 28*(1), 1–12.

Marks, T., & Le, A. (2017). Increasing article findability online: The four Cs of search engine optimization. *Law Library Journal, 109*(1), 83–100.

Matošević, G., Dobša, J., & Mladenić, D. (2021). Using machine learning for web page classification in search engine optimization (article 9). *Future Internet, 13*(1), 1–20.

Palanisamy, R. & Liu, Y. (2018). Users' search satisfaction in search engine optimization. *ICCBI Proceedings*, 1035–1053, Springer.

Schultheiß, S., & Lewandowski, D. (2021). "Outside the industry, nobody knows what we do" SEO as seen by search engine optimizers and content providers. *Journal of Documentation, 77*(2), 542–557.

Zhang, S., & Cabage, N. (2017). Search engine optimization: Comparison of link building and social sharing. *Journal of Computer Information Systems, 57*(2), 148–159.

Sentiment Analysis and Opinion Mining (Business Intelligence 1)

7

This chapter covers the first part of our business intelligence discussion and gives the reader insights into opinion mining and sentiment analysis. Social media are seen as big data in the sense that they provide a massive amount of online reviews and ratings that can be collected and analyzed in order to consider the impact these data may have on organizations. Particularly, several studies have shown that more positive reviews and higher rates for an organization (and its products or services) may lead to a significantly higher number of desired business actions (e.g., higher sales or more subscriptions to an online newsletter). This chapter explains characteristics such as subjectivity and tone in opinions and shows how a sentiment model can be built. The chapter concludes with challenges faced by this research field today.

This chapter is primarily situated in the IT department of an organization. This means that the technical execution or implementation of business intelligence techniques will be conducted by IT people or engineers rather than business people. Nonetheless, input or involvement of business users is still relevant for successful business intelligence applications because fully automated analyses may lead to inappropriate conclusions or business decisions (Fig. 7.1).

> **Teaser Question**
> - How can social media adjust your opinion?

7.1 Introduction to Opinion Mining and Sentiment Analysis

One way to illustrate the impact of social media on our daily lives is by looking at online reviews and ratings. This UGC is omnipresent via discussion platforms, product review websites, e-commerce, and social media tools. For instance, think about the different ways people can look for a restaurant. In the 1990s, i.e., when

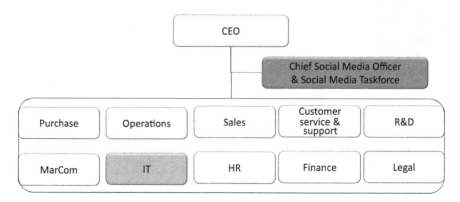

Fig. 7.1 The multidisciplinary approach of opinion mining and sentiment analysis

social media were not omnipresent, people could choose a restaurant after asking advice from other people they know (e.g., relatives, friends, or neighbors). Or for more sophisticated advice, official review institutions published books in which restaurants were scored (e.g., the Michelin™ Guides: https://guide.michelin.com/en). The first option could result in less experienced advice than the second option, but it was easier and also considered to be trusted. Although both options are still valid nowadays, an increasing number of people will rather look for information on the Internet. Additionally, different social media tools now exist in which (unknown) people can share their experience. For instance, regarding restaurants and holiday-related topics, a social media tool such as TripAdvisor™ can be consulted to find and/or post reviews and ratings (e.g., as a score out of five on a Likert scale). Similar to the principle of SEO (see Chap. 6), restaurants will then be ranked based on the reviews and ratings posted by Internet users. Even though the users are strangers with subjective opinions, they can influence others because people are more likely to visit a restaurant with many positive comments and which is ranked in the top 5 or top 10 of restaurants at a certain location.

Take a few moments to reflect on the degree to which you rely on online reviews and/or ratings when buying a certain product or service.

- Would you rely on the reviews of others? If so, rather on the negative reviews or on the positive ones? Would you also take into account the number of reviews? For example, would you buy a product or service with only a few negative reviews (let us say five to ten negative reviews)?
- Would you rely on visual ratings and rankings of others? If so, which ratings do you prefer? For example, regarding a score out of five, would you only buy a product or service if it has 5-star reviews, or do you also allow 4-star or 3-star reviews? Would you also take into account the variation among ratings, or do you only trust products and services with high ratings and without any negative comments?

- Would you rely on other review-related aspects too, e.g., the identity, personal information, or popularity of the reviewers?
- And what about organization-related features, such as the brand name of the product or service?

For quite some time, the literature has widely recognized and demonstrated that organizations with better reviews and ratings have more desired business actions (e.g., higher purchase likelihood, sales, and stock performance) (Zhu and Shang 2010). Although sentiment analysis studies agree on the existence of a correlation or relationship between reviews, ratings, and the desired business actions, they still disagree on the direction of this correlation (Al-Natour and Turetken 2020). Particularly, they disagree on whether this relationship is direct or whether some intermediate factors do count (e.g., brand popularity, review length, and the number of positive and negative reviews).

Edelman's annual and international trust barometer (2020) confirms that people tend to perceive experts and peers as highly trusted or credible sources (rather than a CEO or a government official) when forming an opinion about an organization with regard to employee engagement. Similarly, before deciding whether to buy a certain product or service, the majority of consumers tend to go online to read user reviews and ratings (besides commercial information) and possibly choose for another purchase if negative information is found. The growing power of online reviews and ratings is confirmed by several academia and consultants who refer to the strong influence of social media and the fact that many consumers go online to verify recommendations before buying products or services. Some studies even claim that a large majority of Internet users make use of online reviews and ratings to find product/service/brand information and rely on them before making purchase decisions. Many of them have already written a review or assigned a rating themselves (Jain et al. 2021; Pang and Lee 2008). Moreover, Internet users who read and write recommendations are usually willing to pay more for a 5-star product or service (Pang and Lee 2008). This means that online recommendations count and can possibly result in a higher value per purchase for an organization. On the other hand, negative recommendations can have negative consequences for an organization.

Consequently, for organizations, it is worth monitoring social media tools that collect user reviews and ratings, e.g., on TripAdvisor™, Yelp™, Foursquare™, or the Internet Movie Database™ (IMDb). This topic of opinion mining and sentiment analysis is closely linked to the impact of word of mouth (WOM) and the chapter about social CRM (see Chap. 5), which emphasizes that organizations should constantly keep track of social media posts that deal with keywords related to their brand and products or services.

WOM is any communication about a brand, product, or service that the receiver perceives as a non-commercial action or intention of the sender. It may be available from any place and at any time to a multitude of people (e.g., friends, family, peers) or institutions via the Internet (i.e., electronic WOM), mobile technology (i.e., mobile WOM), or social media (i.e., social WOM). WOM interaction with social media users (as customers or prospects) can highly affect users' satisfaction, perceived control, subjective norms, entertainment, or trust in a brand. This WOM effect is typically larger for new brands, products, or services for which a lack of information exists (e.g., a new skateboard brand). On the other hand, the WOM effect is rather moderate or lower for better known or trusted brands with which we already have a personal experience (e.g., a hotel that you regularly visit with your family).

This chapter covers a multidisciplinary field by combining management angles with people-related aspects (e.g., psychology, sociology) and technical perspectives (e.g., natural language processing and machine learning) (Ligthart et al. 2021). For instance, complaints or negative word of mouth (WOM) can be explained by the following theories.

- **Justice theory or fairness perception theory** (Greenberg 1987): the more people perceive situations of injustice or unfairness, the more they will dissent, create negative WOM intentions, and complain.
- **Attribution theory** (Heider 1958): if a product or service fails, people will feel dissatisfied until a solution is provided. A lack of solution will rather lead to public complaints for directly addressing the brand. If the organization's response is slow but resulting in a proper solution, people tend to complain more to friends and relatives instead of the brand.
- **Self-conceptualization theory** (Turner 1985): people tend to complain more if something is not in accordance with one's identity or self-conceptualization (i.e., similar to the idea of homophily in Chap. 8).

In case of negative reviews or ratings, an organization should react properly and take corrective actions to avoid any reputational damage. While it may take advantage of positive reviews and ratings, an organization can also learn from negative comments to improve its products and services accordingly in order to avoid more negative reviews and to turn them into positive future customer experiences. Some ways to properly manage WOM include respecting different opinions, appreciating negative and positive comments, responding fast, and communicating about updates and this in the customer's language.

7.2   Defining Opinion Mining and Sentiment Analysis

7.2.1   Definitions

Online UGC contains people's sentiments and opinions on different subjects or features (e.g., products, services, issues, events, or other topics and their attributes). It concerns WOM that is typically analyzed automatically using algorithms and datasets in sentiment analysis models (Ligthart et al. 2021). This chapter uses layman's terms to explain the detection of a sentiment (i.e., an emotion) or an opinion (i.e., an attitude) in such unstructured or free-form text, which is actually combining natural language processing (NLP) with information science (Darwich et al. 2020). Moreover, social media data are increasing in volume, subjectivity, and heterogeneity, and thus become challenging to process manually but require business intelligence (Jain et al. 2021).

> Sentiment analysis or opinion mining of social media data covers text mining techniques to analyze users' online content and derive the subjectivity and polarity of their feelings and personal attitudes in order for an organization to act accordingly.

Opinion mining and sentiment analysis can be briefly defined as "the computational study of analyzing people's feelings and opinions for an entity" (Ligthart et al. 2021: p. 4997). Alternatively, a broader definition refers to processing "a set of search results for a given item, generating a list of product attributes (quality, features, etc.) and aggregating opinions about each of them (poor, mixed, good)" (Dave et al. 2003: p. 519). Mining is jargon for analyzing and literally refers to digging for information (or distilling knowledge) that is relevant for a business (i.e., by using business intelligence techniques). The knowledge resulting from this analysis will help to better understand, explain, and predict social phenomena. Moreover, by tracking the mood of Internet users, organizations can create actionable knowledge (e.g., conducting a competitor analysis, enabling the corporate strategy, improving customer satisfaction, identifying trends and key influencers, and ultimately targeting sales or other business benefits) (Ligthart et al. 2021).

Although opinion mining and sentiment analysis are frequently used as synonyms, opinion mining strictly refers to personal opinions (e.g., "I think"), while sentiment analysis rather focuses on feelings or sentiments (e.g., "I like" or "I dislike"). Opinions and sentiments are usually expressed by means of adjectives (e.g., "big" or "boring"). Such opinions or sentiments can be detected in a content analysis of texts, e.g., posts on social media (e.g., Facebook™, Twitter™, blogs, fora) or online newspapers.

The techniques for opinion mining or sentiment analysis can be used for many applications in different domains (e.g., travel, healthcare, finance, crime). One example concerns market share predictions, as an increase in negative buzz about a specific product or service may have a negative impact on the organization's market shares (see the Antennagate crisis of Apple Inc.™, Chap. 5). An example in health care is the detection of depressive children based on the number of positive and negative messages on social media tools (e.g., Facebook™). Further on, the results of political elections could be predicted by the degree to which political parties and individual politicians are covered in online newspapers and social media (e.g., tweets).

Finally, we must note that opinion mining and sentiment analysis are not limited to social media and online text but that a similar content analysis can also be conducted for offline text. Hence, the techniques discussed in this chapter are situated in the overall domain of text mining.

7.2.2   Characteristics

Opinions and sentiments can have a different degree of (1) subjectivity and (2) polarity, as shown in Fig. 7.2.

- Subjectivity ranges from objective to subjective. An objective sentence expresses factual information about the world, while a subjective sentence expresses some personal feelings or beliefs.
- The polarity (i.e., tone or orientation) indicates whether an opinion is positive, neutral, or negative.

Subjectivity and polarity are a continuum, possibly expressed in decimals (instead of an "all-or-nothing" approach with binary values). This means that different degrees of subjectivity exist between factual information and personal feelings or beliefs (Ligthart et al. 2021). Similarly, different degrees of polarity exist between positive, neutral, and negative comments. Examples of (subjective) feelings are "I like the color of the device" (positive) or "I really hate the service given by that organization" (negative). On the other hand, examples of (objective) facts are "the newspaper reported on a tremendous increase in sales for the device" (positive), "I am looking for a good device" (neutral), or "the test has shown some technological problems with the device" (negative). Assessing the positive or negative meaning of facts is, however, more difficult than for opinions or feelings of a certain individual, since it depends on the interpretation of the reader. For instance, an increase in sales of a certain product can be positive for an organization, but negative for the competitors.

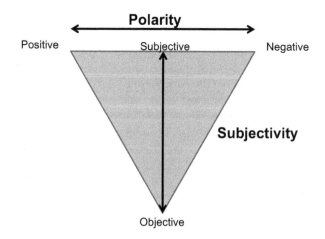

Fig. 7.2 Subjectivity and polarity in opinions

7.3 Building a Sentiment Model

Subjectivity and polarity depend on the sentiment words or opinion words used within a review. It concerns adjectives (e.g., "good," "nice," "fantastic" but also "bad," "poor," "awful") or expressions (e.g., "the more the merrier," "blood, sweat, and tears"). A sentiment analysis is possible at three levels, namely emotions or opinions can be detected on (1) sentence level, (2) document level, or (3) aspect/feature level. Aspect-level sentiment analysis is more difficult because implicit features are harder to extract automatically by algorithms (Ligthart et al. 2021; Nandwani and Verma 2021).

In general, three common approaches can be applied to identify sentiment words (Darwich et al. 2020; Khan et al. 2016; Ligthart et al. 2021): (1) a manual approach, (2) a dictionary-based approach, or (3) a corpus-based approach.

- **Manual.** The manual approach involves a manual screening of the collected reviews to determine their degree of subjectivity and polarity. As the manual approach requires more effort compared to the other approaches, it is frequently used in combination with the other more automated approaches.
- **Dictionary based.** The dictionary-based approach starts with a manual screening to find some sentiment words as "seeds," i.e., words that can be considered as positive or negative. Then, an algorithm searches through online dictionaries (or general lexicons) to find synonyms and antonyms of these seeds to iteratively complete the list of sentiment words. Afterward, a manual check is required to clean up the list. This approach is less time-consuming compared to the manual approach but still needs a manual check afterward. It is particularly useful for general topics, rather than for specific (research) domains in which words may have different meanings depending on the context. For instance, in the sentence "the radio plays quietly," the sentiment word "quietly" can have both a positive and negative meaning depending on where you are (e.g., in a car, at a party). Examples of general lists with sentiment words are publicly available. For instance, SentiWordNet and VADER are popular sentiment lexicons (Nandwani and Verma 2021). Other examples are https://github.com/aesuli/SentiWordNet, https://saifmohammad.com/WebPages/lexicons.html.
- **Corpus based.** While the dictionary-based approach leverages online dictionaries, the corpus-based approach focuses on co-occurrence statistics embedded in text. More specifically, the corpus-based approach aims at building a lexicon that is specific for a certain domain or category. The input are seeds, namely, a small set of category-dependent words (let us say five seeds), supplemented by a list of references that link to domain-specific sources (called a representative text corpus). The output is a ranked list of words associated with that category. A manual screening is only required for the top-ranked words because other words are less typical for the specific category under study. The aim is to compose a sentiment lexicon, i.e., the final list of synonyms and antonyms for a given category. Similar to the dictionary-based approach, different iterations

are needed. However, too many iterations (let us say more than eight) will give a higher risk for general words instead of category-dependent words.

Besides these three approaches, more advanced alternatives exist that rely on machine learning (e.g., using decision trees, Naïve Bayes, Random Forest), deep learning (e.g., using algorithms such as LSTM or CNN), and transfer learning (e.g., using pre-trained models) (Ligthart et al. 2021; Nandwani and Verma 2021). Such techniques for emotion detection are, however, out of scope for this book as they require a stronger technical background from the reader.

A sentiment model is a collection of sentiment words or opinion words that are analyzed to derive the subjectivity and polarity of textual reviews about an organization's product or service.

Once the sentiment words are identified, the collected reviews can be analyzed. As reviews are subjective, it is important to study reviews of many people in order to generalize the findings. A (statistical) summary can be used to reflect the opinions about a product or service (or the features, which give richer information) by means of a percentage or a score, for example:

- "X% of the reviewers are positive/negative about a product/service or about a feature of that product/service."
- "A product/service or a feature of that product/service was reviewed with a score of −0.43" (i.e., a negative decimal close to one/neutral, thus slightly negative).

7.3.1 Example of a Feature-Based Sentiment Analysis

In order to know how many people are positive or negative about which features of a product or service, each review can be analyzed (or mined) as follows.

Example of a user review:

Posted by: Gregory Thurston Posted on: 2022/06/28
"Six months ago, I bought a GStar GPS, particularly the X550 model, whereas my father opted for the TT GO (type 2635). During the first week, I was very pleased with my new gadget. The quality of the screen is very nice with beautiful colors. Now that I am using it more regularly, I experienced that the battery must be recharged quite often and weighs a lot. My father is very enthusiastic about his device, and has no battery problems."

In order to determine what the review is about, each sentence is separately analyzed. The user review can be rewritten as follows.

Posted by: Gregory Thurston Posted on: 2022/06/28
(1) "Six months ago, I bought a GStar GPS, particularly the X550 model, whereas my father opted for the TT GO (type 2635)."
(2) "During the first week, I was very pleased with my new gadget."
(3) "The quality of the screen is very nice with beautiful colors."
(4) "Now that I am using it more regularly, I experienced that the battery must be recharged quite often and weighs a lot."
(5) "My father is very enthusiastic about his device, and has no battery problems."

A feature-based sentiment model can be built by looking at five elements of an opinion: **(e, a, s, h, t)**. The letters respectively refer to e̲ntity, a̲spect, s̲entiment, h̲older, and t̲ime, namely:

- What is the review about (= target entity, e + target aspects, or attributes, a)?
- What is the sentiment (s)?
- To whom does the sentiment belong (= source or sentiment holder, h)?
- When was the sentiment formulated (= time stamp, t)?

The concrete (e, a, s, h, t) elements for the example above are as follows.

- **What is the reviewabout (=target entity, e + target aspects, or attributes, a)?**

The review deals with two types of navigation systems, namely, GStar X550 and TT GO 2635. More particularly, the text refers to different aspects or attributes of a navigation system. For instance, sentence 3 refers to the screen, whereas sentence 4 refers to the battery duration and the battery weight. Such product features can be used for aspect categorization. Therefore, a distinction can be made between explicit and implicit categorization. Explicit (or direct) categorization refers to aspects that are literally mentioned in the text, e.g., the noun "screen" in sentence 3. On the other hand, implicit (or indirect) categorization refers to aspects that can be derived, e.g., sentence 4 refers to the battery duration by indirectly mentioning that "the battery must be recharged quite often." Other examples of implicit categorization are words such as "expensive" (for prize), "it fits my pocket" (for size), or "it can be easily installed" (for installation or ease of use). Also, synonyms can be used for a navigation system, such as "GPS" (sentence 1), "gadget" (sentence 2), or "device" (sentence 5).

- **What is the sentiment (s)?**

Sentence 1 gives a neutral description of a fact, while sentence 2 expresses a sentiment in the past. The message related to the screen of the GStar is positive (sentence 3), while the message related to the duration and the weight of the battery

Table 7.1 An example of a feature-based sentiment model for one review with regular opinions

Target (t): entity (e)	Target (t): aspect (a)	Sentiment/polarity of target (s)	Opinion holder (h)	Date (t)
GStar X550	Screen	Positive	Gregory Thurston	2022/06/28
GStar X550	Battery— duration	Negative	Gregory Thurston	2022/06/28
GStar X550	Battery— weight	Negative	Gregory Thurston	2022/06/28
TT GO 2635	GENERAL	Positive	Father of Gregory Thurston	2022/06/28
TT GO 2635	Battery	Positive	Father of Gregory Thurston	2022/06/28

is rather negative (sentence 4). On the other hand, the message related to the TT GO is generally positive (sentence 5), and also the battery message is positive (sentence 5). The example shows that all sentences must be linked to each other in order to interpret the review correctly. For instance, the father of Gregory Thurston uses a different device than Gregory himself.

- **To whom does the sentiment belong (= source or sentiment holder, h)?**

The review under study mentions two persons, namely, Gregory Thurston and his father. To answer this question, it is also important to consider the perspective of the reader. For instance, if the source is an organization, then it rather concerns an advertisement than a user review. Furthermore, a message can be negative for the sentiment holder, but positive for the reader. For instance, a sentence such as "the price of houses is decreased, which has a negative impact on our economy" might be bad news for sellers but good news for buyers.

- **When was the sentiment formulated (= time stamp, t)?**

Finally, the date of the review should be included in the analysis. In this example, the review was written in June 2022. This information can be used, for instance, to monitor the evolution of similar products over time or to identify trends.

Table 7.1 shows how the unstructured text of a review can be summarized as structured data in a database scheme, based on (e, a, s, h, t).

By bundling all information in a table or a database structure (Table 7.1), an overview is created that can be used to verify how many positive items were involved or to detect a trend over time. For instance, if a new product has technical issues, then the number of negative reviews and ratings may significantly increase within a short amount of time. Such information may alert the organization for a timely intervention.

Alternatively, the data in Table 7.1 can also be written in sentences as follows. Each sentence consists of the same five opinion elements: (e, a, s, h, t).

Table 7.2 An example of a feature-based sentiment model for comparative opinions

Target (t): entity 1 (e1)	Target (t): entity 2 (e2)	Target (t): aspect (a)	Preferred entity (PE)	Opinion holder (h)	Date (t)
Product A	Product B	–	Product A	Gregory Thurston	2022/06/28
Product A	Product B	–	Product A Product B	Gregory Thurston	2022/06/28
Product A	Product B	–	Product A	Gregory Thurston	2022/06/28
Product A	Product B	–	–	Gregory Thurston	2022/06/28

(GStar X550, screen, positive, Gregory Thurston, 2022/06/28)
(GStar X550, battery duration, negative, Gregory Thurston, 2022/06/28)
(GStar X550, battery weight, negative, Gregory Thurston, 2022/06/28)
(TT GO 2635, GENERAL, positive, father of Gregory Thurston, 2022/06/28)
(TT GO 2635, battery, positive, father of Gregory Thurston, 2022/06/28)

The previous example concerned a review with regular opinions. A slightly different approach is used for comparing different entities, i.e., for mining comparative (instead of regular) opinions. In this case, opinions express whether one brand, product, or service is better than another, for instance:

- **Non-equal gradable comparison**: "Product A is <u>better</u> than product B."
- **Equative comparison**: "Product A is about the <u>same</u> as product B."
- **Superlative gradable comparison**: "Product A is the <u>best</u>."
- **Non-gradable comparison**: "Product A is <u>different</u> from product B."

For comparative mining, Table 7.2 shows that the database scheme has one additional column for the second entity and that the sentiment column is replaced by a column for the preferred entity (PE).

7.3.2 Example of a Sentiment Analysis with Reviews and Ratings

While in the previous example the sentences were analyzed in detail, opinions can also be analyzed based on adjectives combined with the corresponding ratings. As an example, suppose that a film (let us say "In Bruges") was reviewed and rated by many users with a score out of five (e.g., on a Likert scale). Such individual ratings can then be used to derive a global score for the film.

Figure 7.3 shows that the stars of a rating system refer to the notion of polarity and represent a continuum from negative to positive values with a neutral center. For a 5-star rating system, the middle or neutral value is obtained by dividing the total

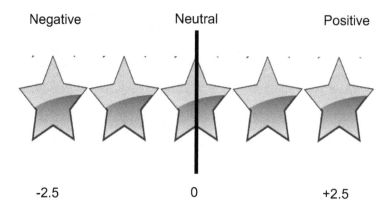

Fig. 7.3 An example of a rating system with five stars

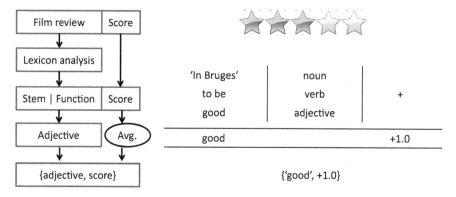

Fig. 7.4 An example of a sentiment model with ratings for a film

number of stars (i.e., five) by two. So in this example, when a reviewer rates the film with 2.5 stars, one actually assigns a polarity score of zero. On the other hand, the most negative rate gets a score of −2.5, and the most positive one gets a score of +2.5. The sign thus refers to a negative or positive opinion and the decimal indicates the degree of polarity.

Suppose that a review looks like this: "In Bruges was good—3/5 stars." Three stars indicate that the review is slightly positive (Fig. 7.3). The review under study contains only one adjective, namely, "good," which means that the assigned stars solely refer to this adjective. It can thus be derived that this adjective may express a slightly positive opinion.

The corresponding sentiment model is presented in Fig. 7.4. When translating to a score, three stars would normally refer to a score of +0.5 (see Fig. 7.3). However, in this example, Fig. 7.4 illustrates that the adjective "good" is associated with a score of +1.0. This can be explained by the fact that many other reviewers have rated films with four stars while describing their opinion with the adjective "good."

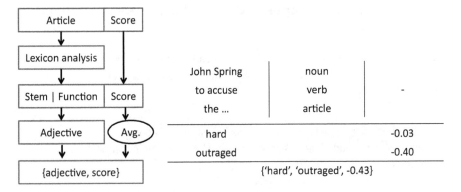

Fig. 7.5 An example of a sentiment model with ratings for a newspaper article

A sentiment model that combines reviews with ratings will first look for a list of adjectives with corresponding scores (based on averages) before assigning global scores, e.g., to particular films. Once such a list of adjectives and scores exists for a certain rating system, it can be reused to conduct a similar sentiment analysis.

Some examples in another context will mine newspaper articles in order to predict positive or negative effects on market shares or the results of political elections, among others. For instance, consider this extract from a (fictive) newspaper article.

> "Politician John Spring accuses the newspaper XYZ of inciting hatred after they published an opinion piece on the new housing code together with a picture of a Nigerian mass grave.
> The editor explains why they will continue to fight Spring's love of segregation **hard**. **Outraged**? Yes, we are first and above all **outraged**."

This extract contains two sentiment words, namely, "hard" and "outraged," with the latter being more negative than the former. The corresponding sentiment model is shown in Fig. 7.5. It is built by searching for the nouns and verbs in the extract and particularly the adjectives and adverbs.

This newspaper example illustrates a sentiment model with multiple sentiment words. In this case, each sentiment word is assigned an average score (as previously defined), and the overall score is the sum of the individual scores (i.e., −0.43 in this example) (Minnaert 2012).

7.4   Big Data Challenges to Opinion Mining and Sentiment Analysis

The introduction section of this chapter already indicated the power of online reviews and ratings. For instance, what would you do as a consumer when reading a review like this?

> "We dined in the restaurant and it was horrible! Wouldn't feed it to my dog! The waiter was rude, and when we told him we were unhappy with our food, we never saw him again."

On the other hand, the restaurant holder would certainly wish to know when such negative reviews go around (see also Chap. 5 on social CRM).

The question remains, however, whether all reviews are sincere, and the answer is unsure. Hence, a critical reflection on the use of text mining techniques is needed. This chapter already started by indicating the importance of human input for successful applications, rather than fully automated mining exercises. Furthermore, as writing online reviews and assigning ratings are cheap (e.g., compared to online ads; see Chap. 4) and can highly influence customers and prospects, some organizations might get tempted to conduct unethical behavior (i.e., comparable to the "black hat"techniques of SEO, Chap. 6). For instance, organizations might write reviews themselves or pay someone else to do so in order to create an impression of peer consensus. Or organizations might pay bloggers for removing a blog post containing a negative review. Other reasons for fake reviews are, among others, to improve the ranking of a product/service, to boost sales of a low-selling product/ service, to boost the visibility of a new product/service/brand, or to balance negative reviews (Jain et al. 2021). On the other hand, unethical behavior is not necessarily initiated by an organization. For instance, former employees may also launch extremely negative comments or false rumors about a brand after they got fired.

Consequently, as a consumer, a critical attitude is required instead of believing everything that is written in user reviews. In order to evaluate a review or rating, it is important to make some of the following considerations:

- Who is the reviewer? Is it written anonymously or is one's identity known?
- What is the purpose of the purchase? For instance, a purchase that is bad for the reviewer can be good or moderate for another user (e.g., different expectations exist for a family dinner with kids or for a romantic dinner with two).
- If the review is extremely positive, be aware that the organization could have written the review itself.
- Or vice versa, if the review is extremely negative, the review could have been written by the competitors of the organization.

Besides the challenge of unethical behavior, the techniques of opinion mining or sentiment analysis are also difficult to apply since subjective language is complex. For instance, citations can use negative words to describe something positive (or vice versa) or citations can start with positive wordings and still have a negative ending. The latter is a challenge for the broader domain of opinion mining techniques and thus not limited to a social media context. Moreover, WOM can also be communicated through audio, video, or pictures (in addition to text) in order to express feelings and viewpoints.

In general, opinion mining techniques have to deal with the following challenges in addition to the typical computational costs and language translation issues (Jain et al. 2021; Nandwani and Verma 2021; Liu 2010, 2012).

- **Literal versus figurative meaning of words**. Words can have different meanings, which makes automated opinion mining more difficult. For instance, the sentence "The activity really sucks" is negative, whereas the sentence "The vacuum cleaner sucks really good" uses the same verb in a positive way.
- **Neutral meaning of words**. Opinion mining is also challenged by words that are used in a neutral meaning. For instance, in the sentence "If I find a good HD television in the shop, I will buy it," the adjective "good" is not referring to something positive (although it usually does). This example shows the importance of context dependency as well.
- **Sarcasm and irony sentences**. Opinion mining has to deal with sarcasm, i.e., if the reviewer means the opposite of what one is writing. Examples of reviews with sarcasm are "What a great tool! It stopped working after two days." and "It was great! Yeah right. . . ."
- **Complex sentences**. Human language is complex to analyze, especially when the message covers web slang (i.e., informal language or new abbreviations used in chat messages), multiple aspects or only implicit aspects, and comparative sentences.
- **Facts without sentiment words**. The fourth challenge indicates that some sentences may look like facts but still have a positive or negative meaning. In the example "The hot tub is heated by much electricity," the message is negative for consumers who will likely have higher utility bills after using the hot tub. Similarly, the sentence "After a few days sleeping in my new bed, the mattress collapsed" does not contain sentiment words and still refers to a negative opinion.
- **Opinion spamming**. The final challenge covers the previous discussion about unethical behavior and emphasizes the need for reliable sources. Opinion spamming refers to the abuse or sabotage by people working at or being related to a certain organization (e.g., competitors, employees, or former employees). It usually results in extremely negative or extremely positive reviews. Three main types of opinion spamming exist: (1) fake reviews by people who have not used the product or service themselves (and which can be positive or negative); (2) brand reviews instead of reviews about a product or service (e.g., "I will never buy any product of company XYZ anymore" after having one problem with

one product), which is a generalization that can harm an organization even more; and (3) non-reviews, which are ads and other texts that express no opinion.

7.5　Takeaways

This chapter discussed the technical side of social media as big data analytics in the field of opinion mining (or sentiment analysis, which we use interchangeably). The related business intelligence techniques can be seen as a content analysis of a massive amount of social media data in order to verify what people are telling about an organization and its products and services. Opinion mining is thus frequently used within the context of social CRM, namely, for monitoring purposes (see Chap. 5).

An organization can profit from monitoring the opinions of users and professionals. For instance, organizations can monitor messages to find out how their brand is perceived, how their products and services can be improved, or if their marketing strategy is working. Further on, messages can be monitored that deal with the market in which they operate in order to find trends, to monitor any shares the organization might have, or to detect what the competitors are doing (right or wrong). Opinion mining and sentiment analysis can also alert an organization when a crisis hits. Think, for instance, about a crisis of smartphones (see Chap. 5) which may give rise to newspaper articles titled like "Exploding smartphone investigated," "Exploding smartphone leaves man in shock" (*The Local*, July 2012), or "Exploding smartphone caught on video" (knowyourmobile.com, July 2012). Such messages may frighten customers and prospects of smartphones and are extremely important to organizations that develop or sell smartphones. When analyzing online reviews and ratings, some negative consequences can be tempered by reacting timely and properly.

This chapter is particularly focused on online reviews and ratings, which can highly impact on sales and the price that people are willing to spend on a specific product or service. Opinion mining thus requires an investment from an organization but has also the potential to pay off in terms of ROI. Given its relevance, more research is needed to overcome the challenges faced by text mining in general, e.g., to automatically detect the correct meaning of words and opinion spamming.

7.6　Self-Test

- What do opinion mining and sentiment analysis mean, and how do they differ?
- Can you explain how opinion mining can create business value from social media?
- What is a sentiment model and how can it be created?
- Can you explain the challenges faced by opinion mining?
- Discuss how the following posts can be managed. Evaluate the positive or negative impact of word of mouth, and suggest possible replies. Tip: respond

by saying sorry, show respect, suggest a private follow-up, appreciate the comment, provide updates, etc.

- – "No response. The fantastic customer service continues! #sarcasm"
- – "Rude cabin staff on flight FR8456... #neveragain"
- – "Saddest part of a holiday is always the flight back: #missyoualready"

• Reflect on what you would do if a competitor or former employee uses black hat methods?

Bibliography

Al-Natour, S., & Turetken, O. (2020). A comparative assessment of sentiment analysis and star ratings for consumer reviews. *International Journal of Information Management, 54*(102132), 1–18.

Dave, K., Lawrence, S., & Pennock, D. M. (2003). Mining the peanut gallery: Opinion extraction and semantic classification of product reviews (pp. 519–528). *Proceedings of the 12th international conference on world wide web.*

Darwich, M., Noah, S. A. M., & Omar, N. (2020). Deriving the sentiment polarity of term senses using dual-step context-aware in-gloss matching. *Information Processing & Management, 57*(6), 1–26.

Edelman. (2020). *Edelman trust barometer 2020.* Retrieved November 22, 2021, from https://www.edelman.com/sites/g/files/aatuss191/files/2020-01/2020%20Edelman%20Trust%20Barometer%20Global%20Report_LIVE.pdf

Greenberg, J. (1987). A taxonomy of organizational justice theories. *Academy of Management Review, 12*(1), 9–22.

Heider, F. (1958). *The psychology of interpersonal relations.* Wiley.

Khan, M. T., Durrani, M., Ali, A., Inayat, I., Khalid, S., & Khan, K. H. (2016). Sentiment analysis and the complex natural language. *Complex Adaptive Systems Modeling, 4*(2), 1–19.

Jain, P. K., Pamula, R., & Srivastava, G. (2021). A systematic literature review on machine learning applications for consumer sentiment analysis using online reviews. *Computer Science Review, 41*, 1–17.

Ligthart, A., Catal, C., & Tekinerdogan, B. (2021). Systematic reviews in sentiment analysis: A tertiary study. *Artificial Intelligence Review, 54*(7), 4997–5053.

Liu, B. (2010). Sentiment analysis and subjectivity. In N. Indurkhya & F. J. Damerau (Eds.), *Handbook of natural language processing* (pp. 627–666). Chapman & Hall, CRC Press.

Liu, B. (2012). *Sentiment analysis and opinion mining.* Morgan & Claypool Publishers.

Minnaert, B. (2012). Guest lecture of Bart Minnaert in the course Creating Value Using Social Media at Ghent University, November 2012.

Nandwani, P., & Verma, R. (2021). A review on sentiment analysis and emotion detection from text. *Social Network Analysis and Mining, 11*(81), 1–19.

Pang, B., & Lee, L. (2008). Opinion mining and sentiment analysis. *Foundations and Trends in Information Retrieval, 2*(2), 1–135.

Turner, J. C. (1985). Social categorization and the self-concept: A social-cognitive theory of group behavior. In E. J. Lawler (Ed.), *Advances in group processes: Theory and research* (Vol. 2, pp. 77–122). JAI Press.

Zhu, F., & Shang, X. M. (2010). Impact of online consumer reviews on sales: The moderating role of product and consumer characteristics. *Journal of Marketing, 74*(2), 133–148.

Social Network Data and Predictive Mining (Business Intelligence 2)

8

This chapter covers the second part of our business intelligence discussion and makes the reader learn how organizations can create business value by analyzing social network data. Diverse information about a certain person can be collected from different social media tools and combined into a database to obtain more complete profiles of employees, customers, or prospects (i.e., social engineering). The latter can supplement the social CRM database (see Chap. 5). Particularly, social media may uncover information about what people post, share, or like but also to whom they are connected. By combining or aggregating such information for many individuals in social networks, organizations can start predicting trends, e.g., to improve their targeted marketing (see Chap. 4) or to predict which people are more likely to churn, fraud, resign, etc. Hence, social media are seen as big data in the sense that they can provide massive amounts of real-time data about many Internet users, which can be used to predict someone's future behavior based on the past behavior of others. This chapter explains how social networks can be built from social media data and introduces concepts such as peer influence and homophily. The chapter concludes with big data challenges to social network data.

Similar to the previous chapter on business intelligence (Chap. 7), this chapter is mainly situated in the IT department of an organization (i.e., especially regarding the technical execution or implementation of business intelligence techniques). However, to ensure successful business intelligence applications, business input and experience are still required to draw appropriate business decisions. In other words, business intelligence should support the (data-driven) decision-making process (Fig. 8.1).

Teaser Question
- How can social media help predict the future?

© The Author(s), under exclusive license to Springer Nature Switzerland AG 2022
A. Van Looy, *Social Media Management*, Springer Texts in Business and
Economics, https://doi.org/10.1007/978-3-030-99094-7_8

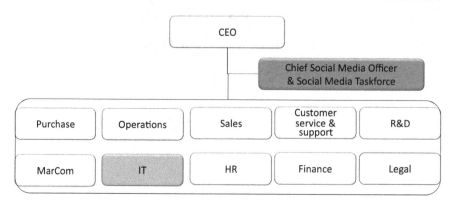

Fig. 8.1 The multidisciplinary approach of social network data

8.1   Introduction to Social Network Data

While Chap. 7 explained how predictions can be made based on one's opinions and sentiments, we now turn to making predictions based on past behaviors of ourselves, of people we know (i.e., acquaintances), and even of people we do not know but who are similar to us (i.e., based on profiling). For this purpose, this chapter also focuses on community detection and recommender systems (Abbas 2021).

In order to introduce the reader to the topic, the use of social network data is first illustrated for targeted marketing before listing applications in other areas.

8.1.1   Examples of Social Network Data in Targeted Marketing

In Chap. 4, we discussed the principle of targeted marketing for brands or purchases, which means that Internet users will rather receive those online ads that fit their personal profile (e.g., related to their specific hobbies, interests, profession, and the city where they live to receive local deals). Targeted marketing can be facilitated by investigating personal information revealed by social media tools, e.g., Facebook™ (with information about a user's personal life such as hobbies), LinkedIn™ (with information about a user's job), or Twitter™ (with information about a user's professional expertise, among others). These different types of user information can be combined per user (e.g., customer or prospect) into a database for the purpose of deriving different client types.

The following examples introduce social network analysis (and predictive analytics in general) for targeted marketing. First, Fig. 8.2 illustrates that if a social media tool reveals that a user (let us say Axl) likes gaming, that user will be more likely to get an online ad for a new game. Similarly for online shops, if browser cookies reveal that a user (let us say Ashley) searched for a specific product in a web shop, that user will be more likely to get an online ad for similar products or similar

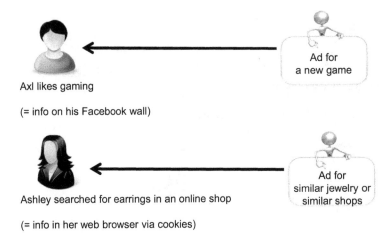

Fig. 8.2 Examples of targeted marketing *without* social network analysis (direct, online)

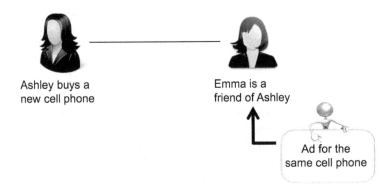

Fig. 8.3 An example of targeted marketing *with* social network analysis (indirect, online)

shops. Targeted marketing can use personal information to better serve people as a (potential) client by trying to predict which products or services the user might be interested in and possibly buy in the near future. However, this kind of (direct) targeted marketing and predictive analytics does not make use of social network data, because predictions of someone's future behavior are limited to the past behavior of oneself.

On the other hand, targeted marketing can also work indirectly, i.e., via a social network. In this case, it tries to predict which products or services a user might be interested in, namely, (1) based on one's relationships with other people or (2) based on similar characteristics with other people. For instance, Fig. 8.3 illustrates that if a user (let us say Ashley) bought a new cell phone online, the user's connections in social media tools (e.g., Emma) are more likely to see an online ad for the same cell phone. This indirect way of targeted marketing tries to estimate the probability that

Axl frequently buys beer

Fig. 8.4 An example of targeted marketing (direct, offline)

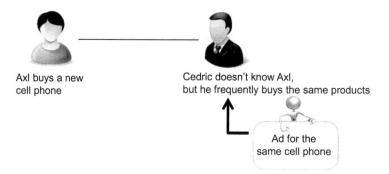

Fig. 8.5 An example of targeted marketing (indirect, offline)

Emma tends to buy the same product as her friend Ashley and which is the topic of this chapter. In particular, social network analysis tries to predict someone's future behavior based on the past behavior of others.

Predictions of future behavior can be based on online information (as seen in the previous examples), but they can also deal with offline information. For instance, shops and supermarkets may give their customers loyalty cards with which they can track the products that are frequently bought (besides personal information, e.g., name and address). Such offline predictions can be direct, as shown in Fig. 8.4. An indirect way to predict future behavior is based on a network of client types (Fig. 8.5) which thus requires network data.

A client type is a collection of customers (or prospects) of an organization who conducted similar behavior in the past. It may concern people who regularly buy similar products, such as Axl and Cedric in Fig. 8.5. In this example, Axl and Cedric do not know each other but share similar characteristics by buying the same products. Those people are more likely to continue buying similar products in the future.

Future behavior can also be predicted based on personal expenses. Ultimately, a bank account may not only reveal personal data (such as a person's name and address) but also in which shops a person frequently buys products or services. Banks currently deal with the issue of commercialization of (anonymous) client information, which enables third-party organizations to derive different client types for targeted marketing. For privacy reasons, the information exchange will be anonymous. For instance, a third-party organization will only know people by an anonymous ID number (e.g., persons X, Y, Z instead of Joe, Harry, or Sandy).

8.1.2 Examples of Social Network Data in Other Areas

This chapter explains how social network data can be analyzed in order to discover relevant knowledge for an organization based on profiles with shared characteristics or attributes. Such knowledge discovery can be applied in diverse areas and is not limited to targeted marketing. Some applications for which organizations can use social network data are Rousidis et al. (2020):

- Customer acquisition and churn prediction (e.g., to predict which customers are more likely to buy or to churn and to send customized recommendations).
- Credit scoring (e.g., to predict which client types are solvable and will likely be able to repay a loan).
- Fraud detection (e.g., to predict which profiles are more likely to be fraudulent in areas such as banking, Internet marketing, telecommunication, or insurance fraud).
- Health care (e.g., to predict which profiles are more likely to bully or to get a certain disease).
- Other (e.g., predictions regarding stock markets, product pricing, real estate pricing, spam detection, phishing, cybercrime, counterterrorism, elections, and public policy outcomes related to natural phenomena).

Moreover, network analysis can go further than merely predicting future behavior. For instance, instead of only suggesting interested products to web shop visitors (i.e., targeted marketing), Amazon™ was the first company to investigate how it can proactively send products to a (loyal) customer (i.e., before one places an order). Already in 2013, Amazon™ received a patent on proactive sending, which was called the "method and system for anticipatory packaging shipping" (patent number US8615473B2) (GooglePatents 2021). The purpose of proactive sending is to guarantee a fast delivery to increase customer service without necessarily having warehouses in every country. Proactive sending makes use of network analysis and data mining technology to predict which products their customers might buy and when. It can therefore analyze online actions, such as previous orders, the keywords that a customer has used in search engines, websites that one has visited, or wish lists in various e-shops that are stored as browser cookies. Additionally, the predictions may rely on what other customers with similar characteristics frequently buy. As such, an organization can collect information of many customers and prospects in big datasets, use data mining techniques to find patterns or client types, and ultimately predict future orders.

8.2   Defining Social Network Data

8.2.1   Social Network Modeling Approaches

Research on social networks can be divided into two groups (Abbas 2021; Cab and Alatas 2019; Yuliansyah et al. 2020): (1) descriptive network modeling for social network analysis and community detection and (2) predictive network modeling for link prediction and attribute prediction.

> A social network is a number of persons or a group of entities that are related to each other in an offline or online context (e.g., relatives, friends, and colleagues).

Descriptive network modeling examines social networks to gain insight into the structure of a network and to identify important people or groups. Community detection involves the discovery of groups or clusters with cohesive characteristics, with a community being "a group of entities that are in proximity of each other when compared to other entities of a dataset" (Cab and Alatas 2019: p. 5). Proximity is measured in terms of similarity or distance between the entities. For instance, in the context of viral campaigns (see Chap. 4), centrality measures can be used to detect social leaders, which is useful information for launching a campaign. In particular, descriptive network modeling tries to detect a network (or community) and its members, and examines how they are linked to each other, as shown in Fig. 8.6. Figure 8.6 also illustrates that networks can be interconnected to each other (e.g., partnerships between organizations). For instance, one network may reinforce the other network by cross-selling to each other products and services, similar to the

Fig. 8.6 Descriptive network modeling

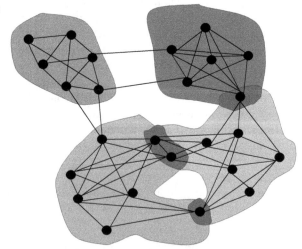

social ripple effect (see Chap. 2). A strong network can also use different channels (e.g., Facebook™, Twitter™, LinkedIn™, and blogs).

On the other hand, predictive network modeling involves link prediction to understand the dynamic changes in a network structure and to predict which connections will be made in the future. More precisely, Yuliansyah et al. (2020) define link prediction as "a technique to forecast new or missing relationships between entities based on the current network information" (p. 183470). Link prediction is frequently used by social media tools to suggest "people you may know" because those people are connected to one or more of your connections (e.g., in Facebook™, LinkedIn™, and Twitter™). Particularly, if more connections are connected to that third person, the more likely it is that you know that person too. Secondly, predictive network modeling involves attribute prediction, which looks for common characteristics or attributes, and is also called "predictive data mining." In particular, it uses historical data (e.g., customer records in a social CRM database; see Chap. 5) to build a predictive model (i.e., a "class probability estimation model") that predicts the unknown value of a class or target variable (e.g., customer acquisition, churn prediction, and credit scoring). Several data mining algorithms exist to automatically build a predictive model, which can be expressed as a mathematical formula (e.g., a linear model for regression or classification) and/or a logical statement (e.g., decision rules). Hence, "mining" literally refers to digging for information to find patterns in big data that can be interpreted in order to distill knowledge that is relevant for a business. Such predictions are typically evaluated by calculating performance measures such as accuracy, precision, recall, or an F1-score (Yuliansyah et al. 2020). Such performance measures are, however, outside the scope of this book.

In sum, descriptive network modeling is often used for a causal understanding of a certain phenomenon (e.g., "How do churning customers typically look like?" or "Why do people churn?"). On the other hand, prescriptive network modeling rather intends to predict or estimate that phenomenon for future use (e.g., "Which other/ new customers are more likely to churn in the future?").

8.2.2 Definitions

Social network analysis is defined as "the process of gathering statistics from the social network data" (Abbas 2021: p. 2), including a huge number of users and a big amount of possibly dynamically changing data (i.e., data that can vary over time). Due to this complexity of big data, the related feature extraction and preprocessing tasks are automatically done using mining techniques (e.g., machine learning such as deep learning algorithms).

> Social network analysis or network-based analysis refers to using (i.e., analyzing, interpreting, evaluating) information about links (i.e., edges, connections, or relationships) in order to predict future behavior and to stimulate desired business actions (e.g., selling products or services).

Given the popularity of social networks, much predictive power is present in the structure of social networks. More specifically, social media tools help organizations build social networks because of their rich user interactions (e.g., joining in the sense of creating and updating a personal profile, defining privacy settings, inviting others to connect, accepting or rejecting invitations by other users, sending and receiving messages, posting content, commenting on posts by others) (Abbas 2021).

When also social media data are used, the social network is called a "social *media* network" (e.g., a group of connected users on Facebook™, Twitter™, LinkedIn™, etc.). Social media network analysis refers to a network-based analysis that uses links in social media tools. The rising popularity of social media gives new opportunities to network-based analysis due to the availability of a large amount of new data to be included.

8.2.3   Graph Representation

The knowledge that can be derived from a social network is used to build a so-called (mathematical or knowledge) graph (Abbas 2021; Cab and Alatas 2019). In other words, a social network is visualized in a graph representation, as shown in Fig. 8.7. A graph consists of circles or nodes for representing entities (e.g., people, animals). The lines between the nodes represent the links, edges, or relationships between two entities (Yuliansyah et al. 2020). Consequently, a social network can also be defined as a network of nodes, representing entities, which are connected by links, representing a relationship between two entities. Subsequently, it will be shown that links may differ in strength, with some links being stronger than others are.

Figure 8.8 illustrates the graph of a social network with people as entities. In this example, the social network consists of three persons, namely, Ashley, Emma, and

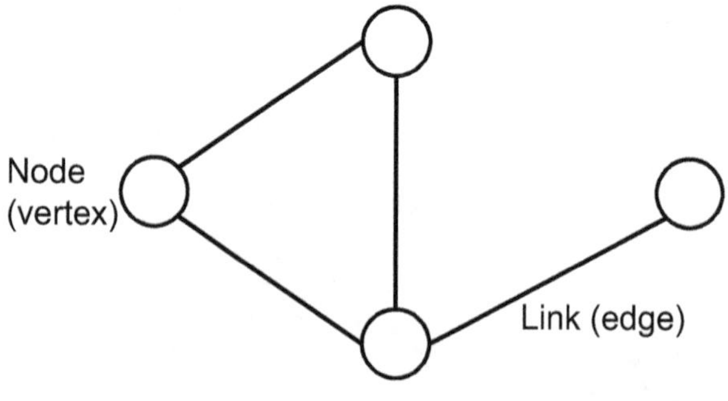

Fig. 8.7 The graph representation of a social network

Fig. 8.8 An example of a
homogeneous social network

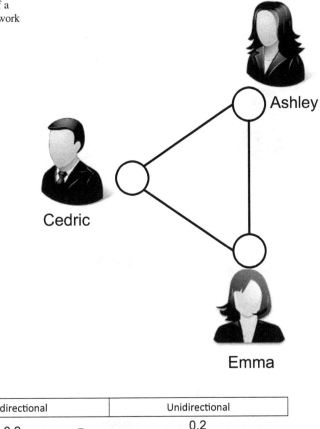

Fig. 8.9 Bidirectional versus unidirectional links in a social network

Cedric. The links between all entities indicate that they might know one another or
that they have similar characteristics, i.e., (1) Ashley and Emma are linked,
(2) Ashley and Cedric are linked, and (3) Emma and Cedric are linked.

In a social network, it frequently occurs that a relationship between two entities is
stronger or weaker than the relationship between two other entities. This strength or
weight of a relationship can be indicated by adding a number to the relationship, for
instance, 0.2 or 1.1. It is, however, also possible to have different weights between
the same entities (e.g., when you feel more connected to your friend than your friend
feels connected to you). In such situations, two weights can be assigned by means of
unidirectional links and arrows that indicate the direction of the relationship. Figure 8.9 presents the difference between bidirectional and unidirectional links. In
sum, bidirectional links can be binary (i.e., they exist or they do not exist) or have a

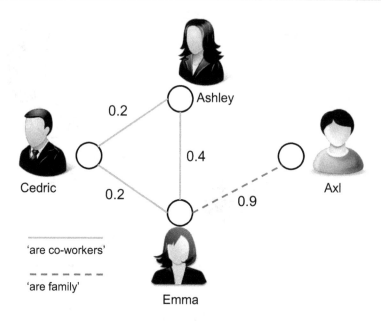

Fig. 8.10 An example of a heterogeneous social network

(positive) weight that represents the strength of the relationship, while also unidirectional links exist to form asymmetric relationships.

Figure 8.10 is an example of a graph with bidirectional links. It contrasts to Fig. 8.8 by having one additional entity (called Axl) who is linked to Emma in order to illustrate a heterogeneous social network (i.e., with different types of connections). In this example, the uninterrupted lines indicate coworkers (i.e., between Ashley, Emma, and Cedric), while the dotted line indicates family (i.e., between Emma and Axl). Emma is simultaneously a relative of Axl and a colleague of Cedric and Ashley. Each link in Fig. 8.10 also has a number that expresses the strength or weight of the relationship. An organization should calculate the weights itself, as the notion of "strength" depends on questions relevant to that organization (e.g., based on the number of products that two entities have in common and the time that two entities stay on the same web page).

8.3   Social Network Analytics

Before social network data can be analyzed, they must be found and collected in a single database. Depending on the type of organization, several ways exist to find datasets to be analyzed as social networks. Besides customer information, organizations can rely on phone logs, health records, government records, and social media interactions (if available). The unique database under study can thus combine offline big data with online big data.

When using the database for a social network application, a predictive model of the target variable will be found based on other attributes available in the database. Therefore, proper attribute identification and selection is important. For instance, predictive network modeling is part of "supervised segmentation" (i.e., by considering a target variable) and tries to iteratively find the most informative attributes on "ever-more-precise" subsets or segments of the database.

The subsequent sections illustrate how a social network analysis can be conducted by looking at concrete applications for reasons of attribute prediction.

8.3.1 Examples of Social Network Applications (with Only Offline Data)

Descriptive and predictive network modeling were originally limited to offline data. For instance, Table 8.1 shows an extract of a customer database.

The final column of Table 8.1 indicates which customers already bought a certain product. In this example, the product was bought by two customers, indicated by the first two rows (i.e., with ID 212 and ID 213). Customer analytics looks for shared attributes or characteristics to predict which other customers (represented by rows) are also likely to buy the same product in the near future. In this example, the customer in the last row of Table 8.1 will probably be interested in the product too as one shares many characteristics with the buyers of the product. In particular, customer ID 216 is in the same age category (i.e., age <30) as the customers who already bought the product and has also placed a high number of orders (order count > 45) of a similar average amount (50 < average amount < 100) and for similar products (i.e., games). These conditions are not met by the other customers in Table 8.1. As customer analytics suggests that customer ID 216 has the same profile as the buyers of the product under study, an organization becomes able to target this customer by proposing a new personalized offer.

The example shows that general rules can be derived from a dataset in order to predict future behavior of others (e.g., future sales, in this example) and this by

Table 8.1 An example of customer analytics based on historical data

ID	Age	Last order	Order count	Average amount	Order interests	Promo	Product purchase
212	25	22/05/31	50	85	Games	X	Yes
213	22	22/02/28	65	73	Games	X	Yes
214	45	22/09/15	12	123	Books, beauty	Y	No
215	50	22/08/17	5	230	Books, beauty	None	No
216	18	22/09/04	66	55	Games	X	No

identifying people who have a high probability of conducting a certain act (e.g., buying a certain product). Deriving such general rules from a dataset in order to create knowledge is called "mining" or "profiling."

The telecommunications sector frequently applies social network analysis based on offline data, e.g., who is calling who and for how long. For instance, for reasons of customer acquisition, a telecommunications organization may wish to answer the following question: "Given that a customer named Axl has bought a certain telecommunications service, what is the probability that Axl's friends will buy the same service too?" The social network for this example can be a network based on the phone calls made, in which:

- Nodes are represented by customers or prospects.
- Links are based on phone calls with a minimum duration (let us say of at least 10 s).
- Weights are based on the aggregate of all phone calls made between the nodes.

The target variable is to know who is more likely to be interested in the service and who might be less interested. Variables to predict this target variable may relate to geographical and demographic data, the level of technological expertise, financial information, and (most importantly) the first-degree connections. In other words, Axl's connections are more likely to buy the same service, and particularly those with similar characteristics on the other variables or attributes (e.g., geography, demography, technological expertise, finances). The resulting predictions will facilitate targeted marketing. Afterward, the social network can be evaluated by verifying how many of the predictions actually turned into sales.

A similar social network can be used for customer churn prediction, which is a relevant business issue (see social CRM, Chap. 5).

8.3.2   Examples of Social Media Network Applications (with Online Data)

Social media data can be added to social networks in order to enhance the dataset. Particularly, social media may supplement corporate data to help find the links (i.e., relationships or connections) between persons. This input is particularly useful for those organizations that do not have their own network data, such as a network of phone calls in the telecommunications sector.

Consider the following example, in which social media reveal connections between users:

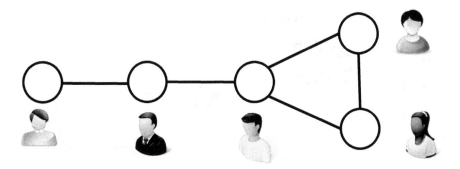

Fig. 8.11 An example of a social media network

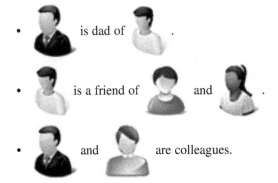

- is dad of .

- is a friend of and .

- and are colleagues.

This social media information can result in a social network, as presented in Fig. 8.11.

Furthermore, social media tools (e.g., Facebook™) do not only record the people who are known by a user (as connections) but also the user's posts and the pages and posts that the user "likes" or "shares." Such personal data can be added to the user's profile, which stimulates social media tools to commercialize their data (i.e., to sell social media data to third-party organizations).

As social media may quickly result in an explosion of data, organizations usually consider the links of the direct connections only (i.e., the first-degree connections, instead of connections of connections of connections).

Figure 8.12 illustrates how online data can create a quasi-social network, starting from Internet users (browsers) visiting web pages with UGC (user-generated content; see Chap. 2).

For instance, since Alex and Ann visited the Facebook™ page of John, it can be derived that they are both linked to John. In addition, Alex and Ann will probably be connected, as Alex and John visited the Facebook™ page of Ann.

Furthermore, it can be derived that Ann, Pete, and Jeff are connected, as they visited the same web pages (i.e., OnlineReviews.com, OrganizationBlog.com, and the Facebook™ page of Company XYZ).

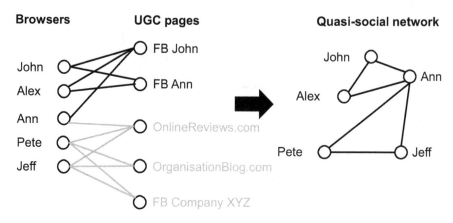

Fig. 8.12 An example of a quasi-social network

The result is a "quasi-social network," because the direct connections are based on assumptions derived from variables (i.e., co-visitations of the same web pages). Nonetheless, it remains unsure whether the persons involved actually know each other in real life, which explains the prefix "quasi-."

The specific procedure to create a quasi-social network is called "bipartite graph mining," because it aims to find bipartite relationships, i.e., a graph with two types of nodes (e.g., browsers versus UGC pages or people versus products, interests, Facebook™ likes, etc.). Thus, a bipartite network is characterized by two node types and links that are only connected to different node types. Besides bipartite networks, other network types exist for indicating temporal links that can (dis)appear over time (i.e., dynamic networks) or for similar nodes across layers (i.e., multiplex networks) (Yuliansyah et al. 2020). The latter are outside the scope of this book.

Predictive mining tries to protect the privacy of social media users by de-identifying both the browser names and the UGC pages by means of (random and unique) ID numbers, as shown in Fig. 8.13. The network is "double de-identified," namely, (1) the ID numbers remain anonymous, and (2) no information on browsers or pages is saved.

The quasi-social network can be improved by adding weights to the links. In this example, a weight or strength refers to the number of UGC pages that a node has in common with its direct neighbors (Yuliansyah et al. 2020). The more pages that are co-visited by two browsers (or individuals), the higher the weight will be. For instance, the link between browser 564,564 and browser 5,884,212 has a strength of 2 (i.e., they co-visited two UGC pages, namely, page 45312 and page 45453), whereas the link between browser 564,564 and browser 8,413,216 has a strength of 1 (i.e., they co-visited one UGC page, namely, page 45312). The former link is thus stronger than the latter, based on the number of co-visitations.

The next section clarifies how a quasi-social network such as Fig. 8.13 can be used for diverse applications.

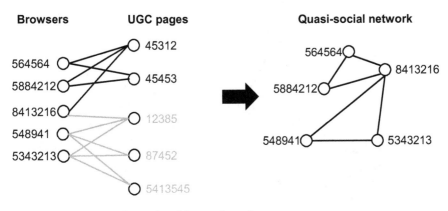

Fig. 8.13   An example of a quasi-social network, made anonymous

8.3.3   Mining Algorithm

In order to make predictions from a (quasi-)social network, a mining algorithm automatically runs to process the massive amount of big (social) data. This section illustrates how an algorithm typically works by means of a case study, based on Minnaert (2012). Although an algorithm normally runs automatically, the different steps are subsequently discussed to explain the process in non-technical language. The case study is as follows.

Assume a situation in which an online ad tries to convince people to act (let us say to buy a product).

You have data from different groups of people that constitute a network, namely:

- People who took action after seeing the ad (i.e., the buyers).
- People who saw the ad without taking action (i.e., the nonbuyers).
- People who have not yet seen the ad.

Try to predict which persons in the third group are more likely to take action after seeing the ad (i.e., to become buyers) in order to improve targeted advertising.

PS We remind the reader that a similar case study can be conducted for other applications, such as credit scoring, fraud detection, spam detection, and predictions regarding stock prices or health issues.

Figure 8.14 shows the start situation of the case study. Suppose that there are:

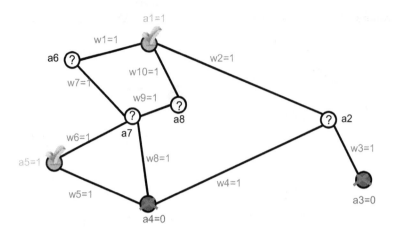

Fig. 8.14 Case study of a mining algorithm (start situation)

- Two buyers (i.e., represented by $a1$ and $a5$).
- Two nonbuyers (i.e., represented by $a3$ and $a4$).
- Four unknown nodes (i.e., represented by $a2$, $a6$, $a7$, and $a8$).

Each of these nodes has a unique ID number, namely determined by clockwise numbering in Fig. 8.14. Each known node also indicates a certain action, namely:

- 1 for action (i.e., buying the product after viewing the ad, e.g., $a1 = 1$)
- 0 for nonaction (i.e., not buying the product after viewing the ad, e.g., $a3 = 0$).

Furthermore, the links between the nodes have a strength or a weight (w). In order to facilitate the example, all connections have an equal strength or a weight of 1 ($w = 1$).

The final aim is to infer a probability distribution for the unknown nodes (i.e., indicated with a question mark) in order to identify which of the unknown nodes are more likely to act. In other words, which ones are potential buyers and which ones are rather not? For this purpose, we need to derive a score for the actions of the unknown nodes, as was already done for the buyers with a score of 1 and for the nonbuyers with a score of 0. Consequently, the probability to be derived will range between 0 and 1, with scores closer to 1 referring to a higher probability of buying a certain product after seeing a particular ad. In fact, probability values always range between 0 and 1.

Figure 8.15 shows the basic prediction, which is the average probability derived from all known "seed" nodes:

- (# buyers)/# seeds $= 2/4 = 1/2 = 0.5$
- $0 < \text{probability} < 1$.

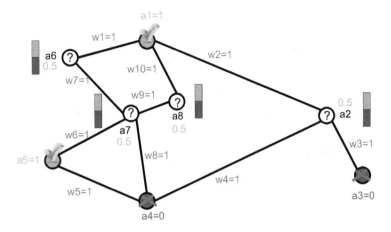

Fig. 8.15 Case study of a mining algorithm (basic prediction)

Seeds are the technical term for referring to the known nodes. In this example, there are two buyers and two nonbuyers, which makes four seeds. As half of the seeds bought the product, the basic prediction results in temporary probabilities of 0.5 (i.e., the number of buyers—which is 2—divided by the number of seeds, which is 4). These temporary probabilities will be refined throughout different iterations and will be reused as direct input for the next iteration by means of a rectangle (as shown in Fig. 8.15). The rectangles have two parts, with the upper part indicating the likelihood of buying and the lower part indicating the likelihood of nonbuying for a specific node. After the basic prediction, the likelihood for all unknown nodes is still 50–50, and the upper part and lower part of the rectangles have equal sizes.

In a first iteration, the basic probabilities are refined by calculating the average probability over all direct neighbors of a particular unknown node (Yuliansyah et al. 2020).

$$[\text{sum of}(\text{neighbors}^*\text{their weights})]/(\text{sum of their weights})$$

As all weights in this example are equal to 1, the calculation is just the sum of the direct neighbors, divided by the sum of their weights. The new probabilities are shown in Fig. 8.16. For instance, node $a2$ has three direct neighbors, namely, one buyer (i.e., $a1$) and two nonbuyers (i.e., $a3$ and $a4$). The sum of the direct neighbors is 1, divided by 3 (or 1 out of 3 was a buyer). This calculation results in a probability of 0.33 for node $a2$. The same reasoning applies to calculate the new probabilities for the other unknown nodes, with $a6$ having 2 direct neighbors, $a7$ with 4 direct neighbors, and $a8$ with two direct neighbors. Remember from Fig. 8.15 that the basic probabilities for all unknown nodes are 0.5, which should be taken into account when calculating the new probabilities for $a6$, $a7$, and $a8$.

In a second iteration, the rectangles and probabilities are adapted to the results of the previous iteration. Fig. 8.17 shows that the starting value for $a7$ is again 0.5,

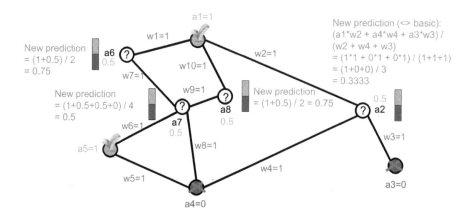

Fig. 8.16 Case study of a mining algorithm (iteration 1)

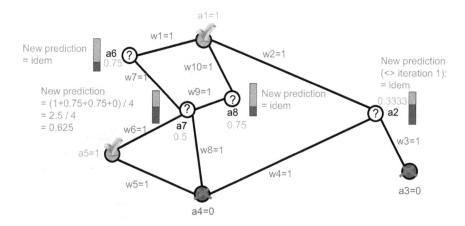

Fig. 8.17 Case study of a mining algorithm (iteration 2)

whereas the starting value for the other unknown nodes has changed (i.e., to 0.33 for *a*2 and 0.75 for *a*6 and *a*8). The same calculation can be redone as in the previous iteration (i.e., the sum of the direct neighbors divided by the sum of the weights), but taking into account the predictions from iteration 1. Figure 8.17 specifies that the new probabilities in iteration 2 do not change for *a*2, *a*6, and *a*8, because the direct neighbors did not change in value throughout iteration 1. Only a new prediction is needed for *a*7, resulting in a probability of 0.625.

We continue iterating until the probabilities remain stable. After a certain number of iterations (let us say x iterations), the probabilities of the unknown nodes will not change anymore and the case has reached an end state (Fig. 8.18).

In real life, the calculations happen automatically by means of an algorithm, but this manual example illustrates how organizations can handle network data to gain knowledge. The final probabilities for the unknown nodes represent a value or a

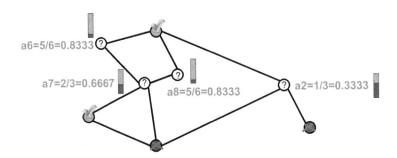

Fig. 8.18 Case study of a mining algorithm (iteration x—end situation)

score between 0 and 1 (i.e., similar to a percentage). Be aware that a probability of 0.33 should not be read as "a chance of 1 out of 3 to buy a product" but rather as a percentage. The goal is to compare the probabilities in order to decide which persons in the third group are potential buyers and are worth targeting in the organization's marketing campaign.

For instance, advertisers can take 10% as a bottom line (i.e., as an under limit), which represents the percentage of nonaction. In other words, they will then target those unknown nodes with a probability between 0.9 and 1. As Fig. 8.18 does not show an unknown node with a value of 0.9 or higher, none of the unknown nodes in our example will be targeted if the bottom line is set at 10%. On the other hand, when the bottom line is 50% or 0.5, for example, all unknown nodes except for $a2$ (which has a probability of 0.33) will be targeted for the ad.

One of the reasons why the previous example is relevant to organizations is because online ads are expensive (see Chap. 4). Therefore, organizations might profit from only showing their ad to those people who seem more responsive to the message of the ad. As explained in Chap. 4, when people (Internet users) navigate to a website, their browser cookies become available to that website. If that website also sells space for ads to a central ad network (e.g., DoubleClick Ad Exchange), a real-time bidding process starts in which organizations with ads that correspond to a user's interest will bid higher. With the business intelligence techniques for predictive mining, an organization can predict which ad must be shown to which user.

For predictive mining, an organization can create and combine different databases. For instance:

- Database of Internet users who clicked on the organization's ad to collect information about one's browser, IP address, and cookies (e.g., to uncover personal interests based on previous clicks, visits of other websites).
- Customer database with information about the buyers of the product or service in the ad (e.g., whether or not they have seen the ad before the purchase). Two browsers can, for instance, be assumed to be connected as neighbors (or quasi-friends) if they have visited the same websites or websites with similar content.

Regarding online brand advertising, organizations best target those people who are part of the 10% best ranked nodes (thus with a probability of 0.90) in order to have good profit from an ad (Provost et al. 2009).

8.4   Triggers for Social Network Data

The previous section clarified that direct neighbors in a social network are targeted in order to make predictions. This method works well because social network mining exploits peer influence and homophily, which concerns two important triggers for mining and business intelligence in general. Peer influence applies when you know the other persons in your network, whereas homophily considers strangers with similar characteristics.

8.4.1   Trigger 1: Peer Influence

The first trigger for targeting network neighbors is peer influence (Aral and Walker 2011). This trigger can be illustrated by wondering about the question: "If my friends jump off a cliff, would I jump too?" The question reflects on the degree to which peers will affect a person in a specific situation. Thus, peer influence refers to how the behavior of one's peers can change the likelihood that a person will engage in a certain behavior. For instance, people can consult relatives and friends before purchasing products (e.g., home electronics).

For an organization, it is important to know the influencers in a social network because behavior can cascade from one node to another (similar to an epidemic or contagion). Peer influence is present in situations related to opinions or rumors, but it can also explain situations related to public health, failures in financial markets, etc. The success of viral campaigns, such as the Hotmail™ campaign in the 1990s (see Chap. 4), can be explained by peer influence as emails are usually sent to people you know. Hotmail™ added a sentence at the bottom of each outgoing mail ("PS: Get your private, free email from Hotmail™ at http://www.hotmail.com"), which resulted in about 12 million new Hotmail™ users within 18 months. Another example relates to book publishers who may rely on peer influence to reach higher sales by giving free copies to influential readers when a new book is released. In sum, peer influence occurs when people in the same network have attributes (e.g., gadgets), and they are no total strangers to each other.

Let us look again at Fig. 8.10, which illustrates a social network with coworkers and family. Suppose that three network neighbors (namely, Ashley, Emma, and Cedric) have a cell phone of the same color and of the same brand, while one other connection (Axl) has a cell phone of another color and of another brand. Axl is connected to only one node in the network, which explains why peer influence is less powerful for him.

8.4.2 Trigger 2: Homophily

Another trigger for targeting network neighbors is homophily, which explains how social relationships arise (McPherson et al. 2001). Homophily means "love of the same" or the tendency of individuals to associate and bond with similar others. This trigger can be illustrated by the expression: "birds of a feather flock together" which indicates that similarity breeds connection. The expression literally refers to groups of birds that pass by. One group always covers the same type of birds (e.g., geese with geese, ducks with ducks, or sparrows with sparrows). It is hard (or even impossible) to find a mixed group of, let us say, sparrows and geese.

Translated to human beings, people with the same characteristics are more likely to form a network (e.g., based on similarities in age, gender, class, values, beliefs, etc.). The phenomenon of homophily regularly takes place because similarity makes communication and relationship formation between people easier. For instance, homophily often leads to homogamy, which is a marriage between people with similar characteristics. Homophily thus explains why people tend to behave similarly or buy similar products and services, even if they are total strangers to each other. The more characteristics they share, the more likely it is that they will conduct similar behavior.

Figure 8.19 illustrates an example of homophily. Assume that the three persons described in Fig. 8.19 sit in the same bar and do not know each other. Who will be more likely to start talking to each other?

All three persons described in Fig. 8.19 are men in the same age category. The two men on the right seem to have a link based on their job and children, whereas the person on the left is unemployed and without kids. Consequently, based on homophily, we can assume that the two men on the right are more likely to influence each other and spontaneously start talking to each other in the bar.

8.4.3 Peer Influence Versus Homophily

Peer influence and homophily can coexist, but one trigger will generally become more decisive to act (or not to act) than another in a specific situation. The effect of

Fig. 8.19 An example of homophily

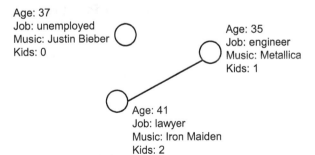

Age: 37
Job: unemployed
Music: Justin Bieber
Kids: 0

Age: 35
Job: engineer
Music: Metallica
Kids: 1

Age: 41
Job: lawyer
Music: Iron Maiden
Kids: 2

homophily also remains longer than peer influence, as the former is based on intrinsic similarities.

As an illustration, think about a situation in which obese children are playing together. Can this situation be described by mainly peer influence or mainly homophily? If the former is true, then obesity is considered as being contagious, meaning that a child will gain weight when playing with obese friends. The situation of obese children playing together is better explained by homophily, meaning that people with similar characteristics are more likely to become friends and to play with each other. Some degree of peer influence plays a role, as friends know each other instead of being strangers. For instance, based on peer influence, one friend can convince another friend to eat more cookies or to drink more soda during a school break. Nonetheless, the degree of homophily is stronger in this situation and is thus the main trigger (e.g., because obese children can be bullied by other children).

Although peer influence and homophily are complementary (and can be present simultaneously), viral marketing generally profits more from high peer influence (e.g., for sharing videos), while direct marketing (e.g., online ads) benefits more from high homophily.

Further, both triggers relate to the theory on the diffusion of innovations (Rogers 2003), which we discussed in Chap. 1. The so-called innovators and early adopters are more likely to have other adopters in their neighborhood because of similar characteristics (i.e., homophily) and will be less influenced by peers. However, also a temporal effect of peer influence can be created, particularly for the "late majority" and "laggards" who are more likely to adopt (or not to adopt) based on peer influence rather than homophily.

What about quasi-social networks? A particular connection becomes stronger when Internet users (browsers) navigate more to the same web pages (frequency), unless it concerns popular pages to which many people navigate (popularity) and unless it concerns older visits (in the past) (Provost et al. 2009). This implies that mainly homophily counts for creating quasi-social networks between users. Peer influence is only present if the users also know each other. Although social media tools can give insight into which users seem to know each other (e.g., as being connections on Facebook™), the degree to which connections know each other remains unsure.

8.5   Big Data Challenges to Social Network Data

This chapter has shown how social network data (as big data) can create business value for organizations by predicting future behavior. The research field of big social data, however, faces some important challenges (Abbas 2021; Cab and Alatas 2019; Rousidis et al. 2020).

First of all, social media give the opportunity to add a lot of data to a network analysis, but it rather concerns personal data (e.g., about interests, hobbies, professions, connections). In the end, privacy remains a big challenge, and efforts have been made to anonymously analyze big data.

Other big data challenges relate to the identification and analysis of social network data. Collecting and getting access to social media data are frequently an issue for organizations. This explains why some sectors make more use of social network data than others do. For instance, predictive mining is frequently done in the telecommunications sector that has access to organization-owned datasets with customer information and lists of phone calls, text messages, mobile data, etc. Regarding the analysis of social network data, tools and algorithms must advance to more accurately deal with the massive amount of big social data and increase prediction success. Technical issues still exist to maximize the computational power (e.g., memory issues of computers) and algorithmic accuracy (e.g., to increase the accuracy of predictions made by algorithms). Furthermore, research may continue to enhance knowledge about visualizing social networks, taking into account the impact of peer influence and homophily.

Consequently, predictive mining can give new opportunities to organizations, but this research field is still open for improvement to facilitate its practical use.

8.6 Takeaways

Predictive mining refers to finding similar characteristics of people in a dataset (e.g., in a customer database and/or in social media data) in order to predict future trends or future behavior of others. Social CRM can be used as input for a customer dataset under study (see Chap. 5), among others.

As the predictions are based on profiles (or types of anonymous people with similar characteristics) instead of individuals, predictive mining can also be called "profiling." These business intelligence techniques are frequently used within the context of online advertisements (see Chap. 4), as it facilitates targeted marketing. For instance, if you know that a certain person already bought a specific product or service, what is the probability or likelihood that one's connections or other people with similar characteristics will be interested in buying the same product or service? But applications of predictive mining are not limited to targeted marketing and can be found in diverse areas, such as predicting customer acquisition and churn, credit scoring, fraud detection, counterterrorism, public policy, and health care.

Social media have drastically changed the way big data are used. They do not only provide organizations with new data (e.g., about interests, hobbies, professions, and connections) but also allow a more personalized approach due to the additional insights that can be gained from social media data. While the previous chapter focused on big (social) data analytics for text mining, this chapter explained why big data analytics is important to predict relevant trends based on peer influence and homophily. Although social media data are immense and network analysis requires an effort, organizations make use of social network data with promising results. In conclusion, a further examination of social network data is worthwhile to overcome current challenges in this research field and to give new opportunities to contemporary organizations in order to perform better.

8.7   Self-Test

- What does social network mining mean?
- Can you explain how social networks are mathematically represented?
- Can you interpret the results of social network mining? For instance, can you give advice to whom an organization best shows a targeted ad in order to save money? Please motivate your choice.
- Are you able to distinguish the degree of peer influence from homophily for a given case description? Think about different situations in which you buy products or services, and evaluate to which degree such situations can be described by homophily and/or peer influence.
    - In a supermarket, travel agency, clothing shop, bank, insurance company, etc.
- Every time when Bricklayers (an R&D company) receives the CV of a job applicant, an in-depth screening starts to determine the degree that this person is likely to fit into the company culture. Can you explain how this screening will benefit from the current chapter?
- Ski-For-U (an insurance company) offers its clients an insurance for ski accidents. The company wants to determine which clients have an increased or decreased risk of a ski accident. If it uses social network data, how can the risk assessment benefit from this chapter?
- Consider the information in Fig. 8.20 in order to find ways to connect both persons.
    - Suppose two persons sit in the same bar and do not know each other. Based on what trigger(s) can a connection be built? For which aspects will this connection be stronger, and for which aspects weaker? Reflect on different types of products and services, as well as the related target groups.
    - Who will influence whom? When not? For instance, in conversations about going to the gym, having a family walk in the park on Sunday, having dinner in a top restaurant on their partner's birthday?

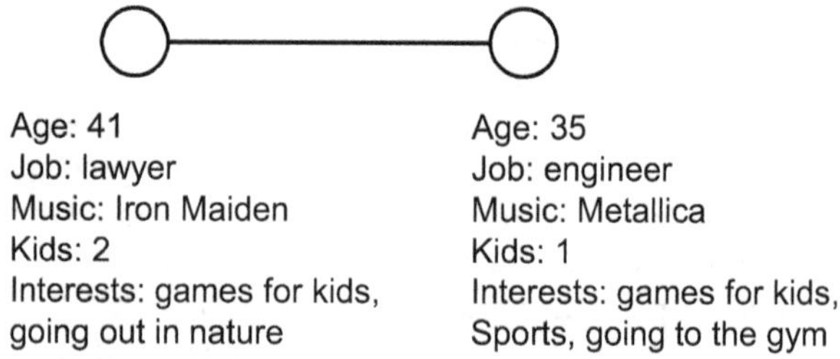

Fig. 8.20 An exercise regarding a potential social network link

Age: 41
Job: lawyer
Music: Iron Maiden
Kids: 2
Interests: games for kids, going out in nature

Age: 35
Job: engineer
Music: Metallica
Kids: 1
Interests: games for kids, Sports, going to the gym

Bibliography

Abbas, A. M. (2021). Social network analysis using deep learning: Applications and schemes. *Social Network Analysis and Mining, 11*(1), 1–21.

Aral, S., & Walker, D. (2011). Identifying social influence in networks using randomized experiments. *IEEE Intelligent Systems, 26*(5), 91–96.

Cab, U., & Alatas, B. (2019). A new direction in social network analysis: Online social network analysis problems and applications. *Physica A, 535*, 1–38.

GooglePatents. (2021). *Method and system for anticipatory package shipping.* Retrieved November 24, 2021, from https://patents.google.com/patent/US8615473B2/en

McPherson, M., Smith-Lovin, L., & Cook, J. M. (2001). Birds of a feather: Homophily in social networks. *Annual Review of Sociology, 27*, 415–444.

Minnaert, B. (2012). Guest lecture of Bart Minnaert in the course Creating Value Using Social Media at Ghent University, November 2012.

Provost, F., Dalessandro, B., Hook, R., Zhang, X., & Murray, A. (2009). Audience selection for on-line brand advertising: Privacy-friendly social network targeting. *Proceedings of the 15th ACM SIGKDD international conference on knowledge discovery and data mining.*

Rogers, E. M. (2003). *The diffusion of innovations* (5th ed.). Free Press.

Rousidis, D., Koukaras, P., & Tjortjis, C. (2020). Social media prediction: A literature review. *Multimedia Tools and Applications, 79*(9–10), 6279–6311.

Yuliansyah, H., Othman, Z. A., & Bakar, A. A. (2020). Taxonomy of link prediction for social network analysis: A review. *IEEE Access, 8*, 183470–183487.

e-Recruitment

9

This chapter clarifies how social media can be used by employers to recruit and by employees to be recruited. Besides general tips and tricks for e-recruitment, the reader will learn about some specific applications of social media tools that are frequently used worldwide. The main focus is on LinkedIn™, which is a social media tool dedicated to recruiting and professional networking, but other social media tools can also support e-recruitment (e.g., Facebook™, Instagram™, or Twitter™). We also delve into dedicated software systems that support the recruiting work. Furthermore, the chapter reflects on legal and ethical consequences that social media can have on hiring and firing.

The chapter of e-recruitment primarily focuses on the human resources (HR) department of an organization (Fig. 9.1).

> **Teaser Question**
> • Which of your private behaviors could jeopardize your job?

9.1 Introduction to e-Recruitment

e-Recruitment is a topic that involves all of us, even students who are not yet fully active on the labor market (e.g., when looking for an internship, a student job, or a first professional experience). The topic was initially limited to job search engines or jobsites that post vacancies and résumés to find a match (e.g., http://www.monster.com/; http://www.stepstone.com/; http://www.indeed.com/; http://www.jobsite.co.uk/; http://jobs.euractiv.com/). Nowadays, social media can also be used for e-recruitment. Additionally, in line with Chap. 7 on opinion mining and sentiment analysis, employees can write reviews and rate a (current or former) employer (e.g., http://www.glassdoor.com/). The latter example also allows us to anonymously compare salaries or to share interview experiences.

© The Author(s), under exclusive license to Springer Nature Switzerland AG 2022
A. Van Looy, *Social Media Management*, Springer Texts in Business and
Economics, https://doi.org/10.1007/978-3-030-99094-7_9

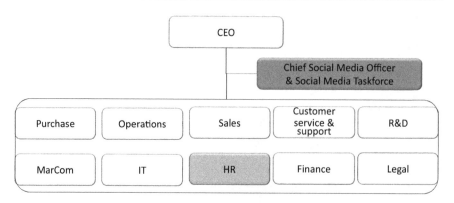

Fig. 9.1 The multidisciplinary approach of e-recruitment

Chapter 1 mentioned that the spread of social media tools may vary from region to region. Consequently, the specific actions for e-recruitment may depend on the social media tool and the region. Therefore, this chapter focuses on general tips and tricks and illustrates specific e-recruitment actions that are typical to the commonly used social media tools of Chap. 2.

e-Recruitment (i.e., electronic, web-based, or online recruitment) involves time and space independent HR activities by using the Internet and social media tools for automating parts of recruitment and selection. It targets to ensure that employees (i.e., as jobholders) have the required skills, experience, knowledge, and attitudes in order to help the organization realize its mission statement and vision.

Recruitment means identifying/sourcing and attracting/acquiring prospective employees or qualified applicants, whereas selection involves deciding whom to hire for a certain job position and thus choosing a suitable and competent candidate from a pool of applicants (Rahman et al. 2020). Afterward, other processes related to human resources (HR) are triggered to train and retain employees, and to improve the organization's employer branding (Mishra and Pavan Kumar 2019; Smythe et al. 2021).

When using social media for e-recruitment, it is important to know which social media tools can be used for which target groups. For instance, LinkedIn™ primarily focuses on higher-educated professionals (from starters to managers), while Facebook™ focuses more on friends. A tool such as Facebook™ can be used when specific target groups and networks of people (i.e., friends groups) need to be reached by employers. For instance, if an organization is looking for electricians, it may try to penetrate in a specific population using social media. On the other hand, many journalists and IT professionals are active on Twitter™, indicating that this social media tool can also be used to find experts in a certain domain or niche.

Furthermore, alternative social media tools can be used for e-recruitment, such as Pinterest™ for creating a résumé (i.e., curriculum vitae or CV) with photos. The latter shows creativity, which is of special interest for vacancies regarding creative jobs (e.g., a marketer or graphical designer). Nonetheless, Pinterest™ can also be used for less creative jobs since a picture is worth a thousand words.

Similar to other social media initiatives (e.g., online ads or viral campaigns; see Chap. 4), e-recruitment should serve the organizational strategy. As a strategy sets some rules and guidelines, the MarCom department will likely attend the human resources (HR) meetings that deal with e-recruitment. The main reasons are cost efficiency and to enrich (not to contradict) each other (e.g., to align specific HR initiatives to the corporate identity and to the general solution chosen for the corporate website). In other words, integration is required between the strategies for e-recruitment and for MarCom and the organization-wide strategy.

Moreover, executives are increasingly aware of the fact that employer branding can be powerful and should be approached and nurtured with actual MarCom skills and tools. Employer branding is a key topic for e-recruitment and relates to the MarCom efforts of an organization in order to create the image of being a "good" employer with a unique identity (Mishra and Pavan Kumar 2019). The notion of "good" can have different meanings and is to be derived from the organizational strategy and mission. It depends on what the organization stands for. For instance, a fast-food restaurant may wish to have an image of being a healthy and sporty employer or may recruit internationally in order to have an international staff.

Finally, e-recruitment means that the Internet and one or more social media tools are used for recruiting or talent acquisition initiatives, in addition to a traditional (electronic or paper-based) approach (Rahman et al. 2020). For an organization, e-recruitment requires combining social media data to create a database with all information available about candidates and employees. On the other hand, (future and current) employees can combine social media data and tools to create a database with information about interesting organizations and their employees. Furthermore, candidates triggered by a concrete vacancy or employer brand will frequently use social media to search for employees they know, which can be positive or negative publicity for the organization.

The subsequent sections take the perspective of organizations and employees in the context of e-recruitment and try to answer the question: "How to recruit or to get recruited by means of social media?"

9.2 Organizations and e-Recruitment: How to e-Recruit?

We start with the perspective of organizations and recruiters to clarify how the HR department can e-recruit employees by applying social media tools in order to perform, speed up, and improve the recruitment and selection work (Rahman et al. 2020). Given the omnipresence of social media and their rich networks of interaction relationships (i.e., nodes or ties; see Chap. 8) between people and organizations, e-recruitment is on the rise (Rahman et al. 2020). An increasing number of employers spread vacancies online and screen the online profiles of candidates who apply for a job.

As an example of e-recruitment, we look at Accenture™ (http://www.accenture. com/), which is an international IT consultancy firm. On its corporate website, the organization has a page dedicated to e-recruitment (http://careers.accenture.com/) that covers links to different social media tools as well. This organization uses, among others, Facebook™ as an active tool to spread direct links to vacancies (https://www.facebook.com/accenture). Such social media initiatives can contribute to a corporate image of being a "good" employer. The organization also tends to use a consistent corporate style, e.g., by using similar pictures on every social media tool and by clearly showing its corporate logo.

More organizations take advantage of e-recruitment and have dedicated job descriptions for online or digital recruiters. Such profiles are, among others, responsible for the HR-related questions and answers on social media. They constantly screen photos and messages, respond to online questions, and keep the online recruiting channels up to date. Also small and medium-sized enterprises (SMEs) use social media for e-recruitment in order to reach more people. However, the latter also depends on the sector in which the organization is active. For instance, smaller organizations in certain niches (e.g., journalists or IT professionals) may have a Facebook™ page, but still prefer relying on physical networking (i.e., during offline social events, besides social media).

Subsequently, we discuss specific e-recruitment initiatives for LinkedIn™ and other social media tools from the perspectives of organizations and recruiters.

9.2.1 LinkedIn™ and e-Recruitment for Organizations

Chapter 2 described LinkedIn™ as a networking website for organizations to list job vacancies and to search for potential candidates. It is a prominent tool for e-recruitment as it only targets professional profiles. The presence of a specialized social media tool such as LinkedIn™ implies that organizations become less dependent on outsourcing to professional agencies with external HR, which may result in higher cost efficiency. Although other professional social network tools exist (e.g., the German-based XING™: https://www.xing.com/en), we now focus on the most popular one to orient the reader to the topic. In particular, LinkedIn™ can help find candidates for vacancies by means of dedicated features such as:

- Create a company page to have a network of followers.
- Create a showcase page per product to have a more targeted network of followers.
- Participate in a group for discussion, knowledge sharing, and guidance.
- Engage in LinkedIn™ virtual events and LinkedIn™ articles.
- Job posting on the LinkedIn™ company page or as an ad.
- Advanced search engine.
- Etc.

These features can be used to let candidates come to the organization, while the traditional search engine acts to actively search for candidates.

First, an organization can decide to create a LinkedIn™ company page to obtain a professional network of followers. Look for an example at the company page of Ghent University (https://www.linkedin.com/school/ghent-university/). Each LinkedIn™ company page has a personalized URL, to which the organization can refer on other social media tools, on the corporate website, or in emails. Vice versa, the LinkedIn™ company page can contain direct links to the corporate website and other social media tools (e.g., in the header to draw the attention of web page visitors). The aim of this LinkedIn™ feature is to get more followers and to inform them properly about all corporate initiatives. Among others, the LinkedIn™ corporate page can be used to post vacancies or to include links to vacancies that are accessible on the corporate website.

Secondly, instead of following an organization, LinkedIn™ allows organizations to launch showcase pages per business area (e.g., per product, per business unit, or per initiative). This means that an organization can also create a showcase page with updates related to a certain product or service. It concerns a dedicated page to highlight different aspects of a business and to build relationships with a more targeted network. As such, people can follow specific products and services in which they are interested. For instance, Microsoft™ has a showcase page for its 365-related functionalities (https://www.linkedin.com/showcase/microsoft-365). Similarly, Adobe™ has a showcase page for its creative cloud (https://www.linkedin.com/showcase/adobe-creative-cloud).

Thirdly, an organization can participate in LinkedIn™ groups for knowledge sharing and discussing questions and answers regarding a certain topic (e.g., digital marketing, process management, entrepreneurship, photography). Professionals and people interested in a similar topic can ask questions or respond to questions in a forum-based way. A LinkedIn™ group also allows the organization to spread links with more information on activities or events. By reading and comparing different LinkedIn™ groups on a certain topic, more candidates can become interested in a brand and its vacancies. Besides e-recruitment, a LinkedIn™ group is thus closely linked to social CRM (see Chap. 5).

Alternatively, LinkedIn™ gives organizations the opportunity to post job vacancies. Vacancies can appear on the LinkedIn™ company page, possibly with a button similar to "Apply with LinkedIn™" to directly apply for the job by sending personal LinkedIn™ information to the organization. Vacancies can also appear as online ads (see Chap. 4). The latter is a more advanced use of LinkedIn™, as a bidding process and a pricing model characterize online ads.

A popular LinkedIn™ feature for e-recruitment relates to an active search engine (see Fig. 9.2). In this feature, the profiles of LinkedIn™ users are used as a database with professional information about potential candidates. One way to actively find candidates is by searching for keywords. This means that users can profit from adding relevant keywords to their individual profile.

In order to look for keywords, a search engine will particularly screen the summary that is on top of a LinkedIn™ user profile. In order to be more findable

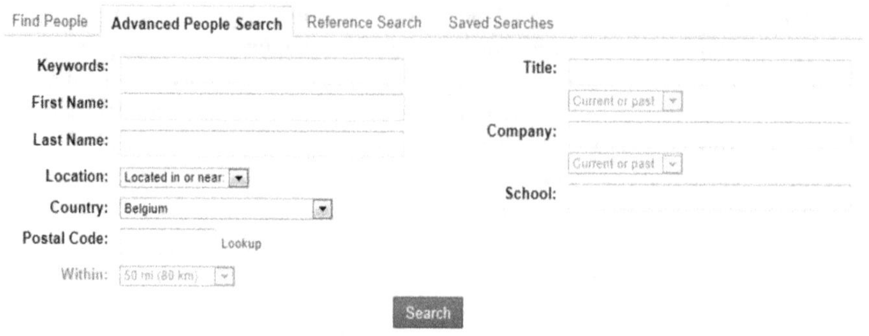

| Find People | **Advanced People Search** | Reference Search | Saved Searches |

Keywords:			Title:	
First Name:				Current or past ▾
Last Name:			Company:	
Location:	Located in or near ▾			Current or past ▾
Country:	Belgium ▾		School:	
Postal Code:		Lookup		
Within:	50 mi (80 km) ▾			

Search

Fig. 9.2 An example of a search engine on LinkedIn™ (LinkedIn™ and the LinkedIn™ logo are registered trademarks of LinkedIn™ Corporation, used with permission)

by a search engine, potential candidates should regularly update their LinkedIn™ profile in order to appear in the latest search lists (see SEO, Chap. 6). The summary of a candidate should also be short, containing the current and previous employers and job titles of the candidate, as well as one's education. For the candidate, the summary of a LinkedIn™ profile is also a good way to promote oneself by using keywords as unique selling points (e.g., why is this candidate different from others and what is one's expertise about?). An example of the summary of a LinkedIn™ user is shown below:

Valentina Boyd.
  Current: Supply chain manager at Organization XYZ.
  Previous: Organization ABC, Organization DEF.
  Education: Ghent University.
  Summary:

- *Supply chain management.*
- *Production planning.*
- *Production strategy.*
- *Total quality management.*
- *Project management.*
- *Change management.*

Once the search engine finds a LinkedIn™ profile, recruiters will screen the profile to prepare for a job interview or an assessment. Recruiters will particularly look at professional expertise, current and previous jobs, contact details, and the professional contacts (i.e., LinkedIn™ connections). The purpose of a social media tool such as LinkedIn™ is providing professional information. Users should better reserve private information (e.g., about hobbies, pets, etc.) for other tools (e.g., Facebook™). Furthermore, recruiters pay attention to details about previous jobs and education and are sensitive for gaps in a résumé. For instance, if a time gap exists between the period of going to high school and university or between jobs, they will very likely ask the candidate what one has been doing meanwhile.

Finally, LinkedIn™ allows highlighting a candidate's skills by means of listing the rewards of a user, as well as by means of recommendations and endorsements. Recruiters appreciate these options as other people then confirm the mentioned skills. Endorsements reveal how many connections confirm that a particular user possesses a certain skill (e.g., "45 people endorse Valentina Boyd for supply chain management"). On the other hand, recommendations are pieces of text in which a user is suggested to be good or suitable for a particular purpose or job. For instance:

> *John Cortes, Production manager at CASIAC.*
> "Valentina is a hardworking person, who functions very well in a team. She came up with an intelligent idea to improve the production process. Valentina was appreciated by the whole team."
> *June 21, 2022, John managed Valentina at Organization ABC.*

9.2.2   Other Social Media Tools for e-Recruitment by Organizations

Besides the professional community of LinkedIn™, other social media tools can be used for e-recruitment. As an illustration, this section looks at some examples of Facebook™, Instagram™, and Twitter™ from the perspective of organizations. Although they are not a professional network, organizations can have other dedicated social media pages that users may "like" or "follow."

Since social media tools such as Facebook™ and Instagram™ offer a private community, the users' "follows" and "likes" allow the organization to get access to personal information and posts. The search engine of Facebook™ and Instagram™ can also be used to find users (e.g., other organizations or professionals, among others). The organization's social media page can be used to announce vacancies but also to prepare for a job interview with targeted questions and to compare a candidate's résumé with the candidate's private Facebook™ or Instagram™ profile in order to find anomalies or inconsistencies. Consequently, given their widespread use (Chap. 1), organizations can use Facebook™ and Instagram™ for e-recruitment in addition to other initiatives such as online ads (Chap. 4), viral campaigns (Chap. 4), or social CRM (Chap. 5).

Additionally, the microblogging tool Twitter™ can be applied for e-recruitment to reach certain niches (e.g., journalists or IT professionals; see supra). For instance, in this publicly available tool, recruiters can "tweet" links to the organization's vacancies in the hope to reach many people when followers start retweeting. Compared to LinkedIn™, Twitter™ relates more to pushing information about a specific content to a target population, and followers deliberately choose what to retweet. Besides posting tweets, organizations can make use of an additional job search engine for Twitter™ (TwitJobSearch: http://www.twitjobsearch.com/, https://

Table 9.1 Examples of Twitter™ hashtags for e-recruitment by organizations

For recruiting in general	For recruiting certain job types
#hiring, #tweetmyjobs, #HR, #jobopening, #jobposting, #employment, #opportunity, #recruiting, #rtjobs, #jobsearch, #joblisting, #job, #jobs	#freelance, #homebusiness, #greenjobs, #dreamjob, #consulting, #consultant, #accounting, #webdesign, #telecom, #legal, #lawyer, #industry, #salesjob

twitter.com/twitjobsearch) to find all Twitter™ messages with certain hashtags (which symbolize the topics), e.g., hashtag "job" and a keyword (#marketingjobBrussels). Examples of frequently used hashtags for recruiters are presented in Table 9.1.

9.2.3   Dedicated e-Recruitment Systems

A growing market exists for tools with CV searching technology and CV parsing technology (i.e., to automatically convert CVs or social media profiles into a candidate profile in the organization's database). Such talent acquisition technologies can help save time in the administrative processing of applications. For instance, international software companies (e.g., Oracle™, SAP™, Kronos™) provide technology that allows organizations to push vacancies from their corporate system or database into social media by clicking just a button, as well as to access network information to search for relevant candidates in return (see also Chap. 8 on social network data). A dedicated corporate database for e-recruitment is also referred to as an "applicant tracking system"or "hiring management system."

Such dedicated e-recruitment systems usually operate comparable to a social CRM database (see Chap. 5), albeit for (potential) employees instead of (potential) customers. Additionally, the SEO-related tips and tricks (see Chap. 6) remain valid since keywords are crucial, such as when searching for profile keywords, for document scanning (i.e., often based on free-text and unstructured natural language in documents of different formats, e.g., .pdf or .doc), and for determining a rating or best-fit ranking with a certain vacancy. Moreover, the software can potentially consider an "over-optimization penalty." In order to make recommendations for matching jobs and candidates, clear links exist with the algorithmic challenges related to textual content analysis (see Chap. 7) and professional social networks (see Chap. 8) using predictive mining (Freire and de Castro 2021; Maree et al. 2019; Ogunniye et al. 2021; Smythe et al. 2021).

An overview of commonly used software functionalities for supporting e-recruitment is, among others:

- Job aggregators or job boards for providing an overview of open job positions (e.g., including the creation and publication of job postings).
- Video interviewing and chatbots.
- Testing or pre-hire assessments to screen a candidate's knowledge and skills.

- AI-based personal assistants to automate the first screenings, to organize the interview scheduling, or to transcribe interview calls.
- Pure applicant tracking features in the sense of creating a CRM-based database of potential candidates.
- Recruitment-based CRM that extends pure applicant tracking with actions for employer branding, career site, and employee referrals.
- Human capital management software that extends the abovementioned features with a full package of talent management for employees as well.

Different pricing models can be applicable, such as a price per user, a price per job opening, or a (monthly) flat fee. Organizations that have trouble in selecting an ATS that fits their business context can use a decision tool such as Capterra (2021) and Matchr (2021), which typically compares functionalities, product ratings, number of users, location, software costs, and deployment options (e.g., web-based or offline).

9.3   Employees and e-Recruitment: How to Get e-Recruited?

This section takes the perspective of (future) employees. The information that an individual posts on the Internet is freely available to some extent and will be used by recruiters. A good exercise for a (future) employee is to regularly check which personal information is revealed when using a search engine with one's name as keyword for the search query (e.g., look for your name in a search engine, and verify which links appear to your social media profiles). Besides the traditional search engines (see Chap. 6), recruiters can benefit from specialized search engines (e.g., Yasni™ http://www.yasni.com/) for specifically browsing through all social media data that are publicly available. The latter are also a free people search that combines all information related to a certain name, which implies that results may contain mixed information when different persons have the same name. Nevertheless, by carefully screening all information available about a certain candidate on the Internet and on social media, recruiters get to know the candidates that apply for a job.

Keeping this in mind, candidates should carefully consider the personal information they reveal on social media. Similarly, they should think twice before posting pictures online without having stipulated access rights. For instance, being a founder of a charity foundation is more professional information than being a stripper or being drunk at a party.

Recruiters will also verify whether a résumé is consistent with the information they find online (e.g., is the birth date correct, are the degrees correct), and they are trained to find incorrect or inconsistent information. The message for candidates is "Manage what you can manage."

Subsequently, specific e-recruitment initiatives are discussed for LinkedIn™ and other social media tools from the perspectives of (future) employees.

9.3.1   LinkedIn™ and e-Recruitment for Employees

Chapter 2 described LinkedIn™ as a networking website for professionals to stay in touch or to find jobs. Similar to organizations, LinkedIn™ allows individuals to create and manage a LinkedIn™ profile. The personalized URL (e.g., http://www.linkedin.com/in/FirstnameSurname) symbolizes the person's online presence or online identity. Individuals can invite professional connections to their network by means of a default message (e.g., "I would like to add you to my professional network—Valentina Boyd"). It is also possible to write a personal note in order to drive contacts in an attempt to have more people that will accept the invitation.

Nonetheless, LinkedIn™ users should manage their contacts strategically. What matters most is not how many contacts someone has (quantity), but to whom one is connected (quality). The quality of connections is more important than the quantity.

LinkedIn™ users can make themselves more visible by adding a profile picture and by strategically choosing relevant keywords (i.e., with which they differentiate themselves from other users and which are relevant to organizations). They can also follow organizations and participate in the LinkedIn™ groups for sharing content and for questions and answers (see Sect. 9.2.1). Furthermore, it is important to regularly update a profile to get higher in the search results (see SEO, Chap. 6). In order to create a consistent and up-to-date profile, old content or incorrect information should be removed. In order to create a consistent message, it is advisable that candidates compare their résumé with their profiles on social media.

On the other hand, LinkedIn™ users can also manage their public profile by means of privacy settings. As such, an individual can decide that the (first-degree) connections have access to more information than people who are not directly connected and might be strangers to the individual. For instance, different privacy control options exist to exclude the profile picture or the list of connections from a user's public profile.

Finally, candidates can use LinkedIn™ information about a certain organization, its employees, and their skills to prepare for a job interview or an assessment. As such, candidates who apply for a job can better prepare themselves, knowing that the recruiters will also be prepared. All information available should be used efficiently as social media can be seen as a big database that contains a lot of information that is used for the same purpose as a traditional database (see business intelligence; Chap. 8). In order to be careful, individuals can keep the following advice in mind:

• Do not lie.
• Do not provide too many details.
• Do not share personal information in a professional community.
• Do not randomly send LinkedIn™ request to connect.

9.3.2   Other Social Media Tools for e-Recruitment of Employees

As many people have an account on nonprofessional social media tools (see Chap. 1), e-recruitment is not necessarily limited to a professional community such as LinkedIn™. We now illustrate some examples of how (future) employees can get recruited by using Facebook™, Instagram™, or Twitter™.

Although private information belongs to a nonprofessional community, social media users should be careful with the information they reveal on such social media tools too. For instance, before posting pictures of a hobby on Facebook™ or Instagram™, users should safely set their privacy settings to decide who can see those posts and pictures. Similarly, when using apps on Facebook™, those apps typically have access to the user's information, pictures, and posts as well. Social media tools thus allow setting privacy settings to manage who can see posts, tags, shares, and contact details. For instance, examples of different sharing options are (1) shares that everyone can see, (2) shares that only "friends" and "friends of friends" can see, or (3) shares that only direct "friends" can see (i.e., which is the safest option). Such privacy settings need to be checked regularly as the social media tool may have changed its privacy policy meanwhile. Facebook™ also offers the option to share personal information, pictures, or posts with only a specific group of friends (e.g., only to relatives and not to acquaintances). This implies that users can organize lists of friends.

Nevertheless, candidates should be fully aware that a rewind button on the Internet does not exist. Similar to other social media tools, Facebook™ and Instagram™ posts are undeletable (see Chap. 1). For instance, the Terms of Service of social media tools can stipulate that even deleted profile pictures can be reused, e.g., for advertising purposes (see Chap. 11 about the ownership of social media content). Therefore, social media users should think twice before revealing information on social media. This implication also emphasizes the need for candidates to create a consistent message and to compare their résumé with their social media profiles.

Furthermore, Twitter™ has some specific features that can be used for e-recruitment. As Twitter™ contains information about various topics based on tweets and retweets, it is important to carefully choose whom to follow in order to avoid an information overload. To find people with similar interests, search queries can be launched with hashtags preceding keywords. Twitter™ can be used for both professional and personal information, but users should keep in mind that tweets and retweets are available in the public domain. For instance, Twitter™ can be used to stay tuned about certain topics that relate to a profession (e.g., for a consultant) or a decent hobby (e.g., for a hobby chef) rather than to share private pictures. This means that users should find a balance between what they tweet and what not (i.e., "give and take") and remember that Twitter™ is rather used to build a network with (unknown) people that share similar interests and to demonstrate a user's expertise. Although Twitter™ is less frequently used than Facebook™ or Instagram™, it can be used for recruiting specific profiles. For instance, depending on the type of job,

Table 9.2 Examples of Twitter™ hashtags for e-recruitment by employees

For getting the attention of recruiters	For educating yourself	For being specific by combining hashtags
#hireme, #MBA, #LinkedIn, #profile, #unemployed, #resume, #CV, #needajob, #jobsearch	#jobtips, #career, #interview, #benefits, #personalbranding, #compensation, #training, #jobhunt, #unemployment, #employers, #jobless	#jobs #CityName #jobhuntchat #resume #IndustryKeyword

Twitter™ can be used for certain niches in which networking is important (e.g., consultants or journalists), albeit without replacing real-life networking.

Some common e-recruitment hashtags for (future) employees are presented in Table 9.2. One tip is to include a city name in the hashtag (#CityName), so recruiters know that the person is looking for a vacancy in New York (#NY), Paris (#Paris), or Ghent (#Ghent). It is also possible to use industry keywords that express an expertise (e.g., #WebDesign, #java, or #SEO). Furthermore, it is interesting to know that #résumé (UK alternative) is more frequently used than #CV (US alternative), although both terms can be used as synonyms.

In sum, as with employer branding by organizations, (future) employees can work on their employee branding by making their résumé look better with accurate information. Some tips to increase employability and to build a professional online identity are:

- Do a search engine search to see what information is publicly available about you.
- Clean up social media profiles and make them consistent.
- Clearly outline a personal description (e.g., correct job title, industry, and skills).
- Subscribe to RSS feeds of organizations.
- For LinkedIn™ users, make connections, get recommendations and endorsements, and import email contacts to find professional connections.
- For Facebook™ and Instagram™ users, specify keywords to facilitate e-recruitment ads and define privacy settings (e.g., which pictures, posts, or comments are publicly available and which are not).
- For Twitter™ users, regularly communicate to build relationships, follow, (re)-tweet, share, etc.

9.4   Legislation Related to e-Recruitment

While Chap. 11 elaborates on legal and ethical issues on social media, this section illustrates possible consequences of social media posts for hiring and firing. Without intending to be legal advice, this section tries to find an answer to the questions:

- "Can I not be recruited for my social media posts?"
- "Can I get fired for my social media posts?"

Regarding the first question, this chapter has shown that social media play an increasing role for recruiters. The law allows recruiters to choose another candidate based on someone's social media profile because organizations can decide who will be recruited as long as the reason is not discrimination. Consequently, the legal answer to the first question is affirmative. However, an organization should have a clear policy and be open about its procedures (see Chap. 11). Some common reasons for not recruiting someone after consulting one's social media profile are:

- The candidate lies about qualifications.
- Low communication skills.
- Negative social media posts or revealing confidential information about former employers or colleagues.
- Inappropriate pictures or comments of the candidate (e.g., excessive use of alcohol or drugs).
- Discriminating posts.

A legendary example deals with a college student who was offered a first job. Directly after the job offering, she was tweeting that she would be paid very well, but that the job content would be terrible. Consequently, the girl lost her job before she could even start it (NBC News 2009). Once hired, employees also risk being fired for things they post on social media. The answer to the second question is thus also affirmative. More specifically, the law allows an organization to fire staff members who insult clients on social media. Private social media use is not allowed during working hours. An organization can also decide to block or restrict access to certain websites on a corporate computer as long as it is clearly communicated on the intranet or in a policy (e.g., a policy on IT use) or contract. Even if social media tools are not blocked, an employee is supposed to use them in an ethical way. For instance, checking private emails can be forbidden, but employees will rather be fired if it occurs excessively. In the end, employers and employees should trust each other. On the other hand, also outside working hours, it is illegal to criticize an employer (e.g., the brand, products, services, or clients) if it can cause economic harm. For instance, a sales manager who publicly posts pictures of himself in a drunk state at a party may rather harm the reputation of the organization than a back-office worker. Additionally, it is illegal to announce business secrets, deals, or confidential information that relate to the user's job. The latter counts for a current job but also for all previous jobs. In conclusion, someone can be fired for social media posts, but generally not for personal posts that do not relate to a job and that are posted during the person's spare time. Nonetheless, it is up to the judge to decide.

Already since the early years of social media, examples have been appearing of people being fired for their social media mistakes (Business Insider 2011; Huffington Post 2010). One notorious example is the Weinergate scandal about an American politician and member of the parliament who tweeted a "selfie" in his underpants (instead of sending a private message to someone), resulting in his dismissal upon request of his political party and President Obama. Another frequently shared example is situated in a pizza place and deals with employees who seemed to add worms into the pizzas (https://www.youtube.com/watch?v=TQqTGBsr_RI). They filmed their actions themselves and posted the video on YouTube™, but were fired afterward.

Finally, employees should consider the consequences of their social media actions for their future career. For instance, in 2013, a girl who worked for a marketing company recorded a video to criticize her boss and publicly posted it on YouTube™. In the video, she argued that only the quantity, clicks, and views of her marketing videos matter and that the organization did not appreciate her long working days. Although the video was created to tell her employer that she is quitting, it already reached more than 19,000,000 views worldwide (http://www.youtube.com/watch?v=Ew_tdY0V4Zo). The girl was dancing in the office building and she was wearing a corporate badge, keeping the corporate name or logo anonymous in the video. Nonetheless, her name is visible on YouTube™ and a company name is easily traceable on the Internet (e.g., in tools such as LinkedIn™ or in search engines). Although the girl is active in the marketing domain (in which creative skills are important), the initiative can be risky for a future career in the sense of potentially harming one's reputation to get recruited elsewhere.

More legal and ethical issues on social media can be found in Chap. 11.

9.5   Takeaways

As e-recruitment matters, organizations should think about their image of being a "good" employer (i.e., employer branding). Similarly, e-recruitment also matters to (future) employees, who should work on their image of being a "good" employee (i.e., employee branding). Career management is thus a serious business.

For recruiters, it is not required to be first-degree connections with a candidate on social media to find various kinds of information about that person on the Internet. Recruiters are eager to take advantage of such an opportunity, possibly supported by advanced e-recruitment systems. In particular, recruiters tend to screen each candidate to prepare for a job interview and expect that candidates do the same regarding an organization's publicly available information. A candidate should profoundly think about one's first impression. In order to be more easily findable or traceable for organizations, a candidate may align different social media tools. For instance, one can opt for using a similar profile picture on LinkedIn™, Facebook™, Instagram™, and Twitter™. This does not mean that a profile picture is necessarily a static one. Instead, profile pictures may symbolize values that are appreciated in a work environment. For instance, a holiday picture of someone reaching a mountaintop also stands for determination, which is a highly appreciated value for many job vacancies. Furthermore, social media content needs to be consistent, which implies that different social media tools should never give contradictory or incorrect information. Particularly, (future) employees should never lie about their education, previous work expertise, or job titles (as recruiters are trained to detect lies).

One of the most important messages of this chapter is to use a particular social media tool for its given purpose. The reader was told to think twice before posting pictures and information on social media and to differentiate professional social media use from private use (i.e., by choosing the most appropriate social media tool depending on the content). For instance, think about where you will post photos of a party (e.g., at a student union) versus information about leading a student union. The former is private information for rather a small number of connections (e.g., friends, but not parents or colleagues), whereas the latter refers to leadership skills which is also relevant to be recruited.

Finally, this chapter has shown direct links to various topics in other chapters. More specifically, with respect to Chap. 6, social media profiles should be regularly updated in order to appear higher in search engines that recruiters use to find appropriate candidates. Thus, tips and tricks for search engine optimization (SEO) also apply to e-recruitment.

9.6   Self-Test

- Which social media tools would you advise for recruiting the following profiles? Please motivate your choice.
  - A Chief Executive Officer, an IT developer, a cleaning lady, etc.
- Think about some situations that may happen in your spare time or during working hours, and evaluate the possible consequences for an employee in the context of e-recruitment.
  - For instance, after a Saturday-night party, an employee posts an obscene picture of himself on Facebook™ in his spare time. Can this person be fired for the post?
  - What if this person would be a salesperson, a back-office worker, a CEO, etc.?
- Search for an online recruiting video. What is positive and negative about the video? Which important elements are covered, and which not? What are the takeaways? Tip: consider elements such as company culture, employee testimonials, unique selling points, and call to action.
- A consultancy company, called ECA, decides to work on its employer branding and launches the idea of an "InstagramTM Takeover." For this initiative, some junior employees are asked to create brand-related content on the official corporate Instagram account for one day in order for the company to discover new channels for communication and hiring. Such junior stories are also sponsored to actually appear in the feeds of adolescents, which is the target audience for such online advertising. Try to properly formulate a goal for this takeover initiative, and explain how it can be monitored and evaluated.

Bibliography

Business Insider. (2011). *13 people who got fired for tweeting*. Retrieved May 28, 2021, from https://www.businessinsider.com/twitter-fired-2011-5?international=true&r=US& IR=T#fired-for-insensitive-jokes-about-japan-3

Capterra. (2021). *Applicant tracking software.* Retrieved December 23, 2021, from https://www.capterra.com/applicant-tracking-software/

Freire, M. N., & de Castro, L. N. (2021). e-Recruitment recommender systems: A systematic review. *Knowledge and Information Systems, 63*(1), 1–20.

Huffington Post. (2010). *Fired over Twitter: 13 tweets that got people canned.* Retrieved July 23, 2021, from https://www.huffpost.com/entry/fired-over-twitter-tweets_n_645884

Maree, M., Kmail, A. B., & Belkhatir, M. (2019). Analysis and shortcomings of e-recruitment systems: Towards a semantics-based approach addressing knowledge incompleteness and limited domain coverage. *Journal of Information Science, 45*(6), 712–735.

Matchr. (2021). *Welcome to our free software match.* Retrieved December 23, 2021, from https://matchr.com/ats-software/

Mishra, S., & Pavan Kumar, S. (2019). e-Recruitment and training comprehensiveness: Untapped antecedents of employer branding. *Industrial & Commercial Training, 51*(2), 125–136.

NBC News. (2009). *Getting the skinny on Twitter's Cisco Fatty.* Retrieved December 16, 2021, from https://www.nbcnews.com/id/wbna29901380

Ogunniye, G., Legastelois, B., Rovatsos, M., Dowthwaite, L., Portillo, V., Vallejos, E. P., Zhao, J., & Jirotka, M. (2021). Understanding user perceptions of trustworthiness in e-recruitment systems. *IEEE Internet Computing, 25*(6), 23–32.

Rahman, M., Aydin, E., Haffar, M., & Nwagbara, U. (2020). The role of social media in e-recruitment process: Empirical evidence from developing countries in social network theory. *Journal of Enterprise Information Management,* (ahead-of-print), 1–22.

Smythe, S., Grotlüschen, A., & Buddeberg, K. (2021). The automated literacies of e-recruitment and online services. *Studies in the Education of Adults, 53*(1), 4–22.

Crowdfunding

10

This chapter elaborates on crowdfunding, which is an alternative funding mechanism for organizations and entrepreneurs to raise small amounts of money from the crowd as micro-investors (instead of a large amount of money from the bank or a few macro-investors). Although crowdfunding may still concern a loan that needs to be paid off, an increasing number of crowdfunding projects only focus on giving rewards in return. This chapter discusses the history and rise of crowdfunding. The reader gets to know the different types of crowdfunding projects, which are linked to different dedicated crowdfunding platforms. Besides providing general tips and tricks for doing a crowdfunding project and the role of social media, this chapter looks at legal issues and risks that are linked to crowdfunding.

This chapter particularly moves to the finance department of an organization by discussing how money can be raised through crowdfunding (Fig. 10.1).

Teaser Question
- Is it legal to borrow me some money?

10.1 Introduction to Crowdfunding

Nowadays, an increasing number of people have innovative ideas that they wish to put on the market. Maybe you are an enterprising person too, who has written a song, book, or film yourself, developed a game, or want to create a start-up to sell handmade items (e.g., jewelry or clothes). Many people have dreamed about it, but they frequently lack money for realizing the dream. Starting a new business or realizing an innovative business project entails some investment risks, and banks or macro-investors are not always willing to throw themselves into an adventure and grant a loan. Nonetheless, from now on, such dreams can come true by means of crowdfunding. In other words, when many people (e.g., relatives, friends,

© The Author(s), under exclusive license to Springer Nature Switzerland AG 2022   207
A. Van Looy, *Social Media Management*, Springer Texts in Business and
Economics, https://doi.org/10.1007/978-3-030-99094-7_10

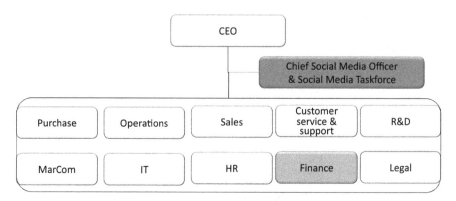

Fig. 10.1 The multidisciplinary approach of crowdfunding

colleagues, acquaintances, etc.) invest a small amount of money in a project, then a large amount of money can be raised too (i.e., without having to rely on a bank or a big investor). Hence, crowdfunding projects will collect money from the crowd and thus differ from the traditional way of investing.

An important challenge faced by crowdfunding projects is finding sufficient investors. Assume that you have €1000 of extra cash on your bank account, which can be spent on other things than taxes, food, or other basic needs. In which novel projects would you probably invest €1000?

- Maybe you will be convinced if the entrepreneur passed a fraud check and can be considered trustworthy or if the project was proposed by an award-winning entrepreneur, let us say "Manager of the Year."
- If not yet convinced, maybe you will invest if the entrepreneur shows a thorough business plan which stipulates the problem to be solved, how the final product can solve that business problem, a calculation of costs, a planning with milestones, and the percentage of equity (ownership) an investor will get.
- Or maybe you will only invest if the entrepreneur is someone you know, such as a relative, friend, or acquaintance.
- What if you can decide to invest a smaller budget, e.g., €500, €50, or €10 (instead of €1000)?

Such arguments may convince people to invest, and that is what crowdfunding is all about.

Crowdfunding tries to raise small amounts of money from a large crowd without gatekeepers. In return, the micro-investors can get a reward (e.g., a T-shirt) or they can even become a shareholder. As anyone can invest, a synonym for crowdfunding is "fan funding." The synonym refers to the fact that an entrepreneur needs to convince people and make them excited about the entrepreneur's idea in order to become a fan and maybe an investor or even an advocate who influences other

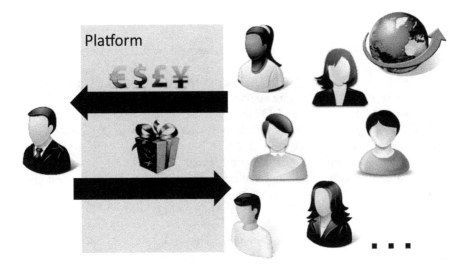

Fig. 10.2 An introduction to crowdfunding

people to invest too. Figure 10.2 illustrates that crowdfunding distinguishes the entrepreneur on one side and many micro-investors on the other side.

The entrepreneur should try to convince the crowd by using the advantages of social media. In other words, one "pitches" the crowd or tries to convince others by clarifying a unique identity, idea, business plan, and what the micro-investor will get in return for the money. The micro-investor has power and can choose whether or not to invest. Particularly, money will only be invested if the micro-investor believes in the idea and the corresponding business plan of the entrepreneur. Therefore, before investing, an open dialogue should be created, in which the crowd can ask questions about the project in order to critically review and rate the entrepreneur's idea.

Crowdfunding is usually characterized by an "all-or-nothing" approach, except for charity projects which will rather use a "keep-it-all" approach. The former means that only if the entrepreneur raises 100% of the funding target, the project is actually funded and money will be exchanged. If an entrepreneur cannot convince enough people to invest in a project, one cannot start working with the funds that are already raised as the risks for failure would be too high and the investors would be more likely to lose their money. As such, the "all-or-nothing" approach of crowdfunding is a guarantee for the micro-investors.

In sum, crowdfunding relies on social networks in which connections can make online payments and this 24/7 (i.e., not limited to office hours). As such, crowdfunding can be an efficient way of finding investors, and it is highly accessible for many people around the world. Moreover, investing in a crowdfunding project is meant to be fun, as the micro-investors can get perks (e.g., rewards or preorders) and feel connected to a project by seeing it grow.

10.2   Defining Crowdfunding

Definitions for crowdfunding share some common elements, as indicated in bold:

- "Crowdfunding is the practice of **funding** a **project or venture** by raising small amounts of **money** from a large number of **people**, in modern times typically via the **Internet**" (Forbes 2012b; Wikipedia 2021b).
- "Crowdfunding is a process in which **individuals or groups** pool **money** and other **resources** to fund **projects** initiated by other **people or organizations** without standard financial intermediaries (Wikipedia 2021a).
- "Crowdfunding is the practice of getting a large number of **people** to each give small amounts of **money** in order to provide the finance for a **business project**, typically using the **internet**" (Cambridge Dictionaries Online 2021).

Based on these definitions, crowdfunding is typically about (1) raising money (2) for funding, financing, or investing in efforts, e.g., a business project or a venture, (3) from a large number of people or individuals and (4) via the Internet. Crowdfunding can be used for a wide variety of activities, e.g., for charity or disaster relief, citizen journalism, supporting artists by fans, political campaigns, start-up company funding, software development, R&D, civic projects, etc.

> Crowdfunding (or fan-funding) is an alternative and approachable way of investing in different types of initiatives (e.g., equity-based, debt-based, good-cause, preorder, reward-based projects) based on an open call on the Internet. Small amounts of money are raised from a large amount of Internet users in exchange for perks. This fund-raising is moderated by a recognized crowdfunding platform, which facilitates the related campaign and collects the pledges of backers by following an all-or-nothing or keep-it-all financing approach.

Crowdfunding is related to the larger concept of **crowdsourcing**, which refers to outsourcing to the crowd in the hope to save money in an organization's way of working. As with traditional outsourcing, crowdsourcing refers to a function that was previously performed by an internal employee (e.g., a translation service) and that will now be performed by an external party. But unlike the traditional outsourcing, an open call is made to the crowd (e.g., on a public forum, instead of to a limited number of potential partners). Crowdsourcing can also be used in the context of social innovations and R&D (see Chap. 5 on social CRM).

The characteristics of crowdsourcing can be directly translated to crowdfunding, namely:

- Instead of a function, crowdfunding implies funding a project.
- Similar to crowdsourcing, crowdfunding relies on the crowd.

- Crowdfunding also refers to an open call on the Internet and by using social media.

Crowdfunding can thus be seen as an application of crowdsourcing. A crowdfunding project typically works as follows.

- First, an entrepreneur wishing to start a crowdfunding project needs a recognized crowdfunding **platform** on which a web page can be created to promote the project. A crowdfunding platform can be considered as a social media tool that offers a "wall" to each user and this "wall" is publicly accessible to the crowd.
- On the project page, the entrepreneur gives **information** about the project (called the "**pitch**"). The more information is given, the greater the chance of funding. The information is not necessarily limited to text but frequently contains pictures and may start with a video to get the attention of potential investors.
- The entrepreneur should stipulate **perks**, which define what people get in return for their investment. Such recognitions can take many forms and usually depend on the amount of money that a person invests in order to stimulate people to invest more money. For instance, in the context of a project on game development, the investor's name can be mentioned in the game credits when investing €5, while the investor can become a beta tester of the game as from €10. For a larger amount of money, the investor can also get a poster or a T-shirt, or a preorder of the game, for instance.
- Next, the entrepreneur should mention the targeted amount of money one needs to raise and how much money has already been raised. The latter are called the **pledges** towards a goal. For instance, suppose that a project needs €13,000 and that €4616 has been pledged so far. This amount of money is invested by 41 micro-investors, called **backers**. This example can be expressed as "41 backers have pledged €4616 of a €13,000 goal, and there are still 27 days to go."
- Most crowdfunding projects use an "**all-or-nothing**" financing approach (instead of a "**keep-it-all**" approach), which means that the backers will only exchange money if the targeted amount is raised within the deadline. As such, the micro-investors are protected from projects with a high risk of failure.
- Finally, a crowdfunding project has a separate section for **comments**, which backers or other people can use to ask questions to the entrepreneurs (e.g., about the business plan). This is an opportunity for the entrepreneur to convince people to invest in the project by building trust. The entrepreneur should create a network of fans who believe in the project by responding to questions and by letting people feel part of the project.

10.3 Origins of Crowdfunding

Crowdfunding has its origins in the mid-2000s. It became more popular during the economic crisis that started around 2008 in the USA and that also spread to the rest of the world in later years. By then, many organizations were facing problems with finding investors. Financial institutions were less likely to grant a loan to novel business ideas, and also government subsidies had been reduced. Consequently, organizations had to find other ways to finance their projects. While the economic crisis resulted in financing problems for many organizations, citizens still had savings on traditional bank accounts with only a low return. As such, crowdfunding was initiated as a win-win situation for organizations and citizens to find each other. Meanwhile, the popularity of crowdfunding has significantly risen worldwide.

Crowdfunding is an alternative funding model that contrasts with the traditional funding sources. The typical funding sources can be arranged according to their amount of money invested and their desire for control and information, ranging from family and friends, over "Seeds" and "Incubators," to "(Super) Angels" and traditional "VCs" (i.e., "venture capitalists" or "venture capital investors"). VCs typically invest the largest amount of money compared to Angels, Incubators, or just family and friends. Being a new funding source that rather targets small amounts of money from many micro-investors, crowdfunding can be classified between family and friends on the one hand and the other traditional funding sources on the other hand. Crowdfunding benefits from the use of social media and viral messages, which can easily reach family and friends but which can also target total strangers who might become fan of a novel business project. Remember the social ripple effect of Chap. 2, which involves multiple social networks. However, as pledges may vary from smaller to larger amounts of money (e.g., from €1 to €1000 or €50,000 or even higher), crowdfunding can still target small and larger investors.

In theory, all categories of investors may benefit from crowdfunding. For instance, if the crowd asks critical questions about the business plan of an entrepreneur, then the traditional investors (e.g., VCs and Angels) can also profit from this information in order to further reduce information asymmetry (Shneor and Vik 2020). Further on, crowdfunding makes investing possible for regular people who are not able to invest large amounts of money. Finally, the entrepreneur can benefit from the critical reflections of the crowd to improve one's business plan and to get validation by wisdom of the crowd. As such, the entrepreneur tries to ensure the existence of a large fan base with fans being more likely to buy a particular product or service and which decreases the risk of failure afterwards.

10.4 Crowdfunding Types and Platforms

The first way to classify crowdfunding projects is by means of the economic domains in which the projects are situated, such as the cultural sector (e.g., art, film, theater, comics, photography, music, dance), the nonprofit sector and social causes (e.g., charity and disaster relief), journalism and publishing, technology and games, food, fashion and design, energy and environment, business and entrepreneurship (e.g., start-ups), etc.

Nonetheless, crowdfunding projects are mostly classified based on different funding models (i.e., based on the reasons why people invest money), namely (Gerber and Hui 2013; Smerik 2012), (1) to obtain equity, (2) to earn interest,

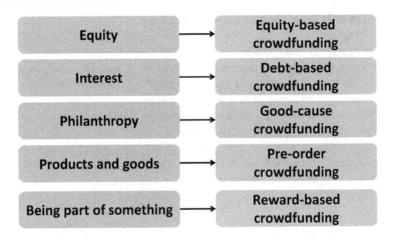

Fig. 10.3 Crowdfunding types: from investment reasons to funding models

(3) for philanthropy (i.e., to give something back to the community), (4) for interesting products or services, or (5) to be part of something (e.g., for fun, passion, or status). Figure 10.3 shows that these five goals are, respectively, linked to five funding models for crowdfunding projects.

In the crowdfunding literature, one can also find an additional classification with four similar crowdfunding types: (1) equity based, (2) lending based or credit based (instead of debt based), (3) donation based (instead of good cause), and (4) reward based. Although these four crowdfunding types are also adopted by the European Commission (Belleflamme 2013; Popescul et al. 2020), this book prefers stipulating five crowdfunding types in order to emphasize the difference between reward-based and preorder crowdfunding.

10.4.1 Type 1: Equity Crowdfunding

The first crowdfunding type emphasizes equity, which refers to ownership, market share, or value of a company that is divided among shareholders. This type of crowdfunding projects is especially related to start-ups that look for regular people who are willing to invest a small amount of money in the company in exchange of equity. This implies that the entrepreneur will provide real ownership of the company to a large group of micro-investors.

As equity crowdfunding makes investing available to the (nonaccredited) crowd instead of only to the high net worth individuals or accredited investors (e.g., VCs or Angels), it entails higher risks than other crowdfunding types. Therefore, it still remains illegal in some situations and countries (see Sect. 10.6).

Crowdfunding platforms such as Republic™ by AngelList™ (https://angel.co/company/republic), LocalStake™ (https://localstake.com/), or Seedrs™ (https://www.seedrs.com/) can be used to launch equity crowdfunding projects.

10.4.2 Type 2: Debt-Based Crowdfunding

The second type of crowdfunding involves a debt-based or lending-based funding model. Instead of going to a financial institution for a loan, the entrepreneur will borrow or lend some money from many individuals. Afterwards, the entrepreneur will pay the investors back, mostly with an additional percentage of interest (i.e., similar to a personal loan in a bank). Synonyms for debt-based crowdfunding are micro-financing or peer-to-peer (P2P) lending.

For supporting debt-based crowdfunding projects, entrepreneurs can use platforms such as LendingClub™ (https://www.lendingclub.com/) or Prosper™ (https://www.prosper.com/), among others.

10.4.3 Type 3: Good-Cause Crowdfunding

The third funding model concerns good-cause crowdfunding, which is frequently done for—but not limited to—not-for-profit projects or in developing countries. It typically involves people who donate (i.e., without a repay) or lend (i.e., with a full or partial repay, and with no or only a marginal percentage of interest) money to a project with good moral or ethical value.

Besides donations (e.g., for charity), this crowdfunding type involves personal loans for low-income individuals and is thus also called "social lending." For instance, in the developing countries, farmers can ask a personal loan to buy seeds, fertilizers, herbicides, and agricultural supplies. Or social lending can also be used to buy water meters, to fix a house, etc. Such social loans usually have a smaller target amount than debt-based crowdfunding.

Good-cause crowdfunding is linked to platforms such as Kiva™ (https://www.kiva.org/), GoFundMe™ (https://www.gofundme.com/) or Panorama™ by FrontStream™ (https://www.frontstream.com/panorama), among others.

10.4.4 Type 4: Preorder Crowdfunding

Frequently, crowdfunding projects relate to a preorder funding model. This means that people make pledges to pre-buy a product or service for later delivery (i.e., when the project is successfully finished). Compared to the previous crowdfunding types, the micro-investors do not get any financial return but become one of the first buyers and thus the first users of a certain product or service.

Kickstarter™ (https://www.kickstarter.com/) and Indiegogo™ (https://www.indiegogo.com/) are typical platforms to illustrate preorder crowdfunding.

10.4.5 Type 5: Reward-Based Crowdfunding

One of the oldest and easiest ways to invest in crowdfunding projects is reward based, in which the micro-investors get a predefined perk or reward, e.g., a T-shirt or another recognition.

This crowdfunding type can be considered as a variation of good-cause and preorder crowdfunding, as the emphasis is not on making money (i.e., equity or interest). Instead, the emphasis is rather on the satisfaction to help someone (as with good-cause crowdfunding), while getting something in return that is perceived as valuable (as with preorder crowdfunding, albeit not necessarily the product or service of the project).

Platforms that can be used for reward-based crowdfunding are, for instance, Kickstarter™ (https://www.kickstarter.com/) or artistShare™ (http://www.artistshare.com/).

10.4.6 Crowdfunding Platforms

A crowdfunding project must always be funded on a recognized crowdfunding platform in order to be conform to legislation. We already referred to some examples of such platforms in the previous sub-sections of Sect. 10.4. Crowdfunding platforms can be pledging platforms that focus on preorders, rewards, or donations (e.g., Kickstarter™) or rather capital marketplaces which focus more on equity or lending (e.g., Republic™ by AngelList™ or LocalStake™), or both.

Nowadays, many crowdfunding platforms exist, while some platforms also come and go over time. An overview and comparison of the most popular crowdfunding platforms can be found at: https://www.crowdfunding.com/.

Many of the crowdfunding platforms are from the USA (as crowdfunding was initiated there, see Sect. 10.3), but an increasing number of country-specific crowdfunding platforms exist. For instance, the 1%Club™ (https://onepercentclub.com/) is a crowdfunding platform for charity projects in the Netherlands, while the Dutch Cinecrowd™ (https://cinecrowd.com/) focuses on films, and OnePlanetCrowd™ (https://www.oneplanetcrowd.com/) focuses on ecology. These examples show that niche platforms are popular as well (e.g., for film, books, music, fashion, ecology, etc.). Nonetheless, most crowdfunding platforms can be used internationally and for different types of crowdfunding projects. For more information, we also refer to the European Crowdfunding Network (http://www.eurocrowd.org/).

Finally, it should be noted that crowdfunding platforms are organizations themselves, charging fees to the entrepreneur or to the micro-investors.

10.5   Tips and Tricks for Crowdfunding

As mentioned before, crowdfunding projects can be situated in diverse domains, even for making potato salad (https://www.kickstarter.com/projects/zackdangerbrown/potato-salad). In the potato salad example, the entrepreneur wished to obtain $10 but ended up with almost $55,500 from approximately 6900 backers. His perks ranged from saying a backer's name out loud while making the potato salad or a "thank you" note on the website, hanging out with the entrepreneur while he is making the dish, to a pizza party or a recipe book.

Nevertheless, approximately half of the launched crowdfunding projects will not be funded, depending on the type of crowdfunding (Filips et al. 2022). For instance, good-cause crowdfunding is likely to have a higher funding probability than equity crowdfunding. Since not all crowdfunding projects successfully raise their funding goal, this section gives general tips and tricks that facilitate the funding of a crowdfunding project (Jelincic and Sveb 2021; Popescul et al. 2020; Shneor and Vik 2020).

The success of a crowdfunding campaign depends on several factors, which can be explained from the perspective of the social capital theory. This theory differentiates between structural social capital (e.g., common links or ties in a social network), relational social capital (e.g., having trust and a common identity, enhanced by the crowdfunding information) and cognitive social capital (e.g., shared goals and cultural values, depending on campaign's region) (Cai et al. 2021; Shneor and Vik 2020). Other theoretical perspectives for crowdfunding success are available in (Shneor and Vik 2020). Social media tools help leverage a community based on the importance of social ties in the respective networks (e.g., to know your audience, to promote a campaign hashtag, to publicize and monitor your crowdfunding efforts). From this perspective, crowdfunding is closely related to Chap. 5 (social CRM) and the big data-related chapters (Chaps. 7 and 8).

10.5.1 Before a Crowdfunding Project

Before a crowdfunding project starts, the entrepreneur can prepare for a **fraud check** by publicly listing one's name and the company name, one's address, social security number or VAT number of the organization, etc. To further protect the micro-investors and to convince the crowd, the entrepreneur should write a **business plan** as a **pitch**. As with a typical business plan, the entrepreneur should clearly describe a problem, how to solve that problem, and how the solution can make money. Furthermore, a business plan should present a financial plan that stipulates how much money is needed (from crowdfunding and/or other investments) and how much money is expected to be earned. Based on this financial information, it is possible to verify whether the project is likely to be successful or at least break even. For instance, the target amount for a crowdfunding project can be defined to cover the expected expenses. Other details to be included in a business plan involve all efforts that must be done to realize the proposed solution and to which degree the requested funds will help with these efforts. In case of equity crowdfunding, the entrepreneur should also specify how much ownership the micro-investors can get. Nonetheless, most crowdfunding projects give perks (rewards).

When defining **perks** for a crowdfunding project, the entrepreneur should reflect on how the crowd can be stimulated. For this purpose, perks should rather be unique, creative, and personal. Particularly, if people start dreaming about the perks, they might become convinced to invest in the project. Usually five to eight perks are required per project, but this may change during the campaign. While creating perks, the entrepreneur should avoid being over-creative because one should be able to finance those perks afterwards. Some ideas for perks are early access to a product or service, discounts or vouchers, limited edition items, free entry to a location, a party, donated perks from local businesses, teaching a class or hosting a tour, personal "thank you" notes, sharing insights, etc.

Before launching the actual crowdfunding project for finding micro-investors, the entrepreneur should start a **pre-campaign**. In particular, it is important to have some first-degree connections who believe in the project and who give early feedback. They can be relatives, friends, or acquaintances but also an external network of fans who are involved in the project as from the start and who might become investors or even advocates afterwards (see social CRM, Chap. 5). During the pre-campaign, the entrepreneur is looking for trust based on interactions, without requesting financial support yet. As the emphasis of the pre-campaign is only on convincing people before they act, it is better to avoid words such as "help," "support," or "fund."

10.5.2 During a Crowdfunding Project

When the crowdfunding project actually starts, the early believers from the pre-campaign phase may become the first investors. This early money matters for the perception of other investors. For instance, projects that already raise a significant part (let us say 20–30%) of the requested money within the first days are likely to convince other people to invest in the project too. Early money may thus create a positive vibe, which is important as the fund-raising period of a crowdfunding project is limited in time (e.g., between 30 and 90 days and ideally between 30 and 45 days to keep the momentum going).

During this campaign period, the entrepreneur can start **pitching**, which involves live fund-raising by organizing meet and greets, showing demonstrations about the product or service involved, responding to questions about the business plan, storytelling, etc. Consequently, the crowdfunding campaign is all about online and offline communication, although the quality of the message is more important than its length. Some suggestions to talk about on the crowdfunding platform are perks, milestones, media coverage, or any update about the organization and the product or service under study. A balanced content mix is needed by combining sales-type posts with informative posts and storytelling. As such, the crowdfunding platform can be used as a blog (see Sect. 2.2.2), e.g., with ideally circa two to five updates per week.

Based on the principles of social CRM (Chap. 5), micro-investors should get the feeling that they are special and belong to an exclusive community. When people feel engaged and the perks are attractive, funders might even invest more than once. An example of how funders can be treated in a more exclusive way is by frequently sending them updates (e.g., daily or weekly), in addition to the publicly available updates that are released to the crowd. Particularly, social media give many opportunities to crowdfunding to communicate about the project, to convince others to invest, and to create an exclusive community. For instance, social media can help people get engaged by asking questions, sending "thank you" notes to micro-investors, doing polls, spreading a link to the crowdfunding page, using specific hashtags, retweeting, etc. Although different social media tools can be integrated, crowdfunding can especially profit from publicly available tools (e.g., Twitter™), because they are not limited to existing connections and generally allow sending both public and private messages. Also traditional e-mails turn out to be efficient ways to communicate.

10.5.3 After a Crowdfunding Project

Some crowdfunding projects succeed with an immense success. A well-known crowdfunding example concerns the Pebble smart watch, for which almost $10,000,000 was raised instead of the targeted $100,000 (https://www.kickstarter. com/projects/getpebble/pebble-e-paper-watch-for-iphone-and-android). This example shows a project that surpassed its goal, namely, with a big difference between the actual pledges and the targeted amount. Also for the web comic "The order of the stick," the final funding was much larger than expected (https://www.kickstarter. com/projects/599092525/the-order-of-the-stick-reprint-drive). If a crowdfunding project raises more money than expected, additional activities can be financed. For instance, an artist might raise enough budget for a tour trip, besides recording the album for which the project was initially launched. To stimulate fans to invest more money, an artist can give special perks such as an online session with the lead singer or a customized song from the artist.

When crowdfunding projects fail to raise the targeted budget, no money will be exchanged when the "all-or-nothing" financing approach is followed in order to protect micro-investors. This means that the backers will not give the promised budget since the project is considered to be too risky. In cases when the funding goals have not been reached, the entrepreneur should take advantage of this failure by rethinking one's idea and by reconsidering the related business plan. After making substantial improvements, a new crowdfunding project can still be launched in an attempt to collect the required money.

Even when a crowdfunding project successfully raised its funding goal, certain risks remain for both the entrepreneur and the micro-investors. It is possible that the entrepreneur will not be able or does not want to reward the perks. Such a situation may, for instance, happen when the project has a delay, when a new product flops, when an organization goes bankrupt, or when the entrepreneur turns out to be a fraudster. Once a project successfully raised its money, the role of a crowdfunding platform generally stops. This means that the final responsibility usually resides with the entrepreneur (i.e., project owner or creator) and the micro-investors, and that legislation should protect them. For instance, crowdfunding platforms may rather refer to "donors" than "investors" as both terms can have different legal consequences. In such cases, the crowdfunding platform may still be used to leave unsatisfied comments on the page of a certain crowdfunding project. For instance, a crowdfunding project on HD video recording glasses was successfully funded, but received negative comments from disappointed backers who did not receive their perks after 1 year or even later (https://www.kickstarter.com/projects/zioneyez/ eyeztm-by-zioneyez-hd-video-recording-glasses-for/comments) (Forbes 2012a). In such unforeseen cases, communication from the entrepreneur to its micro-investors is key to maintain confidence.

10.6 Legislation Related to Crowdfunding

As crowdfunding is a popular mechanism for fund-raising, this section offers a glimpse of the legislation that deals with the matter in hand, without intending to be legal advice.

Legislation about crowdfunding is still complex and rather unclear as it varies from country to country. Moreover, some countries still need to adopt specific legislation that deals with the topic. In such countries, the legislation for traditional fund-raising (e.g., investment laws, banking regulation regarding loans, or e-commerce rules) also applies to crowdfunding. This implies that some forms of crowdfunding can be illegal or ethically less appropriate, especially for equity crowdfunding and debt-based crowdfunding (Mochkabadi and Volkmann 2020; Yazar 2021). A possible problem with debt-based crowdfunding might be that people applying for a loan must usually demonstrate that they are creditworthy, i.e., capable to repay the loan. Further on, the reason why equity crowdfunding can be illegal in some countries is because the traditional investment laws or securities laws want to protect investors for the typical (high) risks of investing. Particularly, in a traditional investment, investors may lose a large amount of money if the organization fails. For security reasons, many traditional investment laws require that investors are accredited, which means that they must have a high salary or net worth. The latter contrasts, however, to crowdfunding which focuses on raising small amounts from a lot of regular people. Also in contrast to equity crowdfunding are those traditional investment laws that stipulate a maximum number of investors (which is called a shareholder cap).

In order to solve the legal issues that are related to crowdfunding, some countries have recognized crowdfunding as an exemption to traditional legislation. For instance, in the USA, the JOBS Act (i.e., Jumpstart Our Business Start-ups) explicitly stipulates the conditions under which equity crowdfunding by unaccredited investors is legalized for start-ups (Title III, the crowdfunding exemption), because it may create new jobs and thus having an economic impact (Investopedia 2021;

Stemler 2013). After an update in November 2020, US-based organizations are allowed to raise up to $five million (instead of the initial $one million) from unaccredited investors in a 12-month period, and allowing accredited investors to invest more (US Securities And Exchange Commission 2020).

Within the European Union, a harmonized European Crowdfunding Network exists (https://www.eurocrowd.org/). Initially, the crowdfunding legislation still differed between European Member States. For instance, a European Member State could traditionally regulate that fund-raising projects only need specific approval by a national authority if they exceed a certain target amount (e.g., €100,000 or €1000,000). This example would imply that smaller European crowdfunding projects (i.e., which are under the nationally determined limit) could be launched without needing approval, while a gray area was present for crowdfunding projects above that limit. However, in response to the still underdeveloped crowdfunding market in the European Union, the **2020/1503 Regulation on European Crowdfunding Service Providers** (ECSP) was created. It entered into force in November 2020, and into application in November 2021. This regulation stipulates uniform rules across all European Member States with respect to especially equity and debt-based crowdfunding. For instance, a prospectus is mandatory once the total amount of raised money is larger than €five million, whereas an information note is needed for lower budgets. This will make it easier for crowdfunding platforms to operate across the European Union with a single authorization while allowing harmonized supervisory powers for the national authorities (European Commission 2021).

Additionally, crowdfunding projects can take some measures to protect the micro-investors. First of all, a crowdfunding project should have a business plan that discloses relevant information about the entrepreneur, the business idea, and a fraud check. Furthermore, a crowdfunding project can only raise money on a registered platform (see Sect. 10.4.6), which also deals with legal reporting, among others. Ultimately, in an "all-or-nothing" crowdfunding project, the entrepreneur should convince the crowd about the business idea in order to raise money. Otherwise, the project remains unfunded. Social media can help convince the crowd as they typically concern many-to-many communication. In particular, social media can be used for free, allow direct feedback from the crowd, and can go viral in a relatively short amount of time. The social media initiatives can also be visible on the crowdfunding platform in order to obtain a total picture and to convince more people (i.e., "wisdom of the crowd").

On the other hand, crowdfunding also entails some risks for the entrepreneur. In general, the entrepreneur should fulfill the promised perks (e.g., equity, interest, preorders, or rewards). Further on, as crowdfunding means convincing people with a business plan, also competitors get access to the entrepreneur's novel ideas. Crowdfunding thus increases the risk of disclosing business secrets. Larger risks are particularly associated with equity crowdfunding, in which investors become shareholders. For instance, a large difference exists between someone who is entitled to a T-shirt and someone who partly owns an organization. Two long-term problems may arise for equity crowdfunding, namely, (1) for decision-making and (2) for follow-up funding. First, depending on whether the majority decides or not, macro-shareholders may be forced to follow the opinions of micro-shareholders. For instance, many micro-investors could get the power to block a sale. To facilitate decision-making, it might be more practical to let the micro-shareholders be represented by a single spokesman or a third party. Secondly, clauses in a crowdfunding contract may contrast to the needs of macro-investors, which makes follow-up funding more difficult in the future. For instance, some terms of micro-investors can make it more difficult for shareholders to exit (while this is what professional VCs or Angels frequently do). In such cases, micro-investors can be bought out to make room for a VC investment (or they can agree to be pooled and represented by a third party). Both long-term risks illustrate that, in worst case, an organization may risk going bankrupt and investors risk losing money after equity crowdfunding. In conclusion, crowdfunding can be a good solution for fund-raising, especially if an organization does not need a VC or Angel and just targets one round of fund-raising.

More legal and ethical issues on social media can be found in Chap. 11.

10.7 Takeaways

Crowdfunding is an approachable way to raise money from the public but should not be considered as the most ideal funding mechanism for all situations. In most business cases, crowdfunding should rather be used as a plan B, i.e., after trying the traditional funding mechanisms. Remember the risks discussed in this chapter for both (micro-)investors and entrepreneurs.

When opting for crowdfunding, entrepreneurs should understand and involve their audience (similar to social CRM, see Chap. 5) and should spend enough time on their business plan (which is also needed for targeting customers). A crowdfunding platform should be chosen that best fits the business plan, such as pledging platforms (e.g., Kickstarter™) or capital marketplaces (e.g., Republic™ by AngelList™ or LocalStake™).

Furthermore, entrepreneurs should be careful with the complex legislation on crowdfunding at hand, which varies from country to country and which still remains unclear to some degree.

10.8 Self-Test

- Can you describe the history and emergence of crowdfunding?
- Reflect on which online brands, social media tools or apps illustrate the notion of crowdsourcing.
- One of the major success factors for crowdfunding is a business plan. From this perspective, the business model canvas (Chap. 3) can be more precisely translated to the context of crowdfunding. For instance, an organization can choose to split its crowdfunding project into several campaigns or crowd sustaining, in order to

profit from ongoing support through the crowd (namely via crowd supporters). Think about appropriate synonyms to label the revenue streams in a business model canvas for crowdfunding projects.

- Look for real-life examples of crowdfunding projects, and explain to which funding model they apply (not).
- What is a pledging platform, and why do you need it in the context of crowdfunding?
- Can you classify a particular crowdfunding platform in one or more social media types, as discussed in Chap. 2? Please motivate your choice.
- Can you classify a particular crowdfunding platform in one or more funding models? Please motivate your choice.
- Can you explain why some types of crowdfunding might be illegal?
- How do you see the future of traditional fund-raising and crowdfunding? Please motivate your choice.
- In Kenya, a farmer asks for a personal loan to buy agricultural supplies, by using the KIVA crowdfunding platform. Explain which funding model can be applied.
- UNIQUE is a small commercial company in the medical industry, which recently completed a successful crowdfunding campaign. On a mission to "let personalization and personality enter into the world of prosthetics and orthotics," this existing company raised €two million. A prosthetic is an extension of a disabled person (i.e., who lost an arm or a leg). UNIQUE succeeded its crowdfunding campaign because it brought new energy to the prosthetics industry by focusing on personalization. Their hook was not functionality or accessibility, which are already qualities that are typically lauded by prosthetic companies. Instead, UNIQUE's unique selling points are self-expression and customization. "We used to focus on making the devices more functional," says CEO Adam Porter. "Now, we are really creating something that people actually like to wear." By offering an angle that is drastically different from other companies in the industry, UNIQUE sets itself up for crowdfunding success using a platform that reached a much broader audience than merely their customer audience. Explain which funding model is most appropriate.

Bibliography

Belleflamme, P. (2013). *Crowdfunding: Tapping the right crowd*. Retrieved June 15, 2013, from http://ec.europa.eu/internal_market/conferences/2013/0603-crowdfunding-workshop/docs/paul-belleflamme_en.pdf

Cai, W., Polzin, F., & Stam, E. (2021). Crowdfunding and social capital: A systematic review using a dynamic perspective. *Technological Forecasting and Social Change, 162*(120412), 1–22.

Cambridge Dictionaries Online. (2021). *Crowdfunding*. Retrieved December 28, 2021, from https://dictionary.cambridge.org/dictionary/english/crowdfunding

European Commission. (2021). *Regulation on European crowdfunding service providers (ECSP) for business*. Retrieved December 15, 2021, from https://ec.europa.eu/info/business-economy-euro/growth-and-investment/financing-investment/crowdfunding_en

Filips, I. J. D. S., Mendes-Da-Silva, W., Leal, C. C., & Santos, D. B. (2022). Reward crowdfunding campaigns: Time-to-success analysis. *Journal of Business Research, 138*, 214–228.

Forbes. (2012a). *The truth about Kickstarter and ZionEyez.* Retrieved June 15, 2021, from http://www.forbes.com/sites/markgibbs/2012/08/20/the-truth-about-kickstarter-and-zioneyez/

Forbes. (2012b). *What is crowdfunding and how does it benefit the economy.* Retrieved June 15, 2021, from http://www.forbes.com/sites/tanyaprive/2012/11/27/what-is-crowdfunding-and-how-does-it-benefit-the-economy/

Gerber, E. M., & Hui, J. (2013). Crowdfunding: motivations and deterrents for participation. *ACM Transactions on Computing-Human Interactions, 20*(6), article number 34.

Investopedia. (2021). *Jumpstart our business startups (JOBS) act.* Retrieved December 15, 2021, from https://www.investopedia.com/terms/j/jumpstart-our-business-startups-act-jobs.asp

Jelincic, D. A., & Sveb, M. (2021). Financial sustainability of cultural heritage: A review of crowdfunding in Europe. *Journal of Risk and Financial Management, 14*(3), 1–16.

Mochkabadi, K., & Volkmann, C. K. (2020). Equity crowdfunding: A systematic review of the literature. *Small Business Economics, 54*(1), 75–118.

Popescul, D., Radu, L. D., Pavaloaia, V. D., & Georgescu, M. R. (2020). Psychological determinants of investor motivation in social media-based crowdfunding projects: A systematic review. *Frontiers in Psychology, 11*(588121), 1–16.

Shneor, R., & Vik, A. A. (2020). Crowdfunding success: A systematic literature review 2010–2017. *Baltic Journal of Management, 15*(2), 149–182.

Smerik, R. (2012). *Crowdfunding. Is there safety in numbers?* Retrieved June 15, 2013, from http://www.Slideshare.net/startupfest/crowdfunding-13723289

Stemler, A. R. (2013). The JOBS Act and crowdfunding: Harnessing the power – and money – of the mass. *Business Horizons, 56*(3), 271–275.

U.S. Securities And Exchange Commission. (2020). *SEC harmonizes and improves "Patchwork" exempt offering framework (press release).* Retrieved December 15, 2021, from https://www.sec.gov/news/press-release/2020-273

Wikipedia. (2021a). *Comparison of crowdfunding services.* Retrieved December 23, 2021, from https://en.wikipedia.org/wiki/Comparison_of_crowdfunding_services

Wikipedia. (2021b). *Crowdfunding.* Retrieved December 23, 2021, from http://en.wikipedia.org/wiki/Crowdfunding

Yazar, B. (2021). The new investment landscape: Equity crowdfunding. *Central Bank Review, 21*(1), 1–16.

Legal and Ethical Issues in Social Media

11

This chapter takes the perspective of legal and ethical issues in social media to complete the multidisciplinary approach of this book. Instead of intending to give legal advice, this chapter encourages the reader to reflect on proper social media use. Previous chapters already looked at how legislation is related to social media. Particularly, the chapter on online ads (Chap. 4) talked about privacy and cookie laws. Furthermore, the chapter on e-recruitment (Chap. 9) discussed some legal practices for organizations not to recruit or to fire someone because of social media posts. The chapter on crowdfunding (Chap. 10) referred to legislation to protect micro-investors. Besides legislation, also ethical concerns have been formulated. For instance, the chapter on SEO mentioned the use of black hat SEO techniques (Chap. 6), and the chapters on business intelligence considered the impact of fake customer reviews (Chap. 7) and privacy concerns for big data analysis (Chap. 8). This chapter supplements the previous chapters by discussing social media ethics from the perspective of organizations, as well as the perspective of individual employees and influencers as social media users. The reader learns about the role of a social media policy, Terms of Service, copyright or intellectual property, a digital afterlife, and password security, among others.

This chapter turns to the legal department within an organization in order to complete the multidisciplinary approach of social media (Fig. 11.1).

> **Teaser Question**
> - What is the best age for a social media manager or chief social media officer?

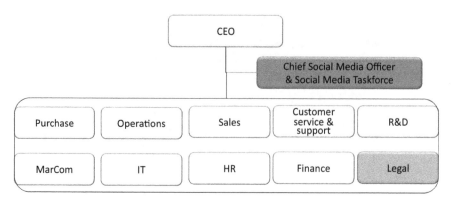

Fig. 11.1 The multidisciplinary approach of legal and ethical issues in social media

11.1   Introduction to Legal and Ethical Issues in Social Media

Suppose you are a blogger who frequently blogs about new technologies. Being a key influencer in the IT community, you are contacted by a software company that asks you to write a supporting blog post about its new product. What would you do?

In order to act in an ethical way, a supporting blog post can still be published if you mention that the company requested for this (or even paid for it). Or, as an independent blogger, you can write personal opinions about the offered product, which possibly contain negative aspects too. Similar to online ads, a writer's affiliation should be disclosed in every type of supportive message that could influence the purchasing decisions of customers. In this example, disclosure of relationship is relevant to the blog readers who might be influenced to purchase the product.

Social media ethics imply that a social media user should be honest about one's relationship, opinion, and identity. For instance, some examples of nonethical behavior from the perspective of organizations are:

- Blog posts or brand reviews paid by marketers, who are hired by an organization and without disclaimer.
- Ghost tweeters.
- Fake customer reviews.
- Fake chat room members.
- Viral campaigns that pretend to be user videos.
- Etc.

Also employees can act in an unethical way, for instance, by:

- Revealing business information online.
- Insulting clients or colleagues online.

- Posting obscene photos about their spare time.
- Etc.

Such examples may seem obvious at first sight, but many people post information online without giving it a lot of thought. In both professional and private situations, unethical social media use can harm the employer (see e-recruitment, Sect. 9.4). Therefore, individuals should always be careful when posting pictures about their hobby as a stripper, being drunk at a party, "liking" posts that deal with alcohol or drug abuse, etc.

Social media ethics have become a highly important topic, because social media are rapidly increasing in use and tend to blur the boundary between someone's private life and professional life. An unclear line also exists between freedom of speech and inappropriate posts. Due to the potential dangers related to social media, the need for education about proper social media use is increasing. Examples of potential dangers of social media use for organizations and employees are as follows:

- **Privacy**: See Chaps. 4, 8, and 9. It is more difficult to control one's personal information in online communication than in face-to-face communication (See Sect. 11.3.3).
- **Discrimination**: See Chap. 9. Social media posts can give digital evidence of discrimination or harassment.
- **Copyright**: An employee should not just copy and post someone else's work (e.g., text, video, picture, poem, art, etc.) without requesting the owner's permission (see also Sect. 11.3.2 on digital afterlife).
- **Intellectual Property**: This danger refers to the question whether social media content is owned by the employee, the employer, or the social media tool (see also "Terms of Service," Sect. 11.2.2). Furthermore, an employee should not post business secrets online. Another example concerns the ownership of online contacts that a recruiter or salesperson has while performing one's job. Particularly, an agreement can be made that stipulates who will get a copy of the social media contacts when this employee leaves the organization.
- **Terms of Service**: If an organization opens an account on one or another social media tool, it needs to accept the tool's Terms of Service (see Sect. 11.2.2). In order to fully understand what the organization actually signs and which legal consequences are related, a legal advisor can be consulted first.
- **Disclosure of Relationship:** When posting information online, an employee should disclose whether or not one acts as an employee of the organization and thus gets paid to create online ads, viral campaigns, blog posts, reviews, etc. (see supra).
- **Disclosure of Location:** an employee or employer can also indirectly reveal business secrets by mentioning one's location online (see also "intellectual property"). For instance, by using a geolocation-based tool such as Swarm™, social media connections may know when the employee is at work and not at home (e.g., if burglars are followers) or how many times an employer checks in at a certain airport or in a certain city. For instance, journalists can derive when

strategic discussions are going on with competitors or suppliers who are located on a specific location.

- **Defamation**: If an employee publishes false information or lies about someone to damage the reputation of that person, the organization can be liable for it in some situations (e.g., if the information is published on the corporate website).
- **Office Drama**: As social media posts can be easily sent (also outside working hours), an employee may post something without common sense and so hurt or embarrass colleagues (e.g., when the employee is angry, sad, tired, drunk, etc.).
- Etc.

It is important that both employers and employees are aware of the potential dangers that directly or indirectly relate to social media use and that may affect an organization's reputation. Although ethical behavior strongly depends on a relationship of trust, organizations can also educate their employees to recognize such dangers and teach them how to act professionally in diverse situations. A possible way to discipline employees is by means of a social media policy, supplemented by training.

Consequently, a secret to success in social media (and business ethics in general) is building trust. As discussed in Chap. 5 on social CRM, it concerns trust between the employer and its employees but also with its suppliers and customers and above all, with its fans on social media (i.e., who are different from customers, but may be prospects or influencers). By building trust, the organization will be more likely to save its brand, reputation, and jobs when, for instance, a crisis hits. Particularly, good relationships with stakeholders can serve as a buffer in times of crisis. This means that an ethical use of social media can facilitate online reputation management and even crisis management afterwards. Furthermore, SEO (see Chap. 6) can help reputation management in order to facilitate sharing (ethically correct) corporate information (e.g., press releases) and to make the corporate website more adapted to the requirements of search engines, social media, and smartphones.

11.2   Social Media Ethics by Organizations

This section elaborates on the explicit actions that an organization can take in order to encourage ethical behavior on social media. Particularly, in addition to building trust, an organization can create a social media policy (or a social media code of ethics) with a corresponding training program. Furthermore, it should take into account the Terms of Service of social media tools. We subsequently discuss these actions.

11.2.1 Social Media Policy and Training

A social media policy is often part of a larger IT policy on business conduct. An organization can create a social media policy from scratch, or it can rely on ethical communication guidelines of industry associations. Templates, guidelines, and examples of social media policies can also be found in a social media policy database, such as:

- https://insidesocialmedia.com/social-media-policies/

Just one example concerns IBM™'s social computing guidelines, which were created by means of crowdsourcing (see Chap. 10) among the employees. These guidelines are part of the organization's global business conduct guidelines:

- https://www.ibm.com/investor/att/pdf/BCG_accessible_2019.pdf

> A social media policy is a corporate code of conduct with official guidelines that stipulate how employees should behave online and appropriately use social media during and outside the business hours (i.e., on behalf of the organization and as a private person). Its main purpose is to avoid legal problems or undesired business implications and to inspire employees how to advocate the organization in an online setting.

Besides addressing the potential dangers mentioned in the introduction section, a social media policy may consider the following elements (Institute of Business Ethics 2022; SocialMedia.org 2015):

- **Social Media (Policy) Audit**. Chapter 3 explained that social media use should follow a social media strategy, which serves the organizational strategy. Social media should only be used if they can help reach the business objectives or solve business problems. In order to know which problems are to be solved and by which principles, a social media audit can be performed with a survey and/or in-depth interviews of employees. An audit may, for instance, also uncover whether employees use social media in an ethical way, whether they are aware of the social media policy in the organization, or whether the managers have an accurate idea of the online behavior of employees. Such insights may be used to set a social media policy or to recommend additional training. An example of a social media policy audit survey is given in (Flynn 2012).
- **Communication Principles and Standards**. A social media policy contains principles about the way employees are ought to act, which should be consistent with the corporate values. For instance, a social media policy can be explicitly driven by corporate values, e.g., collaboration, transparency, diversity, respect, and quality (e.g., https://www.coca-colacompany.com/policies-and-practices/responsible-digital-media-principles). Furthermore, a social media policy can set the organization's online voice and tone. For instance, it can define the expected response time (e.g., an organization can commit itself to respond to answers on Facebook™ within 16 h, on Twitter™ within 2 h, and to emails

within 24 h). In addition, possible characteristics of the organization's voice can be defined. For instance, if the voice is set to approachability, curiosity, and knowledge, then social media posts will rather be conversational, using exciting words and providing casual information.

- **Chief Social Media Officer.** As discussed in Sect. 1.3, a dedicated job description for a Chief Social Media Officer is rising in organizations. Having the right people in charge of social media is crucial. It does not necessarily concern people under the age of 25 who use social media a lot because older people may have relevant experience with marketing principles and knowledge about the business. An organization should hire someone who has both business savvy and social media savvy (e.g., great writers and storytellers), regardless of their age.
- **Social Media Monitoring and Training.** In line with Chap. 3 on social media strategy and ROI and with Chap. 5 on social CRM, an organization should regularly review its social media dashboard metrics. Monitoring social media conversations also enables an organization to correct people's misstatements related to the organization. For instance, see Chap. 7 on opinion mining. Monitoring can generally be considered as an ethically correct action, as long as it is announced in a (social media) policy and that the people involved are aware that monitoring takes place. Similarly, if an organization blocks certain websites or social media tools, it should be clearly stated in a policy. However, trusting employees might be an alternative to actually blocking sites, e.g., by hiring people that fit the organization and by regularly training them.
- **Disclaimers.** It should be clear whether an employee is either representing oneself or one's organization when using social media to talk about the organization and its products or services. The former would imply that the social media content represents one's personal opinion or contribution. In case of the latter, an employee is participating in social media on behalf of the organization and should rather get the manager's approval first. For transparency reasons, an employee should particularly provide a disclaimer if using a tool that is not sponsored by the organization, even if disclaimers are not explicitly requested by an organization in the organization's social media policy. A disclaimer is a disclosure of relationship and can be seen as a declaration whether the social media user represents or has an interest in a specific organization (SocialMedia.org 2015). In the end, it should be clear whether social media are used by the organization or privately by an employee for personal use. Aspects that can be mentioned in a disclaimer are the person's name, whether one was paid for posting the related content and thus represents the organization's point of view, or whether it concerns one's opinion based on a real experience. Some examples of disclaimers are given for the reader's information in Table 11.1.

11.2.2 Terms of Service of Social Media Tools

While organizations can set their own social media policy, each social media tool can set its own Terms of Service. As mentioned in the introduction of this chapter,

Table 11.1 Examples of disclaimers

Example for social mediaposts in general:
"Hello! My name is Valentina and I work for organization XYZ."
"These posts are my own, not those of organization XYZ."

Example for a blog sponsored by organization XYZ:
"Some of the authors contributing to this site, [including the moderators,] work for organization XYZ. Opinions expressed here and in any corresponding comments are the personal opinions of the original authors, not those of organization XYZ."

Example for a third-party blog:
"The opinions expressed in this blog are my own views and not those of organization XYZ."
or
"I received product X or information Y from Organization ABC. #paid"

Example for the personal blog of an employee:
"This blog is a personal blog written and edited by myself. For questions about this blog, please contact me.
This blog does not accept any form of cash advertising, sponsorship or paid topic insertions. However, I accept and keep free products, services, and travel or event tickets from organizations. However, those free products, services, travel or event tickets will never influence the content, topics, or posts made in this blog.
The views and opinions expressed on this blog are purely those of the blog owner. I will only endorse products or services that I believe, based on my expertise, are worthy of such endorsement. Any product claim, statistic, quote or other representation about a product or service should be verified with the manufacturer or provider.
This blog does not contain any content which might present a conflict of interest."

organizations or individuals can only make use of a social media tool after accepting the tool's Terms of Service.

Terms of Service define what the social media tool can offer (i.e., as a service) and how it should be used by the Internet users.

The notion "Terms of Service" can also be called the "Terms of Use" and generally stipulates the policy agreements regarding privacy, copyright, cookie use, safety, etc. As an illustration, we hereby give the link to some examples of Terms of Service:

- https://www.facebook.com/terms.php
- https://policy.pinterest.com/en/terms-of-service
- https://help.instagram.com/581066165581870
- https://www.linkedin.com/legal/user-agreement
- https://twitter.com/en/tos

While the Terms of Service can be considered as general information for the users, additional guidelines for law enforcement authorities can be given on a separate web page (e.g., https://help.twitter.com/en/rules-and-policies/twitter-law-enforcement-support).

According to the user rights initiative "Terms of Service; Didn't Read" (2022), most people do not read the Terms of Service when signing up for an online mailbox or a social media tool or when downloading an app, and just give their approval. Although the Terms of Service may affect someone's online privacy, people tend to agree because the Terms are often perceived as too long and written in legal terms. Therefore, the initiative "Terms of Service; Didn't Read" (2022) has developed a rating and labeling systems for Terms of Service and privacy policies on the Internet. The ratings vary from very good (class A) to very bad (class E). Many social media tools are regularly rated, and the results are publicly available. This initiative allows people to become more aware of what they sign up for.

An important issue related to the Terms of Service of social media tools concerns **intellectual property**. This broader issue relates to the ownership of social media data, i.e., whether the published content is actually owned by the social media tool, the employee, or the employer. Most social media tools give nonexclusive rights to its users, which means that a user may retain all rights and is solely responsible for one's UGC. Nonetheless, many social media tools also stipulate that they can reuse a user's content and pictures for commercial and audit purposes, even when the content or picture is removed by the user. Also other users who have shared specific content or a picture might still be able to make use of it after deletion by the user. This implication illustrates that social media posts can be considered as undeletable (see Sect. 1.2).

Another topic related to intellectual property is **copyright infringement** and implies that a social media user should never copy any content that is created by other people or organizations without acknowledging the original source. Still, the ease of posting on social media tools entails the risk for a user to pretend that a certain post is one's own creation (e.g., a slogan, a video, or an article), even if it does not concern the user's original work. Particularly, pictures on Google™ Images, YouTube™ videos, or lyrics are not there for the taking, and at least the original source should be mentioned. When the original source believes one's copyright-protected work was posted on social media without authorization, a copyright infringement notification can be submitted to the social media tool (e.g., https://www.youtube.com/howyoutubeworks/policies/copyright/). We note that a copyright infringement differs from just "sharing" or "liking" information, which generally does not need prior approval.

11.3 Social Media Ethics by Employees

From the perspective of employees, it is interesting to regularly check which online information is publicly available about yourself as an individual. For instance, in Chap. 9 on e-recruitment, the reader was invited to look for one's own name in a search engine and to take actions if necessary. Such personal searches are not merely conducted by recruiters. Also other jurors can and will screen someone's online identity (e.g., colleagues, customers, suppliers, competitors, etc.). By doing regular "me" searches, employees can manage which personal information can be found by other people. Hence, online reputation management is also important to employees.

Different theoretical approaches exist to assess whether something is ethically correct or not. Ethical frameworks generally distinguish the following approaches (Markkula Center for Applied Ethics 2021):

- **Utilitarian Approach**: Ethical decisions will choose for a certain behavior that maximizes utility, i.e., which is *most useful* or *most positive* with regard to its outcomes or consequences for all stakeholders ("the greatest good to the greatest number").
- **Rights Approach**: Ethical decisions will choose for a certain behavior that *best protects and respects* the rights of all stakeholders.
- **Fairness and Justice Approach**: Ethical decisions will choose for a certain behavior that treats stakeholders *equally or proportionally*.
- **Common Good Approach**: Ethical decisions will choose for a certain behavior that best serves the *community as a whole*, instead of only the stakeholders.
- **Virtue Approach**: Ethical decisions will choose for a certain behavior that best reflects some *virtues or ideals* in order to reach an individual's highest potential (e.g., honesty, courage, compassion, integrity, generosity, tolerance, etc.).
- **Principle Approach (Or Care Ethics Approach)**: Ethical decisions will choose for a certain behavior that best fits a *specific code of ethics*, i.e., by applying personal, professional, or global ethics.

Subsequently, this chapter provides the reader with practical considerations regarding an individual's online behavior.

11.3.1 Do's and Don'ts for Social Media Use

Online behavior of individuals may refer to business use or personal use. In both situations, employees should respect some general do's and don'ts (Institute of Business Ethics 2022).

Examples of ethical do's and don'ts for employees are:

- **Policy**. When communicating anything related to the organization, employees should act in accordance to the organization's code of ethics (i.e., the social media policy and more generally the policies on IT and business conduct).
- **Permission**. When communicating anything related to the organization, employees should first ask their manager for (oral or written) permission. Written permission is particularly required when it concerns confidential or copyrighted material (i.e., that belongs to current or former employers or third parties). Furthermore, identifiable client information should not be posted online without client's permission.
- **Confidentiality and Professionalism**. Additional to the policies, some organizations can ask their employees or interns to sign a nondisclosure

agreement. Nonetheless, confidentiality should always be contained regarding "internal use" information, and business secrets should not be publicly revealed. Similarly, employees should avoid public statements about the financial performance of current or former organizations.

- **Reputation Management.** Employees should contribute to online reputation management to protect both the organization's and their own reputation. Also private social media use should be considered from this perspective (e.g., when clients or colleagues are personal connections or when personal social media posts are in the public domain).

- **Privacy.** Individuals should set privacy settings to safeguard private content. Employees should act professionally, also in their spare time. In order to maintain appropriate professional boundaries, different accounts can be created to separate their private use of social media from their professional use (i.e., a personal online identity versus a professional online identity).

- **Discrimination or Harassment.** During and outside working hours, employees should avoid vulgar, discriminating, or unflattering content on any website or account. Discrimination has a broad interpretation, among others disrespect for someone based on age, race, gender, ethnicity, sexual orientation, etc. Furthermore, caution is required for content that relates to (an abuse of) alcohol and drugs.

- **Informal Social Control.** Employees should bring unethical content or behavior to the attention of a manager or the colleague involved.

- **Influencers.** Everyone who recommends or endorses products should comply with the law when making recommendations. This obligation applies to influencer marketing in general and is based on traditional legislation to avoid unfair commercial practices, such as the **FTC Act** of 1914 in the USA and the **Unfair Commercial Practice Directive 2005/29/EC** in the European Union (Boerman et al. 2018). These corresponding laws have been further interpreted, developed, such as through the **US FTC guidelines** (Federal Trade Commission 2019) and through case law and self-regulative provisions in the EU. One key is to make a good disclosure of your relationship to the brand. For instance, the US FTC (Federal Trade Commission 2019) has published an ethical guide with 101 disclosures for social media influencers to protect consumers. On the other hand, self-regulation of European Member States remains important for defining how to comply with the Unfair Commercial Practice Directive 2005/29/EC in order to enhance transparency for consumers on social media tools (Graetz et al. 2021). This matter is also essential to create a digital single market (e.g., European Commission's communication about a new deal for consumers, COM/2018/0183). Such guidelines and self-regulative provisions help avoid deceptive ads, and offer details about how advertisers but also endorsers can act in an ethically correct manner.

11.3.2 Digital Afterlife

A topic indirectly linked to social media is the digital afterlife of individuals (Öhman and Floridi 2018), i.e., what happens with someone's social media content and accounts when that person dies? To have their digital data properly managed, social media users (or Internet users in general) can take some precautions in a so-called digital will. Although this topic may seem awkward at first, some things in life should be given a thought from time to time.

A first question to be considered is whether your legal heirs (i.e., your loved ones) are aware of all your social media profiles and content. If so, can they also access them? Or maybe the content is not readable anymore because the file format has changed over time (e.g., from PDF files to a new document extension in the future)? Another question concerns the ownership of social media data. The latter question deals with copyright issues and the discussion on Terms of Service (see Sect. 11.2.2). Copyright can last for the life of an individual creator plus 50–70 years (Wikipedia 2021). This implies that social media content (e.g., pictures or recordings) can be registered together with other valuable assets (such as a house, furniture, or personal properties).

Social media tools do not necessarily give legal heirs access to the profile of a deceased person. A relatively safe solution is to provide a list of network usernames and passwords to a trusted relative or friend. Some commercial organizations try to make money in this area and let you (regularly) pay for their service (e.g., for information management, posthumous messaging, online memorials or even re-creation as an AI avatar or chat bot-like application that generates new messages based on one's past social behavior) (Öhman and Floridi 2018). Meanwhile, social media tools are also having a policy about account settings. For instance, Google™ has its "Inactive Account Manager" feature to proactively create a digital will related to one's Google™ services in use. This feature allows, for instance, to set a time-out period (e.g., after 3–12 months of inactivity) and to send automatic notifications to the user and/or trusted contacts when the time-out period ends, including the possibility to automatically delete the user's account after a predefined period of time (https://support.google.com/accounts/answer/3036546). Also other social media tools increasingly offer solutions to a user's digital afterlife.

11.3.3 Privacy and Passwords

Since privacy is essential for Internet users, this section elaborates on the topic from two perspectives. The first perspective recalls that social media tools can sell personal data of users to third parties as part of their business model (e.g., not only for targeted advertising but also for predictive mining, sentiment analysis, etc., See Chap. 3). The second perspective delves deeper into situations during which others use (or misuse) your passwords of social media pages.

In general, privacy is the right to have one's private or family life respected. Information privacy then refers to one's right to have some control over how others collect, share, and use personal information. It concerns a selective control because the law determines exceptions. With regard to social media tools, privacy relates to an individual user's ability to control personal information and the related information sharing.

The first perspective acknowledges the fact that online data have become one of the most valuable commodities (White and Boatwright 2020). Since social media are operating in a data economy that aggregates and sells users' personal information to third parties, strict privacy restrictions can be in the disadvantage of social media tools (White and Boatwright 2020). More specifically, social media tools operate through datafication, which might struggle with one's privacy (e.g., when users have a feeling of being continuously tracked) (Bagger 2021). Nevertheless, the **privacy paradox** explains that, although users have concerns about the increased datafication of everyday life, they do not really take concrete actions against their own datafication. This can be due to a rational exchange, a digital resignation (e.g., because privacy violations seem inevitable) or ignorance (e.g., because Terms of Service are not read) (Bagger 2021). Consequently, social media users face the challenge of balancing between self-disclosure and privacy. They should carefully think of which behaviors will lead to gratifications and which revelations can be harmful for them (Krämer and Schäwel 2020). In other words, while the notion of privacy is closely related to control, social media users cannot easily control their personal information because data exchange occurs between many parties and applications (Trepte 2021). The literature refers to "consumer alienation" to describe the distance between users and a social media tool with respect to its business ethics (e.g., norms and ideas) (Chung et al. 2021). Social media users should feel able to adjust their privacy settings. Otherwise, they are likely to withdraw from social media because of distrust. For instance, studies have shown that factors such as users' information security awareness, perceived privacy control, self-efficacy and perceived usefulness positively affect one's self-disclosure and negatively affect one's privacy-protection behavior (Baker-Eveleth et al. 2021; Chung et al. 2021). This means that the more users trust a social media tool, the more they are likely to share personal information.

One example of a data privacy scandal happened to Facebook™ in 2018, namely when the British political consulting company Cambridge Analytica™ collected personal data from US users after doing a personality quiz for the sake of political advertising in favor of Donald Trump. The link between the personality quiz and the political objectives was not clearly communicated. Once Facebook™ identified this violation, it asked Cambridge Analytica™ to delete the data but without thoroughly checking whether this was actually done (Financial Times 2018). The scandal resulted in a negative public perception and a tremendous #DeleteFacebook user campaign, as well as a company closure of Cambridge Analytica™ (Fortune 2018).

This data privacy issue happened along with other trust crises, such as a news feed integrity issue (i.e., whether users can trust online news feeds after so-called fake news) and a broader cultural issue about smartphone addiction and FOMO (Chap. 1). Consequently, Facebook™'s stock price drastically declined in one month (cfr. Similar to the Antennagate crisis, see Chap. 5). Afterwards, Mark Zuckerberg apologized and asked for stronger regulations during interviews in the American Congress and in the European Parliament (ABC News 2018). Remember that the GDPR legislation (i.e., covering strict privacy restrictions in the EU) started about the same time as the election period of Donald Trump and this trust crisis (see Chap. 4).

The second perspective covers the use of one's passwords by others (i.e., either trusted ones or maliciously). For instance, following the section on digital afterlife, an option exists to look at your online presence and to list up all your online memberships with corresponding username and password. If this option is chosen, the list should be regularly updated as login details need to change over regularly. The list should also be safely stored and only for your trusted ones to be found. Such a paper-based list might be the easiest way to manage a digital afterlife without additional costs, but should not be saved on a computer (i.e., due to the related security risks).

Given the relevance of passwords for proper social media use, this section gives some general tips and tricks to create strong passwords.

- **Creation**. Internet users should choose passwords of at least eight or ten characters long, which are rather non-words instead of names (e.g., not your pet's name), instead of dictionary words (e.g., not "password"or not "admin"), or instead of words spelled backward (e.g., not "drowssap" which refers to "password"). Also avoid common character sequences (e.g., not "azerty," not "0123456789," or not "abc123"), but try to combine lower- and uppercases with numbers and special characters (e.g., with a question mark or dashes). Alternatively, a combination of words or even a sentence can be used.
- **Unique Use**. Internet users should use a unique password per account and update it regularly, even if it will result in a long list of passwords. In order to remember all different passwords of all online accounts, an online trusted password manager tool is preferably used (instead of saving them in a text file on your computer). Many online tools also allow their users to proactively add recovery options in case someone forgets one's password.
- **Extra**. Ideally, Internet users should use a multistep or multifactor authentication process (e.g., with a unique code to be received on a cell phone) or even biometrics (e.g., a scan of their iris or fingerprint) to log in, in addition to the password).
- **Privacy**. When using social media on someone else's computer, make sure to uncheck the "remember my password"function, and never let an account opened without the user's surveillance. Extra caution is needed when using public computers.

Strong and unique passwords are crucial in a social era where someone's digital life is an extension of one's offline life. For instance, passwords are needed for all types of online activities, such as online banking or e-commerce, but also to get access to a computer, a cell phone, social media tools, or services in the cloud. The following videos are meant to make people aware that their entire life can be found online (i.e., by collecting information about a certain individual from different social media tools by means of social engineering) and that online information can be used against you:

- Example 1: amazing mind reader reveals his gift (https://www.youtube.com/watch?v=F7pYHN9iC9I).
- Example 2: how freaks can easily take over someone's life (https://www.youtube.com/watch?v=Rn4Rupla11M).

Consequently, it is highly important for Internet users to use social media and other online services in a privacy-friendly way. Social engineering also explains why Internet users should not use passwords that contain the name of their pet, child, or favorite movie, as those data might be easy to find on social media. Regarding emerging technologies, social media tools increasingly use technologies such as AI and IoT to prevent privacy leaking (Chung et al. 2021).

11.4   Takeaways

A final ethical note is dedicated to the reader in particular. As a social media user, each individual remains responsible for one's social media behavior. Though, an organization can discipline its employees by means of a policy related to social media and IT in general. Nonetheless, proper use of social media and IT should be built on a relationship of mutual respect, trust, and loyalty.

Social media users have the right to get privacy and freedom of speech, albeit only to a certain extent. For instance, if information is really private, then you should not post it on social media and create digital evidence for it. Or as a matter of common sense, never insult others or never harm current and former employers. If necessary, the police will be able to track and trace online users, even if they have an anonymous account (e.g., based on the IP address of a computer, cookies in a browser, etc.). The latter is also true for online abuse outside a business context, such as cyberbullying among teenagers or pedophilia. The indirect or distant use of social media might give users a false sense of omnipotence.

Consequently, the message of this chapter is to act professionally and then a proper use of social media is likely to follow. Although an ethical behavior on social media contributes to online reputation management, the reader is encouraged to meet one's online connections also in real life. As such, online and offline relationships can reinforce one another. In order to have more time for offline relationships and avoid a social media addiction, the reader might consider to check social media updates only at fixed moments in time (e.g., once in the morning, once at noon, and/or once in the evening).

11.5 Self-Test

- Can you explain the dangers related to social media use for organizations and employees?
- Do you know what a social media policy consists of?
- Can you recognize the difference between ethical and unethical use of social media in real-life situations?
  - Is it ethical for an organization to counter online criticism and defend its online reputation?
  - What if an employee has blogged about his colleagues without mentioning any names?
  - What would you do if your employer asks you to put information on the corporate website and on social media without referencing or acknowledging the original sources?
  - Can an employee present oneself as an official representative of or a spokesperson for an organization?
  - George worked for 5 years as the Chief Social Media Officer at organization XYZ, before becoming a freelance. He intends to write a personal blog post that contains copyrighted information belonging to his former employer, organization XYZ. What should George do to act ethically correct?
- After a drunken Saturday-night party, a sales manager posts an obscene picture of himself on Facebook in his spare time. Can one be fired for this post? Why (not)?
- In a European university hospital called ALMEDICA, doctors are working with a self-employed status. One of the doctor takes a picture of a patient for reasons of diagnosis and treatment (namely a part of the patient's arm or an internal tumor). Afterwards, the doctor wants to use this picture to let research in the field advance, and to share and discuss the findings with peers on social media channels. Reflect on who owns the picture (e.g., the hospital, the doctor or the patient), and which actions can be done with the picture in terms of social media usage.
- Can you think of unethical actions that an organization should avoid when promoting products or services online?
- Do you know the importance of strong passwords for social media?
- Can you explain how password hijackers can profit from social engineering?
- What would you like to happen to your personal social media pages upon your death?
- Compare different organizations based on their social media policy.

- Discuss why a social media policy or privacy policy can be perceived as not important or not accepted by employees? Try to think of possible explanations, and countermeasures. Tip: consider elements such as visibility, readability, understandability, interest, awareness of dangers, etc.
- Reflect on some specific situations and how you (as a potential influencer) can address the 101 statements about disclosures, as stipulated by the US Federal Trade Commission (2019), such as:
  - Disclose when you have any financial, employment, personal, or family relationship with a brand.
  - Tags, likes, pins and similar ways of showing you like a brand or product are endorsements.
  - In case you have no brand relationship and are just telling people about a product you bought and happen to like, it is not required to explicitly declare that you do not have a brand relationship.
  - An explanation like "Thanks to Acme for the free product" is often enough if placed in a way that is hard to miss, but avoid vague terms like "spon," "collab" or just "thanks."

Bibliography

ABC News. (2018). *Marck Zuckerberg speaks out on data scandal.* Retrieved January 6, 2022, from https://www.youtube.com/watch?v=3fS5A_hw2w8

Bagger, C. (2021). An organizational cultivation of digital resignation? Enterprise social media, privacy, and autonomy. *Nordicom Review, 42*(S4), 185–198.

Baker-Eveleth, L., Stone, R., & Eveleth, D. (2021). Understanding social media users' privacy-protection behaviors. *Information & Computer Security,* 1–22.

Boerman, S. C., van Noort, G., Helberger, N., & Hoofnagie, J. (2018). *Sponsored blog content: What do the regulations say? And what do bloggers say.* Retrieved January 8, 2022, from https://www.jipitec.eu/issues/jipitec-9-2-2018/4730

Chung, K.-C., Chen, C.-H., Tsai, H.-H., & Chuang, Y.-H. (2021). Social media privacy management strategies: A SEM analysis of user privacy behaviors. *Computer Communications, 174,* 122–130.

Federal Trade Commission. (2019). *Disclosures 101 for social media influencers.* Retrieved January 8, 2022, from https://www.ftc.gov/tips-advice/business-center/guidance/disclosures-101-social-media-influencers

Financial Times. (2018). *Facebook privacy breach.* Retrieved January 6, 2022, from https://www.ft.com/content/87184c40-2cfe-11e8-9b4b-bc4b9f08f381

Flynn, N. (2012). *The social media handbook: Rules, policies, and best practices.* New Riders.

Fortune. (2018). *Commentary: #DeleteFacebook is just the beginning. Here's the movement we could see next.* Retrieved January 6, 2022, from https://fortune.com/2018/04/16/delete-facebook-data-privacy-movement/

Graetz, D., Hieronimus, L., & Bachman, F. (2021). *To disclose or not to disclose... That is the question!* Retrieved January 8, 2022, from https://www.maastrichtuniversity.nl/blog/2021/07/disclose-or-not-disclose%E2%80%A6-question

Institute of Business Ethics. (2022). *Social media.* Retrieved January 8, 2022, from https://www.ibe.org.uk/knowledge-hub/technology/social-media.html

Krämer, N. C., & Schäwel, J. (2020). Mastering the challenge of balancing self-disclosure and privacy in social media. *Current Opinion in Psychology, 31,* 67–71.

Markkula Center for Applied Ethics. (2021). *A framework for ethical decision making.* Retrieved January 8, 2022, from https://www.scu.edu/ethics/ethics-resources/a-framework-for-ethical-decision-making/

Öhman, C., & Floridi, L. (2018). An ethical framework for the digital afterlife industry. *Nature Human Behaviour, 2*(5), 318–320.

SocialMedia.org. (2015). *The SocialMedia.org disclosure toolkit.* Retrieved June 15, 2021, from: http://socialmedia.org/disclosure/

Terms of Service; Didn't Read. (2022). *"I have read and agree to the Terms" is the biggest lie on the web. We aim to fix that.* Retrieved January 8, 2022, from https://tosdr.org/en/frontpage

Trepte, S. (2021). The social media privacy model: Privacy and communication in the light of social media affordances. *Communication Theory, 31*(4), 549–570.

White, C. L., & Boatwright, B. (2020). Social media ethics in the data economy: Issues of social responsibility for using Facebook for public relations. *Public Relations Review, 46*(5), 1–7.

Wikipedia. (2021). *Copyright.* Retrieved December 28, 2021, from https://en.wikipedia.org/wiki/Copyright

Wrap-Up: Integration Exercises

12

This chapter concludes the book by combining the perspectives of previous chapters in various integration exercises. Diverse insights and knowledge obtained throughout the book are now applied in multidisciplinary case studies, assignments, and brainstorming exercises. The latter are not intended to be comprehensive or to apply the entire book at once. Instead, the reader is encouraged to carefully think through which knowledge and reflections may apply to certain business situations. The purpose of this final chapter is to encourage the reader to critically discuss how specific organizations can take advantage of social media and create business value. Together with the self-tests offered in previous chapters, this chapter illustrates the extent to which the reader meets the book's learning objectives (as presented in Chap. 1), namely, about (1) proper use, (2) knowledge, (3) strategic insights, (4) critical reasoning, and (5) lifelong learning in the context of social media.

> **Teaser Question**
> • Can you give me social media advice?

12.1 Case Study

The different perspectives taken in this book are now applied to the context of an existing organization. The case study describes how the organization under study determines, executes, and evaluates its internal and external social media strategies. In other words, the case study investigates the degree to which the organization addresses each topic (i.e., chapter) presented in this book and motivates why. The information is based on Borremans (2014) and Forbes (2013), and is written with permission.

To orient the reader to the study, some general information about the organization is given in Table 12.1.

© The Author(s), under exclusive license to Springer Nature Switzerland AG 2022
A. Van Looy, *Social Media Management*, Springer Texts in Business and
Economics, https://doi.org/10.1007/978-3-030-99094-7_12

Table 12.1   General information about the case study (2014)

Name:	Van Marcke™ (http://www.vanmarcke.com/)
Location:	Europe and the USA (headquarters in Belgium)
Sector:	Manufacturer, wholesaler, and seller of sanitary facilities, kitchens, and heating systems
Client types:	B2C: individuals B2B: professional installers (e.g., plumbers)
Organization size:	Large sized (circa 1500 employees)
Organization's social media budget:	Every department has its own budget Plus € 20,000 per year for the overall coordination by the Chief Social Media Officer (e.g., for the monitoring platform, online relationship management, nonpaid campaigns, translation costs)
Organization's social media experience:	Since mid-2009

12.1.1   Organogram and the Role of a Chief Social Media Officer

Van Marcke™ is a family-owned organization with a complex matrix organization chart. As shown in Fig. 12.1, the organization has product-related pillars with operational and supporting departments organized in regional divisions.

Van Marcke™ is one of the first organizations to introduce a Chief Social Media Officer (CSO). In contrast to Chap. 1, the CSO is not included in the executive committee of CxOs, but reports to the Chief HR Officer and the Chief Operations Officer (instead of to the CEO). More specifically, the CSO initially reported to the CEO during the first 3 years. This reporting line changed when the CSO function was broadened with corporate social responsibility. Since then, the CSO reports to (1) the Chief Operations Officer (also called the Chief Efficiency and Organization Officer at Van Marcke™) for the (internal) use of social media and to (2) the Chief HR Officer for Corporate Social Responsibility. Van Marcke™ thus adapted the CSO role to its specific context, including specific business processes, structure, and culture.

A nonhierarchical relationship exists between the CSO and the other departments at Van Marcke™, i.e., similar to a "hub and spoke" model (Altimeter Group 2013) in which the CSO acts as a central Center of Excellence for social activities. Figure 12.2 illustrates that the CSO is positioned in the middle, with a direct relationship to each department manager separately.

The CSO aims at coordinating and transferring the necessary tools, skills, experience, knowledge, and methodologies to the different departments. From this perspective, the role of the CSO is rather a temporary position at Van Marcke™. Once the tools, skills, experience, knowledge, and methodologies are transferred, the CSO as an enabler becomes superfluous.

In particular, the CSO job description at Van Marcke™ can be summarized as follows:

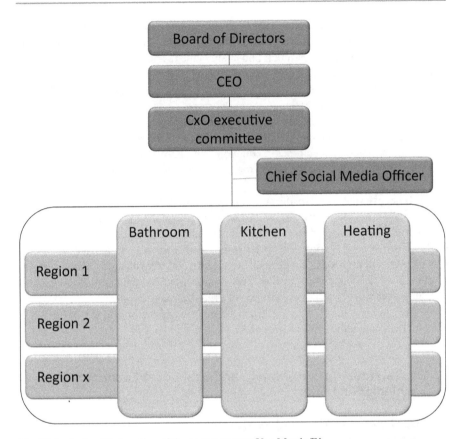

Fig. 12.1   A simplified version of the organogram at Van Marcke™

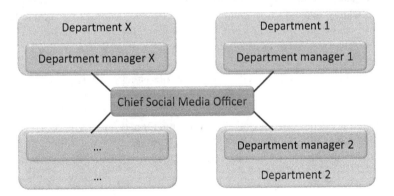

Fig. 12.2   A simplified version of the "hub and spoke" model at Van Marcke™, based on Altimeter Group (2013)

- Responsible for all aspects of (internal and external) social media communication and collaboration across the different divisions and departments of Van Marcke™, as well as for reputation management and stakeholder outreach in the context of corporate social responsibility.
- Create and roll out the internal and external social media communication strategies at Van Marcke™.
- Apply social media communication to public relations and outreach programs in the area of sustainable energy, green economy, and innovation areas.
- Roll out an internal social media collaboration platform to all employees of Van Marcke™, including the strategies for change management, communication, and learning/adoption.
- Establish external social media communication strategies and execute them for all sales channels and corporate staff functions, e.g., the departments of public relations, HR, customer service and support, and MarCom.
- Responsible for the corporate social responsibility strategy in close relationship with different divisions, departmental functions, and sales channels. This includes regular audits, change management, communication, and managing relationships with stakeholders and nongovernmental organizations.
- Project manager to roll out client-focused mobile applications in the context of a new financial credit services project.

12.1.2 Determining, Monitoring, and Evaluating External Social Media Strategies

In order to illustrate some external social media strategies at Van Marcke™, we start by taking the perspective of one division. It concerns "Big Blue," which is an education and training center regarding sustainable or renewable energy. The strategies highly depend on monitoring activities, such as tracking the number of daily mentions (Fig. 12.3) or listing Twitter™ users whose status updates about Van Marcke™ have been most retweeted by others.

- When "Big Blue" was created in 2009, the objective was to position Van Marcke™ as a **thought leader on sustainable energy**. Therefore, social media were monitored to identify influencers in the domain. For instance, daily mentions in online newspapers, blogs, and other social media tools were tracked, as well as the most retweeted and most mentioned Twitter™ users in status updates about Van Marcke™. This influencer tracking uncovered that many engineers, architects, and clients were then active on Twitter™. Besides a corporate presence on **Twitter**™ (https://twitter.com/bigbluebelgium), Van Marcke™ also decided to start a **blog** with knowledge articles to show expertise on sustainable energy (http://www.bigblue.be/nl). For instance, blog posts reported on the calculation of energy loss, sustainable buildings, or trade fairs. Only indirectly, the blog posts dealt with Van Marcke™'s products (e.g., heating systems). This blog was also available on the corporate website and could be used for reasons of community management (i.e., similar to social CRM). In

Fig. 12.3 An extract of the monitoring dashboard at Van Marcke™

2012, a corporate Facebook™ page was created (https://www.facebook.com/BigBlueBelgium/). Additionally, "The Big Blue Channel" account was created on YouTube™, as well as a photo stream on Flickr™.

- The business priorities at Van Marcke™ have changed from thought leadership to **cost savings**. The focus now is less on Twitter™ and the corporate blog. Instead, in line with social responsibility, Van Marcke™ has invested in a **document management system**, called "Issuu" (http://issuu.com/vanmarcke). Van Marcke™ will print only a small amount of glossaries and encourages people to download an electronic copy from "Issuu" for free.

Next, more general examples of external social media strategies at Van Marcke™ are as follows:

- In order to **manage media relations and to directly communicate with the target audience**, Van Marcke™ launched a "social media news room" (http://press.vanmarcke.com/). Instead of sending press releases to journalists by email, anyone can now freely find press releases online (including high-definition pictures for newspapers, video clips for television, audio fragments for radio stations, podcasts, etc.). No account or password is needed in order to reach as many people as possible. Furthermore, people can start retweeting or commenting on the press releases and so creating a social media ripple effect. Another advantage is that the online press releases are keyword driven and thus SEO friendly.
- To achieve a **better and quicker customer service and support**, the corporate Twitter™ page is monitored for complaints or queries. Van Marcke™ tries to take advantage of external complaints to improve its internal way of working (i.e., its business processes or workflows). For instance, in 2012, a customer was complaining that his boiler was still under warranty, but after several phone calls and visits, no one seemed to help him. The customer even posted evidence (including invoices) online. In response, Van Marcke™ changed its workflow so

Table 12.2 Some results after evaluating the external social media strategies at Van Marcke™

Social media strategies	Social media tactics	Results
To become a thought leader on sustainable energy	Blog	• Average of 30 face-to-face meetings through the website • Average of 60 email contacts through the website
To become a thought leader on sustainable energy To achieve a better and quicker customer service and support	Twitter™	• Customer insights have changed procedures • Rapid and transparent response led to positive customer experiences • Be the number 10 source of traffic to the website
To achieve cost savings	Issuu	• More than 10,000,000 catalogue views
To manage media relations and directly communicate with the target audience	Social media newsroom	• Average of more than 500 views of press releases • Interactive comments on press releases • Positive impact on search result rankings

that every boiler under warranty will be directly replaced, without trying to fix the product at the customer's house first.

After the external social media strategies were determined and monitored, an evaluation phase at Van Marcke™ led to the results described in Table 12.2.

12.1.3 Determining, Monitoring, and Evaluating Internal Social Media Strategies

Together with an external consultant, the CSO at Van Marcke™ started with an internal communication and collaboration audit at the end of 2009. The audit assessed the situation to identify the problems to be solved. Based on this input, KPIs were linked to concrete solutions.

The audit entailed an online survey for all knowledge workers (i.e., employees working with a computer, thus not the factory workers), followed by face-to-face interviews with a small subset of knowledge workers on a two-on-one basis. The audit uncovered several unproductivity issues, such as:

- 37% of the knowledge workers needed 1 h per day to manage their inbox.
- 31% of the knowledge workers needed 1 h per client request.
- 82% of the knowledge workers used emails to share documents internally.
- 56% of the knowledge workers did 20 or more internal phone calls per day.

- 20% of the knowledge workers spent 30 min per day to find the right internal information.
- 42% of the knowledge workers spent 10 min on average to find the right colleague.

Several KPIs were defined per area of improvement, aiming at increasing overall ROI. Some examples are given below (albeit not in a SMART way):

- Reduce the respond cycle time of projects and requests for proposal.
- Reduce the cost of losing employees before the end of the probation period.
- Improve employee productivity through more effective organizational collaboration.
- Increase employee productivity through a faster access to role-specific information.
- Improve email management.
- Reduce the cost of manual data collection, consolidation, and reporting.
- Reduce the lost time spent on leaving voice mails.
- Reduce the internal conversation telephone calls and related cost.
- Reduce the cost of the IT helpdesk by providing self-service access to IT support.
- Reduce the printing and distribution cost.
- Reduce the volume of email attachments.

Until then, Van Marcke™ worked with a static intranet with online folders, which was primarily based on emails for internal communication and collaboration in a complex matrix organization (Fig. 12.1). The problem was that the initial intranet relied too much on paper-based information, and employees experienced difficulties in finding the right information and people in the organization and therefore were more likely to resign.

The solution proposed by the CSO was to replace the static intranet by a more personalized intranet with a collaboration tool for all employees worldwide. The time frame set for this initiative was three years, because of the need for change management and to overcome resistance. For instance:

- To improve **employee productivity through more effective organizational collaboration**, the landing page of the collaboration tool was an aggregator with widgets personalized per employee (e.g., showing updates in one's communities, wikis, activities, bookmarks, blogs, feeds).
- To increase **employee productivity through faster access to role-specific information**, the collaboration tool offered a profile per employee with one's name, picture profile, job title, working address, contact details, and other background information.
- To reduce **the volume of email attachments**, the collaboration tool worked with personal and public wikis. This initiative also helped to improve **email management** by reducing the cost of manual data collection, consolidation, and reporting.

- To reduce **the general cycle time of projects and the cycle time to respond to project offers**, specific communities were launched in which projects and offers were discussed.

The knowledge workers were carefully trained to work with the collaboration tool. Even when the 3-year project was finished, ongoing productivity and refreshing and specialized training are given.

Not all KPIs were met after the project, but Van Marcke™ experienced an increased use in collaborative spaces and less email-based work. About 40% of all employees now regularly use the collaboration tool (i.e., once a day or more frequently).

In the meantime, Van Marcke™ has changed the collaboration tool for a supplier reorientation.

12.1.4 Other Topics

As the other topics of the book are covered to a limited extent at Van Marcke™, they are briefly discussed to complete the case study.

- **Online advertising and viral campaigns**. Some online ads have been launched on the initiative of the MarCom department at Van Marcke™. The focus is less on viral campaigns, because B2C clients typically buy a bathroom, kitchen, or heating system only a few times. On the other hand, most B2B clients are loyal to a local shop of Van Marcke™, which reduces the need for specific viral campaigns.
- **Social customer relationship management (social CRM)**. Van Marcke™ does not have a real CRM system in 1.0 or 2.0, but plans are being made. For instance, a CRM 1.0 system may contain invoice-related data. The most important B2B clients are already approached as partners in order to strengthen customer relationships and stimulate loyalty and brand advocacy. Next, the use of "Issuu" can help refine CRM information about prospects, e.g., when people provide personal information for downloading an electronic glossary. However, the Facebook™ pages of local B2B shops are working and reflect a real form of community that already exists offline. For instance, B2B clients feel at home in their local shop. Also, the local shop managers update their Facebook™ pages themselves, ensuring a familiar tone of voice and recognizable images. In sum, since the local shops of Van Marcke™ profit from a strong offline community of B2B clients, some shops have already virtualized their community with a dedicated Facebook™ group. Furthermore, the "Big Blue" community is situated in the domain of social CRM.
- **Search engine optimization (SEO)**. The corporate website of Van Marcke™ is keyword driven. Additionally, press releases are publicly available in the "social media news room" to directly reach the target audience and to obtain a higher ranking in search engines for certain keywords.

- **Opinion mining and sentiment analysis.** Van Marcke™ has a monitoring tool that detects brand-related posts. An advanced use of opinion mining is not present in the organization.
- **Social network data and predictive mining.** Van Marcke™ does not apply predictive mining, mainly because an advanced CRM system is still lacking.
- **e-Recruitment.** Van Marcke™ uses an ATS 1.0 system without storage or link to social media data. Vacancies are usually published on Facebook™ and Twitter™. LinkedIn™ is used to publish news and vacancies on the LinkedIn™ company page, but the professional paid features of LinkedIn™ are deemed too expensive by the HR department.
- **Crowdfunding.** Van Marcke™ is a family-owned organization which focuses on traditional funding mechanisms. As it does not face funding problems, the need for crowdfunding has not been risen so far.
- **Legal and ethical issues in social media and a social media policy.** Van Marcke™ has established corporate social media guidelines (not rules) in order to protect itself and its employees. The guidelines build upon common sense and trust. For instance, the public Internet was initially blocked for all employees, but the CSO requested for an open access to build internal relationships based on trust. The idea behind this change was: "No point being 2.0 outside if you are not even 1.0 inside."

12.2 Social Media Bloopers and Lessons Learned

From a successful case study, we now turn to situations in which social media are used rather inappropriately or less successful.

As explained in Sect. 1.2, the technological evolution graph of Gartner Inc. (2021) can be used to explain the social media bloopers (i.e., failures or mistakes) of organizations. Although organizations get more acquainted with social media, they should continue to learn from mistakes along their journey toward a yet more mature and advanced use of social media. Therefore, this section looks at some reported social media bloopers in order to distill the corresponding lessons learned.

When the first edition looked for "social media bloopers" in a search engine such as Google™, almost 2.5 million search results appeared in 2015. When redoing the same search in 2021, the number of search results had significantly dropped to a several thousand. This small exercise clearly demonstrates the learning curve of many organizations in the past few years. Nonetheless, other challenges have appeared which relate to new ways of using social media, such as the use of influencers (e.g., the risks of social media takeovers) and automated replies (e.g., the risks of using robots), and the changing norms and values in society with an increased awareness for certain sensitive issues (e.g., environmental sustainability, racism, or stereotypes).

Cases are not limited to organizations, but also individual users should think twice before posting something online and take responsibility. In particular, also on social media, sources should be carefully checked before "liking" or "sharing" information as anyone can spread any message. In recent years, there has been an increase in fake news messages (e.g., related to political elections or the COVID-19 pandemic), and which are stimulated by today's information overload (Menczer 2020).

As this book deals with social media use by organizations, the next paragraphs illustrate some lessons learned from the perspective of organizations. The intention is not to give an overview of lessons learned and best practices or to focus on specific organizations, but to encourage the reader to critically reflect on particular situations with an eye on suggestions for improvement.

12.2.1 Example: Monitoring and Support Are Important

This section illustrates that proper customer support and dedicated communities can strongly contribute to a positive customer experience and positive reviews (see Chap. 5 on social CRM). If any issue rises on social media, 24/7 monitoring efforts may notice negative messages before a crisis hits (see Chaps. 3 and 5).

Sources for the DELL™ Case
- http://www.theguardian.com/technology/2005/aug/29/mondaymediasection. blogging
- https://notesmatic.com/dell-social-media-strategy/

Case Description
The computer company DELL™ faced a serious social media blooper in 2005, when a journalist posted negative messages on a blog. His new computer had technical issues and the customer service at the organization took too long. As a journalist, this customer had a high impact on others, directly resulting in lower profit for the organization. In response, the organization committed itself to help customers in a more proactive way. Meanwhile, DELL™ has a global social media policy (https://www.delltechnologies.com/en-us/policies/social-media-policy.htm). For support issues, DELL™ can be contacted on various social media tools and its own community, which includes a knowledge base and an open forum for customers to ask questions (https://www.dell.com/community/Dell-Community/ct-p/English). Even today, this example illustrates a best practice for many organizations with continued efforts.

Lessons Learned
The organization heavily invests in social CRM (see Chap. 5). This example showed that customers with a negative experience can influence others, resulting in lower profit for the organization.

12.2.2 Example: Anticipate Opposite Behavior

In the context of social CRM (Chap. 5), new and diverse initiatives can be launched to encourage customer loyalty and conversation. However, an organization can try to influence (but not totally control) the conversations by anticipating opposite behavior. And sometimes, competitors take advantage of such failures to promote themselves.

A/ Sources for the #DareToCreate Jersey Trolls
- https://www.forbes.com/sites/masonsands/2019/07/02/adidas-arsenal-jersey-twitter-campaign-was-flawed-from-the-start/?sh=3c1e069e14cd
- https://www.dailymail.co.uk/sport/sportsnews/article-7204475/Adidas-face-backlash-social-media-campaign-launch-Arsenal-kit.html
- https://www.theguardian.com/technology/2019/jul/02/adidas-under-fire-racist-offensive-tweets-arsenal-new-shirt-launch

Case Description
In 2019, Adidas™ started a social media campaign to promote a new football jersey based on customized pictures. Followers could request an automatically generated picture of the jersey with a self-created text. Nonetheless, Internet trolls started using this automatic customization to spread negative messages about offensive and sensitive topics. The campaign was quickly stopped because this was not in line with the intended message for diversity and inclusion.

Lessons Learned
The conclusion in this example is that AI can offer new opportunities to engage with customers, but that an unfiltered use of AI may lead to undesired side effects instead of true customer engagement. An organization should only start a campaign if it has public support within a specific social media tool. Otherwise, it may result in a boycott (e.g., similar to what can happen by a vocal minority on a publicly available tool such as Twitter™). By monitoring 24/7 (see Chaps. 3 and 5), an organization can try to resolve negative comments and be part of the conversation. It can also apologize, tell the organization's position on the issue, and try to respond personally to each customer in order to rebuild trust. Furthermore, a crisis plan helps to manage any backlash. Finally, in this example, an alternative initiative could have been to reward customer loyalty instead.

B/ Sources for the #iPhone6plus #bendgate crisis
- https://www.zdnet.com/article/apple-to-replace-bent-iphone-6-plus-models/
- https://www.forbes.com/sites/gordonkelly/2018/05/24/apple-iphone-problem-iphone-6-iphone-6-plus-bend-touchscreen/?sh=67681dd8115c
- https://www.theverge.com/circuitbreaker/2018/5/24/17389220/apple-bendgate-internal-documents-iphone-6-plus

Case Description

In 2014, customers contacted Apple™ because their new smartphone handsets had bent in pockets. In response, replacements were offered based on a visual mechanical inspection only. Other companies profited from this crisis by posting jokes on social media. For instance, a picture of a Kit Kat™ wafer stated: "We do not bend, we break." Similarly, Heineken™ posted a crown cap of their beer bottles with the slogan: "No worries, it happens to us all the time."

Lessons Learned

This example illustrates that organizations cannot control social media messages, but they can only try to influence them. While this was bad news for the smartphone producer, it remains crucial to respond and offer a solution soon.

12.2.3 Example: Do Not Insult Customers

Social CRM (Chap. 5) encourages organizations to truly listen to the needs of customers and prospects in order to stimulate customer loyalty. The latter implies that an organization should view all stakeholders as equal partners and also in times when customers ask for advice or post complaints.

Sources for the "Thin and Gorgeous" Shoe Crisis
- https://www.teenvogue.com/story/dolce-gabbana-thin-and-gorgeous-shoes
- https://www.harpersbazaar.com/fashion/designers/a9565191/dolce-and-gabbana-thin-and-gorgeous-sneakers/
- https://edition.cnn.com/2018/11/24/business/dolce-gabbana-china/index.html
- https://bettermarketing.pub/how-dolce-gabbana-lost-98-of-their-chinese-market-with-one-video-cb2baacb4a10

Case Description

In 2017, a luxury fashion brand designed a sneaker that showed the slogan: "Thin and Gorgeous." Many fans felt attacked because this slogan was provoking customers, and they were referring to an irresponsible message with body shaming. Also groups (e.g., related to eating disorders) reacted to this controversial message. In response, the designer personally commented with negative messages and so insulting the fans even more. Moreover, controversial statements had already been made in the past. Also one year later, in 2018, the same brand faced an even greater backlash after showing a controversial video (i.e., about an Asian model eating Italian food with chopsticks), which was perceived by the Chinese market as disrespectful and racist. Again, the co-founder personally reacted with inappropriate comments instead of showing sympathy, resulting in a boycott of many Chinese e-commerce websites. According to an official brand statement, this personal account was hacked.

Lessons Learned

An important message in this example is never to insult customers but to truly understand customer needs (see social CRM, Chap. 5) and, above all, to show respect and apologize. Given the series of controversial events, the brand may profit from crisis communication to build more consistent messages on their social media pages, and should try to avoid controversial statements on personal accounts as well.

12.2.4 Example: Highly Sensitive Issues

Highly sensitive issues can be used to improve an organization's image, such as for the sake of corporate social responsibility (see Chap. 3 on social media strategy). However, organizations should also be extremely careful if social media campaigns are attached to it because of the risks for (cultural) misinterpretations. This also applies to accidental references with respect to highly sensitive issues.

A/ Sources for the Stereotyping Case

- https://medium.com/@jilliandowden/german-appliance-manufacturer-miele-publishes-sexist-facebook-post-1e38b250d3e4
- https://www.channelnews.com.au/miele-slammed-for-shocking-female-video/

Case Description

In the light of the 2018 International Women's Day, Miele™ posted a picture of women having a party while sitting on a washing machine and a dryer, with the slogan: "May all women always remember to embrace what makes them unique." This image let many followers think of the typical stereotype that existed many decades ago, namely of "women in the home." The brand misinterpreted how customers would react, and only a few hours after receiving negative comments, the post was down without clear apologies.

Lessons Learned

This example makes the reader learn that stereotyping is a highly sensitive issue. Organizations should especially think twice on such initiatives, and possibly test their message more carefully before launching it to a wide audience. Moreover, an organization should also explicitly apologize for any misunderstanding in order to gain trust.

B/ Sources for the Racism Case

- https://www.theguardian.com/world/2017/oct/08/dove-apologises-for-ad-showing-black-woman-turning-into-white-one
- https://www.businessinsider.nl/doves-racist-ad-10-9-2017-10?international=true&r=US
- https://www.bbc.com/news/newsbeat-42603960

- https://www.theguardian.com/fashion/2019/feb/08/courting-controversy-from-hms-coolest-monkey-to-guccis-blackface-jumper

Case Description

The following example involves another highly sensitive topic, namely racism. We go back to 2017, when Dove™ launched a "Real Beauty" transformation project. In a campaign for promoting body lotion, three transformation phases were shown: (1) a black woman wearing a brown shirt, (2) a white man pulling off a brown shirt but keeping a white shirt, and (3) a white woman wearing a white shirt. After this misstep became clear, the video was removed. Unfortunately, the credibility of also earlier investments in beauty diversity messages was harmed, such as "You are more beautiful than you think."

Lessons Learned

Similar lessons learned apply to this example. Even if the intention is sincere, perceptions on social media can be totally different. Such failures may also come unintentionally, for instance when fashion brands allow for customized slogans (Sect. 12.2.2: #DareToCreate jersey trolls). Also the choice for properly selected models counts, as experienced by H&M™ after showing a black boy in a hoodie with the slogan "Coolest monkey in the jungle." Consequently, even when organizations get more acquainted with the use of social media, careful actions remain crucial.

12.3   Assignment

After describing some (successful and less successful) case studies in the previous sections, we now encourage the reader to conduct a case study based on an assignment.

Case Description

A large company develops, sells, and repairs customized earplugs for noise protection. Earplugs are small pieces of soft material (such as wax, cotton, or plastic) that someone can put into one's ears to keep out noise. Besides a headquarters, the company owns 100 local hearing shops across three European countries.

Thanks to its own laboratory and technical service, a direct and fast service can be guaranteed. Nevertheless, the company faces strong competition, as an increasing number of students and musicians suffer from tinnitus or even hearing loss after parties with loud music and heavy beats. On the other hand, tinnitus is an emerging issue, and many doctors still feel ill-informed about its treatment and prevention.

(continued)

The company focuses on a customer-oriented approach. In contrast to its competitors, it does not publish any price list on the corporate website. Instead, it explicitly recognizes that every problem is different by inviting people with hearing problems for a personal test and advice in a local shop.

The organization's mission and some corresponding business goals are listed in Fig. 12.4. As the company is a large player on the market, it also has a large marketing budget.

Assignment

Give advice on the company's B2C and B2B use of social media.
    In this case:

- B2C mainly covers adolescents and musicians, who profit from earplugs on parties or concerts in order to avoid hearing problems afterward.
- B2B mainly covers doctors, such as general practitioners and specialists treating hearing diseases.

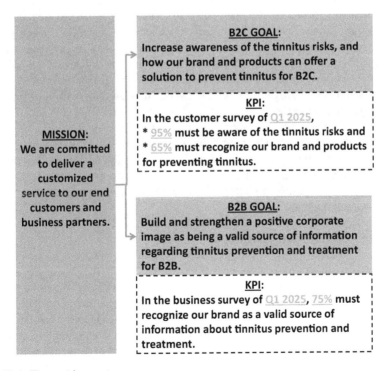

Fig. 12.4 Home assignment

12.3.1 Advice on Social Media Use for B2C

Question

Choose two topics (i.e., chapters) presented in this book that best fit your B2C advice. Please explain your choice.

- Online advertising.
- Viral campaigns.
- Social CRM.
- SEO.
- Business intelligence (sentiment analysis).
- Business intelligence (social network analysis).
- e-Recruitment,
- Crowdfunding.
- Legal and ethical issues in social media.

Possible Topic 1: Social CRM

As customer orientation is a unique selling point for the organization under study, a first possible topic involves social CRM. Particularly, social CRM aims at engaging and creating long-term relationships with (potential) customers and social media connections in general, e.g., by truly listening to their needs, showing expertise by answering questions, and having mutually beneficial conversations. When people are treated in a personalized way and feel appreciated, they might even become brand advocates who indirectly motivate others to buy the organization's products (albeit not a primary goal). As the organization's B2C goal is to create tinnitus awareness and brand recognition, social CRM could be used for reasons of storytelling instead of direct sales, e.g., by sharing stories of (both regular and famous) people with hearing problems or people who already wear earplugs. The organization could also create a brand community which serves as a knowledge base with articles on hearing problems, solutions, and prevention initiatives (besides product information). For instance, people with hearing problems could use the proposed community to find trustworthy information about their problems and ask questions to qualified employees.

Possible Topic 2: Viral Campaigns

In general, mouth-to-mouth communication is more convincing than advertising (e.g., because of ad avoidance or ad blindness). From this perspective, viral campaigns (which are also called "word-of-mouth advertising") could be used, because they require that the corporate message is voluntarily shared by the Internet users in order to cause a social ripple effect. The target group of adolescents and musicians also consists of people who are eager to share online information and may create awareness due to peer pressure. One example of a viral campaign is to create videos in which tinnitus risks and prevention are explained in real-life situations or in which experiments are conducted. As tinnitus and hearing loss may happen to anyone who regularly visits places with loud music, the videos may shock and evoke emotions of the people involved or stimulate curiosity of people with little knowledge about the topic. In order to have more influence, the videos may also cover testimonies of recognized musicians or celebrities wearing earplugs. The videos could end with a positive note, i.e., by giving solutions and prevention tips (without emphasizing direct selling). Moreover, influencers, musicians, or celebrities may act as trendsetters who stimulate sharing to a larger audience.

Note

- Online advertising could be an alternative for or a complement to viral campaigns, as long as the emphasis is not on direct selling and dependent on the budget willing to spend on particular pricing models. Nonetheless, ads focus more on one-to-many communication than on supporting conversations. If ads are preferred, possible websites to buy ad space are festival websites, websites that sell tickets for music events or music stores. Also, an audio publishing tool such as Spotify™ can be used to reach a target group that frequently listens to music. As customized earplugs are niche products, the organization could potentially benefit from targeted marketing in the short run.
- The organization could also opt to focus on search engine marketing by combining SEO with SEA. For instance, for reasons of reputation management and to increase the visibility of the brand, it can offer links to external websites with trustworthy information about tinnitus risks and prevention (e.g., Wikipedia™). Nonetheless, if SEO is advised for B2C as the most important topic, then the organization rather assumes that its (potential) customers are already aware of tinnitus and try to find information about the topic by looking for relevant keywords (e.g., "festival," "music," "tinnitus," "hearing loss," or "earplug"). Therefore, the results of SEO will be less proactive than the other initiatives and more likely to reach musicians or people already suffering from tinnitus (i.e., dependent on the keywords chosen).
- Sentiment analysis in the sense of analyzing product reviews and product ratings is rather related to product feedback for reasons of innovation and direct sales (i.e., which are not primary goals in this assignment). Since the actions to be taken are closely related to social CRM, the latter seems more suitable for the organization under study.
- Social network analysis is generally more expensive than viral campaigns, because personal data need to be collected and analyzed first (e.g., by means of social engineering, plus customer data and possibly medical data). Also privacy issues may arise. If the network data are not yet available (e.g., to identify trendsetters), this investment will rather be used for reasons of direct selling than for brand awareness.

Question

Which social media *types and tools* would you suggest for *B2C*? Please explain your choice.

Possible Answer

Although the organization seems to have access to a relatively large marketing budget, it should not necessarily apply all social media types and tools. For instance, based on the social media trinity (see Chap. 2), the organization may start with (1) social communities, (2) text publishing tools, and (3) microblogging. The organization's choice should be guided by the results of an internal and external audit. For instance, if the audit uncovers that many customers (particularly adolescents) are active on Instagram™, then this social community could be used to create a corporate Instagram™ profile. Another alternative (in line with social CRM) is to create a brand community owned by the organization itself. Regarding text publishing tools, the organization could opt to create a corporate blog, which can also be promoted within the proposed brand community and other social media tools in use. Regarding microblogging, Twitter™ could be particularly used to reach musicians as a niche.

Note

- Another possibility is to use video publishing tools, e.g., YouTube™ videos to share testimonies.
- Please note that Wikipedia™'s online encyclopedia cannot be used for commercial information. For instance, in this case, Wikipedia™ could be used for sharing general information about tinnitus or hearing problems, but not for product information of the organization under study.
- We also remind the reader that search engines and emails are not part of a social media type or tool.

Question

Give an example of one social media strategy that you advise for *B2C*, including two corresponding tactics. Do not forget to apply the SMART rule.

Possible Answer

In line with Fig. 3.2, an extract of a possible B2C social media strategic plan is proposed in Fig. 12.5.

Similar to Chap. 3, the SMART elements are underlined and refer to a certain time interval, social media tool, and/or amount or percentage to measure success.

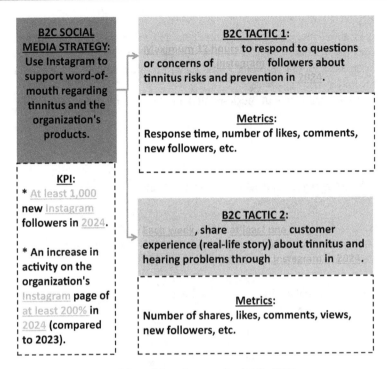

Fig. 12.5 An extract of a possible social media strategic plan for B2C

Note

- Remember that the social media strategy should not focus on direct selling (e.g., no discount vouchers or a targeted number of new customers), but on tinnitus awareness and brand recognition. The aim is to build trust instead of spreading commercial talk.
- Giving away free earplugs seems to be less appropriate for the organization under study, as it highly values customization. Free tests better fit the organization's way of working but are also more focused on direct selling than awareness (though such hearing tests should rather be conducted by a qualified employee than a quick test through a free mobile app or any other social media tool).
- Alternative tactics exist, for instance:
  - To organize a contest in which people who follow the organization's Instagram™ page can win free festival tickets.
  - To organize a contest to collect creative videos with testimonies or pictures of people wearing earplugs, e.g., with festival tickets as a reward.
  - To create a survey in which people can test the effect of their lifestyle and their knowledge about hearing issues.
  - To organize a quiz in tinnitus risks.

- To post general messages that are relevant for the target audience, such as posts about music, upcoming concerts, and information about musicians, in order to stimulate people to follow the organization's Instagram™ page.
- To create a mobile app that warns when noise seems to reach a critical level that may cause ear damage.
- To ask questions about music-related and hearing-related topics.
- Etc.

12.3.2 Advice on Social Media Use for B2B

Question

Choose two topics (i.e., chapters) presented in this book that best fit your B2B advice. Please explain your choice.

- Online advertising.
- Viral campaigns.
- Social CRM.
- SEO.
- Business intelligence (sentiment analysis).
- Business intelligence (social network analysis).
- e-Recruitment,
- Crowdfunding.
- Legal and ethical issues in social media.

Possible Topic 1: Social CRM

Social CRM is a way to build long-term relationships with doctors and to learn from their experience in practice. Besides participating in existing medical blogs, the organization can create a brand community dedicated to doctors, which serves as a corporate fan base and a knowledge base for professional questions and answers (Q&A) about tinnitus risks and prevention tips. As the B2B goal involves brand recognition, the brand community should rather focus on (proactive as well as reactive) information sharing about the issue than on sales talk (i.e., no direct sales offers nor pushing product information). The focus should rather be on social collaboration than social marketing or social sales. As doctors are generally considered as trustworthy, their noncommittal product recommendations are frequently followed by the patients. Doctors' insights can also be valuable for the organization for reasons of product innovation. The brand community should encourage an open discussion forum between specialists and may offer additional services, such as free access to external webinars or keynote presentations on international conferences. For instance, the brand community can be used to share corporate research but also to link to medical news articles (e.g., http://www.medscape.com/) or to other

medical blogs and communities (e.g., http://www.sermo.com/, http://en.meltingdoc.
com/, https://www.doximity.com/, http://www.imedexchange.com/).

Possible Topic 2: SEO

Investing in SEO may help the organization get its corporate website, blog, or other
social media pages higher on a search engine results page and to get more traffic to
the corporate website in the long run. A higher ranking or visibility generally implies
that doctors will find the corporate information on relevant keywords more easily by
means of natural or nonpaid search traffic (i.e., when doctors feel the need for more
information themselves). Possible SEO adjustments are adding relevant keywords
(e.g., "tinnitus," "hearing loss," or "earplug") in the URL of the corporate website,
repeating those keywords in the content of the corporate web pages, and try to make
other social media pages refer to the corporate URL, Furthermore, the content of the
corporate website should be professional and with relevant information. Besides
optimizing for regular search engines (e.g., Google™, Bing™, or Yahoo!™), also
medical-related engines exist (e.g., http://www.imedisearch.com/ or http://pogofrog.
com/).

Note

- Please note that doctors should act independently of any commercial organization. They cannot become a representative or salesman of the organization nor
  directly prescribe the organization's products. Only a noncommittal recommen-
  dation is possible, driven by product quality. Thus, doctors are not customers or
  clients (i.e., not B2C), but rather partners who do not sell and who do not
  necessarily use the products themselves.
- Online advertising (as paid search traffic) could be an alternative to SEO, if the
  targeted content is not focused on direct selling and depending on the budget for
  pricing models. Nonetheless, another content is preferable for B2C and B2B, as
  the interests of the target groups differ. For instance, the ad may contain an input
  field for doctors to register their email address and receive more information
  about tinnitus. The B2B ads may also appear on different websites, such as
  medical encyclopedias or associations.
- A viral campaign could be launched to share an e-book about the topic or a video
  that reports on a professional (panel) discussion about the problems and risks of
  tinnitus. Moreover, doctors can indirectly be reached by a B2C viral campaign.
- Similar to B2C, opinion mining of product reviews and product ratings seems less
  appropriate for information sharing regarding tinnitus (but rather for product
  feedback, innovation, and direct sales).
- An expensive social network analysis is not necessarily required for the identification of doctors, since simple lists of doctors and their specialism are likely to
  exist (e.g., on hospital websites, in the Yellow Pages). Moreover, doctors cannot
  be equated with sellers and help protect privacy of patient information.
- Since the assignment does not mention a lack of expertise or budget, the topics of
  e-recruitment and crowdfunding are less suitable for the given organization.

Question
Which social media *types and tools* would you suggest for *B2B*? Please explain your choice.

Possible Answer
Similar to the B2C advice, the possible social media types and tools should depend on an internal and external audit (Chap. 3) and may follow the social media trilogy (Chap. 2). For instance, the organization should verify whether doctor profiles are generally present on microblogging tools (e.g., Twitter™) or social communities. Regarding the latter, a professional community (e.g., LinkedIn™) may be more appropriate than a nonprofessional community (e.g., Facebook™). The choice for one or another social media tool may also differ from region to region. Nonetheless, for reasons of social CRM, the organization can also create its own brand community which may serve as a knowledge base for doctors (i.e., as a social community), as well as using an exclusive corporate blog and a wiki or Slideshare™ (i.e., text publishing tools) with knowledge articles about health issues and corporate products (i.e., as a solution to the issues). The organization can try to position itself as an expert or authority in the field of tinnitus and hearing loss. Furthermore, RSS technology can be used to timely spread newly added knowledge and insights to the subscribed community members.

Note
• Remember from Chap. 2 that search engines (e.g., Google™, Bing™, Yahoo!™) and emails cannot be considered as social media types or tools.

Question
Give an example of one social media strategy that you advise for *B2B*, including two corresponding tactics. Do not forget to apply the SMART rule.

Possible Answer
See Fig. 12.6.
Again, the SMART elements are underlined and refer to a certain time interval, social media tool, and/or amount or percentage to measure success.

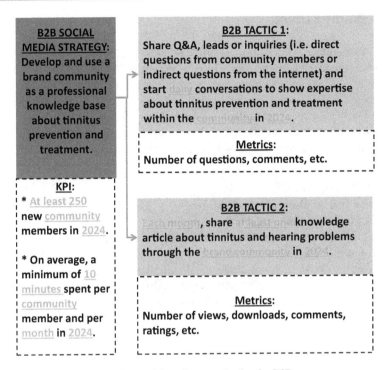

Fig. 12.6 An extract of a possible social media strategic plan for B2B

Note

- Please note that doctors are not customers of the organization. As they do not directly sell earplugs to their patients (i.e., they can only give independent advice to go to a local shop), free (i.e., not customized) samples, or discount vouchers for direct selling approaches seem less appropriate for independent doctors.
- Alternative tactics exist, for instance:
  - To share a virtual visit in the corporate laboratory to provide doctors with inside information about tinnitus prevention and research.
  - To acquire brand-related recommendations or endorsements for being a valid source of information and research center regarding tinnitus (e.g., on LinkedIn™).
  - To start a discussion forum within the community for doctors to interact with each other and share experience.
  - To broadcast medical conferences related to tinnitus or hearing problems.
  - Etc.

12.4   Brainstorming

Finally, to facilitate a brainstorming exercise, this section offers a protocol with questions to guide open discussions. Since the purpose of this exercise is to reflect on alternative scenarios that combine all chapters in a consistent manner, we start with a defined scope but without suggesting predefined responses. The following questions thus only serve as a checklist to allow for a structured way of thinking. The scope of this brainstorming is described first. Subsequently, you are invited to start brainstorming about the application of each chapter within this given scope.

> **Scope Description**
> Suppose you are the CEO of an innovative organization. Think about a new product or service that is original and unique.
> For instance, in this example, we can consider an **app on traveling**. It can be an entirely new social media tool or app (e.g., a traveling platform), or extensions to existing social media tools with new functionalities (e.g., extra RSS features or private fora on public tools). Also decide on your target group (e.g., young people, disabled people, hikers). You can also consider side-products or –services (e.g., selling or renting clothes, equipment, books).

Brainstorm about Chap. 2 by reflecting on possible alternatives for getting the message through. Remember that it is important to create word of mouth (e.g., online, mobile, or tablet WoM). Therefore, you can ideally take ideas or topics where people talk about.

- What type of messages will you communicate?
- How will you create collaboration?
- If you also wish to educate, which initiatives can be interesting?
- Which options exist to entertain?

The following questions help you to think about social media strategies and the related monitoring efforts (Chap. 3).

- Which alternative social media strategies are possible?
- To which business objectives do these alternative social media strategies relate?
- What will be your social actions and business actions?
- Are you working with SMART formulations?
- Which monitoring tools will you use?
- How will the alternative social media strategies be evaluated?

Next, for Chap. 4, we distinguish questions for online ads and viral campaigns. You can start with alternatives for online ads.

- How will you start an online ad?
- What will be its content (e.g., as a text ad or banner, using which keywords, and including which landing page)?
- Which pricing model will you prefer, and why?
- What is your preferred position on a website to be shown?

For your viral campaigns, you can think of the following issues.

- What will be the viral content?
- How will you try to stimulate a social ripple effect?

We continue by brainstorming about social CRM (Chap. 5).

- Which alternative (or combination of alternatives) is most appropriate: social marketing, social sales, or social service?
- What about the other SCRM type, such as social innovation, social collaboration, or social customer experience?
- How will you develop your chosen SCRM initiative?
- Which type of SCRM software tools will you use?

Reflections on SEO (Chap. 6) can be facilitated as follows.

- On which search engines will you focus? And why?
- Who will be your target audience?
- Which SEO initiatives will you take regarding architecture?
- Which SEO initiatives will you take regarding content?
- Which SEO initiatives will you take regarding links?
- Which SEO initiatives will you take regarding user improvements?

We now consider questions related to Chap. 7. Discuss possible alternatives for dealing with opinions and sentiments on the Internet.

- How will you identify opinions and sentiments about the organization or the new product/service?
- How will you react to positive messages?
- What about complaints?

The following questions help you to brainstorm about the opportunities for social network analysis (Chap. 8).

- How will you describe a relevant social network for your product/service?
- How will you make predictions?
- How does peer influence play a role?
- What about the role of homophily?

Another perspective can be added by considering e-recruitment (Chap. 9).

- Which social media tools will you use for which roles (e.g., web developer, salesperson, cleaning lady, Chief Social Media Officer)?
- How will you screen candidates?
- Which type of ATS will you use?
- If you opt for creating a video: how will you introduce the corporate culture and the different departments, use employee testimonials, show your organization is unique?

Regarding the financial implications, we apply our insights from Chap. 10 to discuss alternative possibilities for getting funded. In order to make the brainstorming more concrete, we will set an initial target amount at 75,000 euro.

- What is your business plan?
- Will you rely on traditional funding, crowdfunding, or both?

The next questions apply to those cases in which crowdfunding is considered.

- Which crowdfunding type will you use?
- Which crowdfunding platform will you use?
- What are the possible perks?
- What will you do during the pre-campaign and actual crowdfunding campaign?

Finally, Chap. 11 helps you to respect the related legal and ethical issues. At this stage, we reflect on options to establish a social media policy.

- Who will be involved in creating a social media policy?
- For whom will you create a social media policy?
- Which topics will be included?
- How will you perform a social media audit?
- How will the social media policy be monitored?
- How will you ensure that strong passwords are used by all users?

12.5   Self-Test

- Elaborate on a topic discussed in one of the chapters.
    - Find at least two academic studies and two commercial studies, and discuss in more detail.
    - Conduct a literature study (e.g., what is SEO, why is it used, how).
- Write an essay that answers the question whether social media are good or bad for doing business. According to your opinion, what are the positive and negative implications of social media? Please critically think through your response and motivate your choice.

- Find one article in a newspaper or commercial magazine that positively/negatively covers the value of social media for organizations in general (e.g., regarding the initial public offerings (IPOs) of social media tools, privacy or security risks, click fraud, bidding wars).
  - Please argue why the tone of the article is positive/negative.
  - Why did you opt for this article?
  - Can you relate this article to one or more chapters in this book?
- Search online for an example of how a particular organization makes good/bad use of social media (e.g., specific examples of online ads, viral campaigns, or social CRM for a certain organization).
  - To which social media type does it relate?
  - Why is this a successful or failed initiative? Evaluate the example.
- Search for real-life examples of online ads and viral campaigns. Can you think of a possible social media strategy (with KPIs) and two possible corresponding social media tactics (with metrics) that might be realized by each example? Do not forget to apply the SMART rule.
- Conduct a case study in a particular organization (e.g., by means of an in-depth interview with the person responsible for social media, supplemented by publicly available information on the organization).
  - To which degree does the organization address each topic (i.e., chapter) presented in this book?
  - Do you think the organization makes sufficient use of social media and this by considering its particular context? Formulate suggestions for improvement, if appropriate.
- If a case study is given for a specific organization, can you advise on its social media use and strategy for business to consumer (B2C) and/or business to business (B2B), for instance, regarding an SME with a small marketing budget or regarding different business goals (e.g., higher sales, brand awareness, image building, product innovation, an improved way of working, better internal collaboration—see Chap. 3)?
  - Please explain which topics (chapters) best fit your B2C/B2B advice, and why?
  - Which social media types and tools would you suggest for B2C/B2B?
  - Can you give an example of one possible social media strategy that you advise for B2C/B2B (with KPIs) and two possible corresponding social media tactics (with metrics)? Do not forget to apply the SMART rule.
- The OECD has proposed restrictive requirements to define UGC. For instance, it states that UGC must be created outside the professional routines and practices. Nonetheless, an increasing number of popular YouTube™ users can live with the money earned by their self-made videos. Hence, influencers (both paid and unpaid) have a crucial role in social media management, among others for viral campaigns, and social media should thus be defined in a broader sense. Explain which social media strategy primarily helps detect influencers to better profit from the social ripple effect.

- A small and medium-sized enterprise has a small marketing budget for social media initiatives. As it is still a start-up, its business goal is to drive store traffic in order to increase sales and profit. The organization asks for some high-level advice, without too much risks. Reflect on which social media strategy best covers this situation.

Bibliography

Altimeter Group. (2013). *The evolution of social business: Six stages of social business transformation.* Retrieved November 27, 2014, from http://www.Slideshare.net/Altimeter/the-evolution-of-social-business-six-stages-of-social-media-transformation

Borremans, P. (2014). Guest lecture of Philippe Borremans in the course Creating Value Using Social media at Ghent University, November 2014.

Forbes. (2013). *European companies stay the long-term course towards social business.* Retrieved November 27, 2014, from http://www.forbes.com/sites/rawnshah/2013/04/04/european-companies-stay-the-long-term-course-towards-social-business/

Gartner, Inc. (2021). *Hype cycle.* Retrieved July 14, 2021, from https://www.gartner.com/en/research/methodologies/gartner-hype-cycle

Menczer, F. (2020). *Information overload helps fake news spread, and social media knows it.* Retrieved July 14, 2021, from https://www.scientificamerican.com/article/information-overload-helps-fake-news-spread-and-social-media-knows-it/

Index

U

Unboxing videos, 92, 94
Uniform resource locator (URL), 16, 127, 131,
    135–138, 141, 142, 195, 200, 263
User-generated content (UGC), 21, 26–28,
    31–33, 48, 103, 115, 147, 150, 177, 178,
    232, 269

V

Value creation, 11, 14, 19, 108–111
Venture capitalist (VC), 212, 213, 221
Viral campaigns, 2, 10, 13, 15, 18, 19, 27, 28,
    45–47, 51, 64–66, 69–95, 99, 109, 114,
    120, 121, 170, 184, 193, 197, 226, 227,
    250, 258, 259, 262, 263, 266, 267, 269
Virtual reality (VR), 24, 39, 59, 62
Virtual tours, 85
Vlogs, 13, 34

W

Web
    1.0, 22, 23, 25, 47
    2.0, 21–26, 28, 29, 47, 103
    3.0, 23, 24, 47
    4.0, 21, 23, 24, 47
    5.0, 23, 24
    6.0, 23
    analytics, 62–64, 83, 115
White hat, 132, 145
Word-of-mouth (WoM), 86, 87, 90, 92, 149,
    150, 161, 258

Y

Your money or your life (YMYL), 132

Printed in the USA
CPSIA information can be obtained
at www.ICGtesting.com
LVHW011524030923
757103LV00005B/77